Blackmaled by Academia

Larry, I love You
2021

Blackmaled by Academia
Edited by G. Strohschen and K.B. Elazier

American Scholars Press
Atlanta, Georgia
http://www.americanscholarspress.us/about.php

ISBN: 978-1-7337122-5-5

Printed in the United States of America

Blackmaled by Academia

CONTENT

CONTENT

PROLOGUE

Blackmaled by Academia

"Though the colored man is no longer subject to barter and sale, he is surrounded by an adverse sentiment which fetters all his movements. In his downward course he meets with no resistance, but his course upward is resented and resisted at every step of his progress. If he comes in ignorance, rags and wretchedness he conforms to the popular belief of his character, and in that character, he is welcome; but if he shall come as a gentleman, a scholar and a statesman, he is hailed as a contradiction to the national faith concerning his race, and his coming is resented as impudence. In one case he may provoke contempt and derision, but in the other he is an affront to pride and provokes malice."

Frederick Douglass
September 25, 1883

They regret to say that although well qualified, I
don't get the job.
Am I angry? You're damned straight I am! Go polish my
knob.
The committee decided to choose someone else
And, sure as shooting, they don't look like myself

Angry black men are no longer en vogue
They'd rather you be a sycophantic pogue
And take it, and bear it, and suck up the sin
Of being male and smart, but in a black skin.

'Twas a competitive opening of this I'm sure
It's just they don't hire the nigger du jour.
I guess it was something they couldn't explain
It certainly wasn't based on my credentials or name
It couldn't be color, race, gender, or sex
Because I'm supposed to be equal when compared to the
rest.

And despite all the professing of searching for best
It seems I'm unable to pass their opaque test.

But checking their roster, I see something's amiss

In all of their pictures, and profiles, and lists
I look in my mirror and see nothing like this.

More sympathetic than warmed over Pablum.
These progressive, socialist, liberals all surely protest
Look among our faculties, we have Black women, Latinas
and yet
Despite best intentions, do they fully represent?

Scenes familiar, you must admit
But I'm really getting tired of this discrimination shit.
I'm ready to kick ass on the academic block
To make sure these suckers don't turn back the clock.

Blackmailed by academia
By souls in white anemia
Don't blurt out the obvious
Or risk being seen as loud and obnoxious

Going through the interview motions is just a protocol
Because they really have no intentions of hiring you at all
So, make your great impression or make yourself a fool
It simply doesn't matter; you'll not be at this school.

So where are all the black men in academia? Why such a
dearth?
One can only surmise that he's the "Wretched of the
Earth."

The few black men in AE are either gay or effete,
So, the message seems to not threaten, but be sweet.
To protect fragile white women and lesbian queers,
Strong black males draw nothing but sneers.
Oh, you'll see a black African male or two
But when his contract period nears
He'll be shuffled back across the ocean blue

If you're reading this, then it is by a miracle.
It means it got past the gatekeeper's uncritical gaze
In early times I'd have a serving plate filled with petits-fours
But even now, as a free man, I still don't rate
In post-black Obama I am considered a Boor.
Now I risk getting shot trying to enter either door

Perhaps an extended party metaphor would serve to illustrate
How much the folks in academe have tried to block the gate
I'm not trying to crash someone else's party
I know that would be unwise
But I am determined to get my portion
Of the employment opportunities that **all** of our taxes subsidize.

I am expected to have the social decorum to know just where to stand
And to know I'm not wanted and keep the conversation bland

That the only job open for me is to be their security
At least my father or grandfather was allowed the dignity...of servant's tray
Now the message is just, stay away!

I am to have the good graces not to embarrass my host and guests
I can ill afford to attend or be allowed to work the fest.
I am to stand by and swallow the indelicacies and try not to digest
The crumbs and bums and social scum, but keep my tongue at rest.

All their research and scholarship has come with a score
Subsidized by tax dollars and federal grants galore
To practice up on people from near and distant shores
They took their wives and lovers and kids and pets
They wined in hotel rooms and high-powered jets
They hoard their obtuse findings in journals and in books
And present it to each other and steal it back like crooks.

They issue subsidized tuition loans to burden the poor
And create obstacles to learning you can be sure
And they keep piling up useless work so you're forever in debt for more
But the smart niggas that peep the game, get shown straight to the door
Look around the room, you'll see them no more
In order to keep the education franchise safe and secure

They cry social justice and equity for all
But ask them for some and then watch them stall

In this thought I'd be remiss
If I failed to help you realize this
These jobs are reserved for the chosen few:
Whitey's wife, consultant, and Ashkenazi Jew

And if you think I'm making or faking this
Just take a look at the faculty list
Maybe a spick, a chink, a spook, or wop
Might even have a nigga sittin' at the top

But it's all designed to put to a stop
To the claim that we discriminate
Yet black males singly suffer their state
And truth for them remains a hollow fake.

Epilogue:
"In the opinion of the court, the legislation and histories of the times, and the language used in the Declaration of Independence, show, that neither the class of persons who had been imported as slaves, nor their descendants, whether they had become free or not, were then acknowledged as a part of the people, nor intended to be included in the general words used in that memorable instrument...They had for more than a century before been regarded as beings of an inferior order, and altogether unfit to associate with the white race, either in social or political relations; and so far inferior, that they had no rights which the white man was bound to respect; and that the negro might justly and lawfully be reduced to slavery for his benefit."
Roger B. Taney, Chief Justice, US Supreme Court 1857

Editor's note: this selection was previously published in: *Dialogues in Social Justice: An Adult Education Journal*, 5(1) Spring, by K. B. Elazier (2020).

Origins of the Book

Perspectives by the Co-Editors

"In these the Chief Justice does not directly assert, but plainly assumes, as a fact, that the public estimate of the black man is more favorable *now* than it was in the days of the Revolution. This assumption is a mistake. In some trifling particulars, the condition of that race has been ameliorated; but as a whole in this country, the change between then and now is decidedly the other way; and their ultimate destiny has never appeared so hopeless as in the last three or four years…All the powers of earth seem rapidly combining against him. Mammon is after him; ambition follows, and philosophy follows, and the Theology of the day is fast joining the cry. They have him in his prison house; they have searched his person and left no prying instrument with him. One after another they have closed the heavy iron doors upon him, and now they have him, as it were, bolted in with a lock of a hundred keys, which can never be unlocked without the concurrent of every key; the keys in the hands of a hundred different men, and they scattered to a hundred different and distant places; and they stand musing as to what invention, in all the dominions of mind and matter, can be produced to make the impossibility of his escape more complete than it is. It is grossly incorrect to say or assume, that the public estimate of the negro is more favorable now than it was at the origin of the government."

Excerpt from the *Speech on the Dred Scott Decision* by Abraham Lincoln, June 26, 1857

The idea for this book has been brewing for several years and crystallized into a poem I wrote for *Dialogues in Social Justice* in 2019; I sought to expand on the concepts and to explain what has been embedded through prose. Since that time, the country has erupted in months-long protests against the killing of blacks --male and female-- by vigilante cops and the neo-slave patrollers. Little did I know how timely the issues in this book would be and any early resistance to its publication is now defeated. Many types of studies on the treatment of blacks in academia are very informative; unfortunately, most have been buried in academic journals, but this book is intended to be different.

It is the result of long observation, some research, and much reflection. The writing is not intended to be in the style of a traditional academic work (more prosaic) nor a typical treatise on the ills of racism and the harmful actions of whites toward non-whites. I intend no usual accusations or sinister motives on the part of whites. To paraphrase Jesus of Nazareth, I recognize this as "the time of the Gentiles." I harbor no ill will or hatred toward whites. I feel that is a waste of time, even if they actually hate me or wish me harm. Time is too short and life too precious to spend it on hating anyone. Yet, I am not a person who thinks we should all just get along; people are different and regardless of race etc. we are allowed our preferences, socially.

But I am concerned here with public and workplace situations, where it is expected that we maintain collegial, professional behaviors and relations toward each other. I know we have enemies; history has borne that out...like the so-termed Jews, lest they forget; that's assertoric. I want to survive and thrive despite them [enemies]. I also feel at this juncture I need to state what is obvious to all: we black men are in a detestable condition. Despite all the protestations from either side, a great number of black men are in peril. Despite real progress on all fronts, including electing Obama president, black men are under constant attack--Blackmaled in America. I wonder how often Obama worried about being shot mistakenly by his own Secret Service men? Four years after his departure from office he is still being berated by his successor. I'll tell you, it's an obsession with these folks!

The introductory quote by Lincoln still rings true today, sometimes, even more so. Black conservatives readily provide stats to prove we are worse off than in previous times, except they blame the black community for its ills, offering themselves as exemplars. Liberals quote similar stats but lay blame on the systems of white supremacy and racist institutions, excluding themselves as exceptions. I believe they are both right. But there's more to it than systems and the sheer force of will to overcome.

With *Blackmaled by Academia*, we do not wish to engage in elaborate descriptions or debates about a racist system and how it affects black men; that should be evident to all thinking people by now. The status quo of racism in the USA has a conditioned prejudice toward US-born black males. The essential purpose of the book is to uncover positive and practical ways to advance the inclusion of Black men in the academy. It's time to look inward, inside the institution. It is again time for a candid reconsideration by the academy of the hostile sentiments toward black males through covert enactments, overt antagonistic actions, and deliberate evasions. It's time for black men to act!

K. B. Elazier,
Hampton, Virginia
Winter 2021.

"It comes with great shock to discover that the country which is your birthplace and to which you owe your life and your identity has not in its whole system of reality evolved any place for you"

(J. Baldwin in Peck, 2016, p.23)

When we sent out the call for this book, we did not expect that it would become a choral symphony of incredibly strong men who collectively cry 'I AM.' This collaboration is not merely a collection of chapters about the discriminatory and racist experiences of Black men in academia. This is an assemblage of the voices of men who are brave enough to shout out to the world what is kept behind the veils in our society, especially in academia.

Like symphonic movements, in the four-part arrangement these men lead us through their world; we see their daily lived realty of tragic discrimination portrayed in briskness and liveliness; with energy, bone-deep honesty, and lyrical narrative. Perhaps most importantly, when it comes to the last movement, the readers have actually become a part of that reality. Why? Because we will have laughed and cried and connected to the events and grasped the feelings of these men. I seriously doubt, that our readers will be able to dismiss the reverberations of the told truths that are sure to keep ringing in our minds. Like in a rollicking finale, this is where the reader has a grand opportunity to become a part of the symphony. When we listen and reflect on the experiences told, we can hear that the voices in *Blackmaled by Academia* chant not only about the tragic and horrific behaviors by a white society that is mirrored in academia; the voices also exemplify resilience, strength, and courage.

It is with deep hope that some of our white readers can seize upon this moment while reading the book, connecting, perhaps, with honesty and acceptance of the authors; standing up for just action in your world; and doing so powerful and unafraid. At least, this is what *Blackmaled by* Academia so strongly expects to accomplish.

Reference

Peck, R. (2016). *I am not your Negro*. Vintage Books)

Gabriele I.E. Strohschen
Chicago, Illinois
December 2020

Introduction to the Book

Beyond the Numbers
But Let's Start There Anyway

K.B. Elazier with Gabriele Strohschen

According to the National Center for Education Statistics (2019) of the 1.5 million faculty in degree-granting post-secondary institutions in the USA, 3 percent each were in the category of Black males, Black females, Hispanic males, and Hispanic females. 45,000 in each of these categories, then, are distributed across the *xx#* of institutions, defined in the NCES report as those granting associate's or higher degrees and participating in the federal Title IV financial aid programs.

In fall of 2017, of the 1.5 million faculty in degree-granting postsecondary institutions, 53 percent were full- time and 47 percent were part-time. Faculty include professors, associate professors, assistant professors, instructors, lecturers, assisting professors, adjunct professors, and interim professors.

Of all full-time faculty in degree-granting postsecondary institutions in fall 2017, 41 percent were White males; 35 percent were White females; 6 percent were Asian/Pacific Islander males; 5 percent were Asian/Pacific Islander females; and 3 percent each were Black males, Black females, Hispanic males, and Hispanic females.[1] Those who were American Indian/Alaska Native and those who were of two or more races each made up 1 percent or less of full-time faculty.

The racial/ethnic and sex distribution of faculty varied by academic rank at degree-granting postsecondary institutions in fall 2017. For example, among full-time professors, 54 percent were White males, 27 percent were White females, 8 percent were Asian/Pacific Islander males, and 3 percent were Asian/Pacific Islander females. Black males, Black females, and Hispanic males each accounted for 2 percent of full-time professors. The following groups each made up 1 percent or less of the total number of full-time professors: Hispanic females, American Indian/Alaska Native individuals, and individuals of Two or more races. In comparison, among full-time assistant professors, 34 percent were White males, 38 percent were White females, 7 percent were Asian/Pacific Islander males, 6 percent were Asian/Pacific Islander females, and 4 percent were Black females. Black males, Hispanic males, and Hispanic females each accounted for three percent of full-time assistant professors, while American, Indian/Alaska Native individuals and individuals of two or more races each made up one percent or less of the total number of full-time assistant professors.

Figure 1

For each academic rank, the percentage distribution of full-time faculty in degree-granting postsecondary institutions, by race/ethnicity and sex. Fall 2017

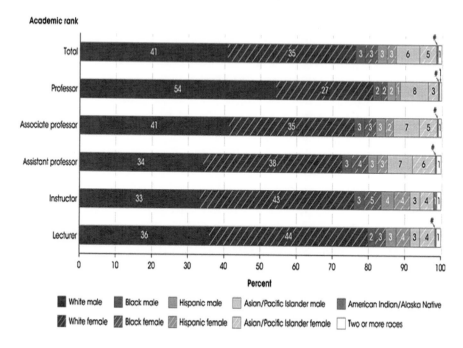

NOTE: Gender breakouts excluded for faculty who were American Indian/Alaska Native and of Two or more races because the percentages were 1 percent or less. Degree-granting institutions grant associate's or higher degrees and participate in Title IV federal financial aid programs. Race categories exclude persons of Hispanic ethnicity. Estimates are based on full-time faculty whose race/ethnicity was known. Detail may not sum to 100 percent due to rounding. Although rounded numbers are displayed, figures are based on unrounded percentages.

[1] Percentages are based on full-time faculty whose race/ethnicity was known.

U.S. Department of Education, (2019).

Clearly, whites are superior in number in the Academy. Reverend. Albert Cleage Jr. through his seminal work, *The Black Messiah*, speaks to the perpetuation of white supremacy through education and religion; these two institutions being most responsible for the destruction of black children. He states the "black church and white school perpetuate and hand down from generation to generation the white man's interpretation of the world, of history, of religion, of God, of everything." (p.228). They are a destructive influence because they teach white supremacy through the curricula, the classes, the teachers, the books, the very power symbols, like the preponderance of white teachers and administrators. Rev. Cleage acknowledges there are white teachers who are committed to the success of blacks. But the subtle message, the question from the student, why is everywhere I look I see nothing but white people running everything? Why is the teacher white, the principal white, the administrator?

This leads to the conclusion that white folks know best how to educate blacks. This message is reinforced to both black and whites! If the school gets too many black teachers, administrators, staff, or students. then both begin to question the quality of that institution and the exodus begins. If the school is a PWI no one has an issue with that imbalance. In fact, it is considered desirable and higher quality. HBCUs aren't the answer because they were created to separate blacks and mimic the PWIs. Their existence maintains the legacy of inferiority of institutions. White oversight and funding drive the administrations. Though faculty might be fully "integrated" the message is the same: black inferiority. This assumption is why they were formed, exist, and are maintained. White power structures determine what is valid to learn, who is validated, and who can validate it. No radical change can occur; in fact, a large percentage of the "Black Bourgeoisie and Boule" emanate from their hallowed halls.

Whites exert disproportionate impact on black communities and institutions they don't live or participate in. Whites exert disproportionate impact on lives that are anathema to them, or at best indifferent to. What can be the impact of a hostile enemy in decision-making roles for blacks?
In a learning environment blacks can help heal but cannot be open and speak freely with whites in the room or leadership positions without consequence. There is a punishment for this frankness, esp. if whites perceive themselves as liberal and friends to blacks. Whites don't understand this. It is a wearisome task. Blacks live duality; it is exhausting. Whites can't handle the unvarnished truth. DeAngelo (2018) calls it "white fragility."

Thoughts on the Matter

From our perspective, there is a direct relationship between and intersection of adult education (AE), social justice and white supremacy. Historically, the idea of social justice and adult education as connected and opposed to oppressive systems, including white supremacist systems, is the mantra by many so-termed radical adult educators in the US. We assert that the practitioners of AE, irrespective of color, are not as sincere in their actions to prevent discrimination as their writings might suggest; that they are hypocrites and work actively to suppress the aspirations of the blacks they profess to serve. For example, one current exploitative action which offers lucrative funding and publishing opportunities to boost their careers is the fad of studying incarcerated black men, whom they would be reluctant to hire as colleagues, if they were similarly qualified. In this, they withhold one of the hundred keys mentioned above.

Much like the "great emancipator" has stated previously, they maintain a sense of superiority in their positionality and application of "standards and rigor" to black students; yet, in true Darwinian fashion they fail to provide the supports and accommodations needed for the students entering with known deficits coming from poor quality, public school systems. They admit them and charge exorbitant fees and tuitions, all while denigrating these students that support their elite, parasitic lifestyles. They, being afraid of appearing illiberal or discriminatory, fail to give the necessary corrective feedback and delude the students into thinking their work measures to standards. These students then fail in real-world tests and are viewed as even more deficient with their useless degrees. Racist caricature and impersonation of *ed-u-ma-ca-ted nigras* are widely accepted tools of white supremacy; AE is complicit in perpetuating this *meme* throughout the academy. Again, they withhold the key.

> "One of the marvels of future history will be that it was counted a small matter, by a majority of our nation, for six million people within it, made by its own decree a component part of it, to be subjected to a system of oppression so rank that nothing could make it seem small except the fact that they had already been ground under it for a century and a half." (G.W. Cable. Excerpt from a commencement address at the University of Alabama on June 18, 1884)

This was written by George Washington Cable over 136 years ago, and We wonder how contemporary white academics would respond to this accusation? Notice he said a system of oppression, not a status of slave…he knew it more insidious than a mere condition; it was a complete and total system-wide affair. Every institution was utilized in the oppression, as identified by Neely Fuller Jr.: education, economics, entertainment, labor, law, religion, politics, sex, and war (see Cress-Welsing, 1991). When did this system of oppression change? When was it abolished? How does one abolish such a system? From one side only? From both the oppressor's side and the oppressed? Equally? Simultaneously? Willingly, Equitably? You say amend? You say reform? Yet, where does the power lie? In the institutions and those who control them. Those entrenched interests of the past still exist and get stronger with each successive generation in this republic. For the majority of our nation, when did they stop oppressing? How can they be exempt when it is not only embedded deeply within the system, when it is, in fact, the system? …And as time progresses will it continue to be counted as a smaller and smaller matter?

> "I have seen a land right merry with the sun, where children sing, and rolling hills lie like passioned women wanton with harvest. And there in the King's Highway sat and sits a figure veiled and bowed, by which the traveler's footsteps hasten as they go. On the tainted air broods fear. Three centuries' thought has been the raising and unveiling of that bowed human heart, and now behold a century new for the duty and the deed. The problem of the Twentieth Century is the problem of the color-line." (DuBois, 2008, p. 378)

Poor Dubois, he said the color line would be the problem of the 20th century…perhaps he was too generous in his appraisal of the character of his countrymen, too optimistic, thinking so ingrained a problem could be solved within a century's time. Perhaps he thought America was big enough to admit and overcome its problems…well here we are in the 21st century and riots are breaking out all over the country in major cities over the killing of a black man by police that once again exposed the rotted roots of racial oppression.

And where lie these rotted roots? Cable gives us a clue:

> "First, then, what are these sentiments? Foremost among them
> stands the idea that he is of necessity an alien. He was brought to our
> shores a naked, brutish, unclean, captive, pagan savage, to be and
> remain a kind of connecting link between man and the beasts of burden.
> The great changes to result from his contact with a superb race of
> masters were not taken into account. As a social factor he was intended
> to be as purely zero as the brute at the other end of his plow line. The
> occasional mingling of his blood with that of the white man worked no
> change in the sentiment; one, two, four, eight multiplied upon or
> divided into zero still gave zero for the result. Generations of American
> nativity made no difference; his children and children's children were
> born in sight of our door, yet the old notion held fast. He increased to
> vast numbers, but it never wavered. He accepted our dress, language,
> religion, all the fundamentals of our civilization, and became forever
> expatriated from his own land; still he remained, to us, an alien. Our
> sentiment went blind. It did not see that gradually, here by force and
> there by choice, he was fulfilling a host of conditions that earned at
> least a solemn moral right to that naturalization which no one at first
> had dreamed of giving him. Frequently he even bought back the
> freedom of which he had been robbed, became a tax-payer, and at times
> an educator of his children at his own expense; but the old idea of
> alienism passed laws to banish him, his wife, and children by thousands
> from the state, and threw him into loathsome jails as a common felon
> for returning to his native land." (Cable, 1898, p. 60)

Again, Cable reports:

> "It will be wise to remember that these were the acts of an enlightened,
> God-fearing people, the great mass of whom have passed beyond all
> earthly accountability. They were our fathers. I am the son and
> grandson of slave-holders. These were their faults; posterity will
> discover ours; but these things must be frankly, fearlessly taken into
> account if we are ever to understand the true interests of our peculiar
> state of society." (Cable, 1898, p. 60)

So, again, we ask the question. White people, when did you change? How did
you escape the transmission of attitudes of white superiority and prejudice so
deeply embedded within your fathers and grandfathers? How was this erasure
so completely accomplished in so short of time? We really would like to know.
When did you "frankly and fearlessly" deal with this "peculiar state of
society?" It is short of miraculous that this structural change could occur so
thoroughly among millions of whites without notice of formal action, attention,
or mandate on everyone's part. Was it some sort of universal unconscious
desire on the part of your millions to have such a complete change of heart
overnight? Was it a zeitgeist that blacks were unconscious of? Where were all
the black men when this change of heart occurred? I, a black man, don't recall
my father or grandfathers re-telling of this miracle. If fact, they reported the
opposite: that things never really changed, they just morphed into more

12

insidious and subtler ways to hold us back and keep us down. History documents your vigorous attempts to thwart our progress at every step. Were you deluded to think a ten-year civil rights struggle and "Landmark" legislation would cure the disease? Were we all lulled to sleep under a cover of post-racial sheets? Well, it seems the recent George Floyd killing pulled back those sheets, exposed the nightmare, and unleashed the pent-up rage against this oppressive system, proving once again the boot on our necks is back out in the open.

So, I ask again. When did you change?

> "…And although we were told the degrees and the jobs and the accomplishments would somehow protect us from being treated like second-class citizens; although we were made to believe that working hard and contributing to society would mean society would treat us like human beings, we've learned the painful truth — that's a lie."(Cadet, 2020, p. 59).

Race and wealth are the two greatest dividers of the classes, and main determinants of success in the USA. One avenue to success proffered to blacks is the attainment of a quality education. For generations of blacks, education was the holy grail to be sought at all costs. It was the one thing the white man could not take away from an individual, once attained.

The field of education and the intellectual community should and could be the great equalizing force for an informed citizenry and a fair, equitable society. But instead, both entities have proven to be exclusionary tools of the wealthy and structural supports of racism. It is most distressing when these actions are perpetrated by those intellectuals espousing platitudes of social justice and liberatory education practices…the liberal professors of adult education: they are the Charlatans. They talk the talk, but balk at the walk. When it's time for them to practice what they preach, they show their true colors and lack of courage and commitment to their credos. The long struggle to prevent blacks from getting even a basic education, the long efforts to deny us entry into higher education, the denial of jobs even after we gain the degree…all done by whom? Your best and brightest. At what cost? And who bears the consequences? Both black and white.

> "Practically, through the great majority of our higher educational officers, we are fairly converted to the imperative necessity of elevating the colored man intellectually and are beginning to see very plainly that the whole community is sinned against in every act or attitude of oppression, however gross or however refined." (Cable, p. 78).

We don't question if it's prejudice and racism, we question why it is, especially among so-called liberals and liberatory "professors" that write about the very thing they oppose yet practice daily. The intellectual elite seem the most intransigent when it comes to walking-the-walk. We just don't understand why. The benefits of full inclusion are myriad, why the resistance? Are they afraid of losing their positions? Fear not, the track record of black male inclusion has the opposite effect: a near explosion of opportunities and markets. Just look at the success of the NBA in China. Little Chinese boys aspire to be NBA players. In international relations, the only US citizen able to access North Korean leadership was an ex-NBA star: Dennis Rodman. Instead of acknowledgement of his accomplishment utilizing the benefits of engagement through sport, he was derided. Regardless of your politics and views on international relations, the truth stares us in the face: a 6-foot, 9-inch, tattooed black man from the NBA standing shoulder to shoulder with Kim engendered hatred and ridicule. If this had been a white anything, the script would have been written differently. To prove the point, the antics of bombastic Trump, who publicly satirized Kim as "rocket man" received acclaim for his daring, personal diplomacy.

For decades the white NFL experts determined that blacks lacked the intelligence to succeed in the quarterback position. Given the chance to compete fairly, five of the top 10, highest-rated quarterbacks are black. They lead teams that place in or near the tops of their divisions. The NFL ranks among the highest-rated TV shows. The players, black and white, are among the highest paid in sports. The Super Bowl commands the most expensive advertising dollars in all of TV. NFL franchises are worth billions of dollars. Employment and earnings for TV executives, divisions, announcers, sports analysts, media personalities, ex-coaches and players, etc. have skyrocketed. The gaming industry, stadium employees, adjacent bars and restaurants, pizza delivery services, sports paraphernalia sales, are examples of indirect beneficiaries of black male inclusion. Corporate sponsorship of stadium construction (e.g., Mercedes Dome, Atlanta, GA cost 1.6 billion) has skyrocketed throughout major cities in the US, providing tremendous benefits to local taxing entities, land developers and the construction industry. The list goes on. The point? Full inclusion of black men escalated the profession from a sleepy, white male pastime to a full-blown dynamic, multi-billion-dollar, world-wide entertainment industry. Everyone's getting paid…including more women!

This pattern and the outcome are repeated in every avenue that blacks are allowed to compete fairly. Isn't it time for higher education to take it to the next level, as well? If white intellectuals worry about displacement through expansion, then the empirical evidence should convince them otherwise. To hold onto irrational prejudice is folly:

"Why, then, did this notion that the man of color must always remain an alien stand so unshaken? We may readily recall how, under ancient systems, he rose not only to high privileges, but often to public station and power. Singularly, with us the trouble lay in a modern principle of liberty. The whole idea of American government rested on all men's equal, inalienable right to secure their life, liberty, and the pursuit of happiness by governments founded in their own consent. Hence, our Southern forefathers, shedding their blood, or ready to shed it, for this principle, yet proposing in equal good conscience to continue holding the American black man and mulatto and quadroon in slavery, had to anchor that conscience, their conduct, and their laws in the conviction that the man of African tincture was, not by his master's arbitrary assertion merely, but by nature and unalterably, an alien…

14

"They abandoned the methods of moral and intellectual reasoning" [Editor's emphasis]. (Cable, pp. 61-62).

Herbert Spencer asserts,

> "There is a principle which is a bar against all information; which is proof against all argument; and which cannot fail to keep a man in everlasting ignorance. This principle is contempt prior to examination." (https://www.forbes.com/quotes/4324/).

Therefore, to harbor prejudice and racist attitudes of mind are antithetical to intelligent and right thinking. Yes, so-called intellectuals, scholars, and scientist have supported racists ideologies and superior/inferior claims. And intelligent thinking people have refuted them, along with providing overwhelming proof of the fallacy of those claims. Blacks have consistently exhibited capacities equal or better to whites and others, that refute those claims. Perhaps that's the real fear: you will discover your structural supports for supremacy, built upon refuted whimsical theories and falsehoods, will be shattered without a safety net of comfort. You will have to face the uncomfortable truth. Otherwise, intelligent and harmonious minds cannot exist in this soil.

Epilogue

I'm not saying you owe me anything or that you should be fair, or even to give a damn about me and how I feel. In fact, I am not asking anything of you; you have nothing to give. It is my inheritance. But you are taking advantage of me. (How? You might ask.) Any advantage you gain in support of white supremacy creates an unequal and opposite disadvantage to me: ipso facto. You are, then, an impediment. And I will no longer tolerate it. I have an equal birthright in this country (i.e., XIV Amendment). The American declaration of equality, in part, rejected the status quo superiority of the nobility and kings. The founders declared themselves equals to sovereigns, that no one has rights superior to those of anyone else. These revolutionaries overthrew oppressive English rule; they were not about to reimpose oppression on themselves. This stance repudiates any advantage or particular privilege over others, based on birth. Sumner, in 1848, argued:

> "No man, nor corporation, or association of men, have any other title to obtain advantages, or particular and exclusive privileges, distinct from those of the community than what arises from the consideration of services rendered to the public; and this title being in nature neither hereditary nor transmissible to children, or descendants or relations by blood, the idea of a man being born a magistrate, lawgiver, or judge, is absurd and unnatural. This language, in its natural signification, condemns every form of inequality in civil and political institutions. We abjure nobility of all kinds; but here is a nobility of the skin. We abjure all hereditary distinctions; but here is a hereditary distinction, founded not on the merit of the ancestor, but on his color. We abjure all privileges from birth; but here is a privilege which depends solely on the accident whether an ancestor is black or white.

15

We abjure all inequality before the law; but here is an
inequality which touches not an individual, but a race.
We revolt at the relation of Caste; but here is a
caste which is established under a Constitution
declaring that all men are born equal." (p. 9)

Yet, forces conspired over subsequent decades to undermine this principle of
equality by the use of "tradition" throughout the South, by "custom" as
practiced in the North, and through "shared governance" within the halls of the
academy. Sumner again states:

"Here nobility cannot exist because it is a
privilege from birth. But the same anathema
which smites and banishes nobility must also
smite and banish every form of discrimination
founded on birth."

This birthright equality also repudiates any attempts by those
who would impose a racial caste system. I will not suffer to be treated
inequitably any longer based on color or race. I expect an equitable
bargain and I will have it. If we are equal (and I believe we are, despite
a system that has built-in inequalities) then I am expected to act as an
equal. I have an equal obligation. This is the "American Way."
However, this sword doesn't cut both ways. I treat you as equal, yet
you act superior and hold a superior position. You support others in
their acts of inequality toward me. You support and defend entrenched
systems of white superiority. Despite my best efforts, sometimes
extraordinary efforts, to assert and maintain my equal right to make a
fair living, to access jobs and benefits, I am individually and
institutionally opposed. I have tried direct appeal, the courts, protests,
and accommodation, all with limited or little long-lasting result. You
chip away at even these minimal concessions my efforts have garnered.
You refuse to accept equality on manly terms. Equality is denied on all
fronts, especially economically. I suffer greatly as a result. I am being
grievously harmed by this gross inequality. By my being
disadvantaged, you are being advantaged. How was this advantage
gained? Not through your achievement, but through a system of
inequality. It's time to take your thumb off the scale. Balance out the
inequality by either removing the added weight from your side of the
scale or adding weight to the other side. This is not affirmative action
when I get my full portion, it is equity. I will no longer be cheated out
of my job. I wish you not to leave, as I take my seat beside you. History
has proved we will both benefit greatly by the association. But if you
insist on remaining the obstacle, you will need to be removed, as I
reclaim my inheritance.

"To be a free man is his still distant goal. Twice
he has been a freedman. In the days of
compulsory reconstruction, he was freed in

the presence of his master by that master's victorious foe. In these days of voluntary reconstruction, he is virtually freed by the consent of his master, but the master retaining the exclusive right to define the bounds of his freedom." (Turner, p. 66)

This is not your world or your country unequally, despite your attempts to maintain an imbalance. We all have an equal right in its existence. You may acquire more or less of its bounty or misery, but in a civilized world you cannot claim rights to another's existence, nor can you claim more than your own existence. You owe your existence to the world and to the country. The world can exist without you; you cannot exist without the world. You cannot exist within the world without one another's existence; we depend on each other for our existence. We equally exist, but do not exist equally:

"What need to say more? The question is answered. Is the freedman a free man? No. We have considered his position in a land whence nothing can, and no man has a shadow of right to, drive him, and where he is multiplying as only oppression can multiply a people. We have carefully analyzed his relations to the finer and prouder race, with which he shares the ownership and citizenship of a region large enough for ten times the number of both. Without accepting one word of his testimony, we have shown that the laws made for his protection against the habits of suspicion and oppression in his late master are being constantly set aside, not for their defects, but for such merit as they possess. We have shown that the very natural source of these oppressions is the surviving sentiments of an extinct and now universally execrated institution; sentiments which no intelligent or moral people should harbor a moment after the admission that slavery was a moral mistake." (Turner, p. 81)

I would hope the words of Cable that follow, written over a hundred years ago, will finally ring true and that the white mental bonds that enslaves them will finally be broken in the halls of academia; that the minds of intellectuals will finally see that they are not free if chained by prejudice. Be superior, then, by dropping the pretense that white academia is the sole franchise for knowledge production and validity of experience. Your existence and relevance to the future depends on it. Show superior character by overcoming ignorance and prejudice, intolerance and superstition, and stand boldly beside your black male academic who is striving to civilize an otherwise uncivil institution before it loses all relevance…

"There is a growing number who see that the one thing we cannot afford to tolerate at large is a class of people less than citizens; and that every interest in the land demands that the freedman be free to become in all things, as far as his own personal gifts will lift and sustain him, the same sort of American citizen he would be if, with the same intellectual and moral caliber, he were white." (Turner, pp. 66-67)

References

Cable, G. W. (1898). *The negro question*. C. Scribner's Sons.

Cadet, D. (2020). This Is Why R29's Unbothered Is

Collaborating with Target. *Refinery
29.*Retrieved from Refinery 29.com
https://www.refinery29.com/en-us/author/danielle-cadet

DiAngelo, R. (2018). *White fragility: Why it's so Hard for white people to talk about racism.* Beacon Press.

Du Bois, W. E. B. (2008). *The souls of black folk.* Oxford University Press.

Elazier, K. B. (Spring 2020). Blackmaled by Academia. *Dialogues in Social Justice. An Adult Education Journal, 5*(1).

U.S. Department of Education, National Center for Education (NCES2019-144), Characteristics of Postsecondary Faculty.

Sumner, C. (1900). Equality before the law: Unconstitutionality. of separate colored schools in Massachusetts. *Charles Summer: His complete works*, 51-100. Lee and Shepard

Turner, A. (1958). *The Negro Question: A selection of writings on civil rights on the South.* Doubleday.

Welsing, F. C. (1991). *The Isis papers: The keys to the colors.* CW Publishing.

Blackmaled in Academia

PART ONE

Life in academia when one's personhood and scholarship are denied due to racist structures, herd mentality, and fragile white colleagues.

CHAPTER ONE

Talking about Race in a Predominantly White Space: White Fragility and A Black Man's Critical Race Theory Dissertation 3-Year Experience at a Predominately White Institution

Dr. George Ligon, IV, Florida State University

Change You Could Believe in

It is important to go back to the year 2013. This was a very transitional year for me. In January, I attended the 57th Presidential inauguration for the second term of President Barack Obama. This was my first presidential inauguration. In May, I graduated with my master's degree. In July, I left K-12 classroom teaching to take a job as a large-scale state assessment developer. I moved out of my apartment in the Trinidad neighborhood of Washington, D.C. to a luxury apartment in Alexandria, VA. I made new friends. I entered new social circles and I enjoyed a golden era of young Black professional socializing.

Unfortunately, the golden era did not last long. Within a year, social circles gave way to new romantic relationships. New friends became lost associates. Old building issues resurfaced in the new apartment. The social life in D.C. became an expensive monthly budget item. Work became demanding and dull, and I was ready to find my next opportunity.

I explored the thought of pursuing a doctorate degree during the commencement ceremony for my masters. I revisited that thought more often as work became more unfulfilling. However, at the time, I did not know what to study or where to attend school. I was interested in changing school policies and structures that influenced student achievement for economically disadvantaged Black students, like me growing up. My experiences, at the time, lead me to believe schools in communities of mostly Black people were producing poor outcomes because of policies and the people governing them. Furthermore, while working as an assessment developer, I had begun to make sense of the disconnection between the alignment of assessment, curriculum, and instruction that made it difficult for many of my past colleagues to have success improving the academic achievement outcomes for their students. All these things seemed policy related. Thus, I leveraged opportunities at work to influence states' interpretations of content standards, and ways to create curriculum supports to help teachers better understand them and assessment items. Unfortunately, my employer was only interested in assessment development. So, I joined an educational policy fellowship program to learn how I could affect education policy to help teachers improve student outcomes. In addition, I began looking more into doctorate programs. I felt I might need a doctorate degree to be heard and taken seriously. I began looking at doctoral programs in the D.C., Maryland, and Virginia area. However, nothing appealed to me. I always wanted to attend Florida State University (FSU), but I could not figure out how to do that from D.C.

In January of 2015, I was asked to join an education initiative in Chicago as an Independent Education Consultant supporting Mathematics, school culture and climate, and teacher leadership development. I left my role as an assessment developer to do the work I was passionate about. The experience was phenomenal, and I grew it into a business venture. I worked with multiple school districts across the country, and through this work I saw trends that helped cultivate my thoughts around education policy. As I supported schools and their communities, my desire to influence education policy grew. I continued searching for the ideal doctorate program and eventually found my dream school.

In July of 2015, I visited FSU's College of Education website and saw they had an online doctorate program for education policy and evaluation. To say I was excited would be an understatement. I immediately emailed the program contact with a resume and cover letter stating my interest to join the next cohort. In response, I was told I sound like I would bring a wealth of knowledge to the program and was directed to the individuals handling the application process. I stayed in communication with the College of Education at FSU over the next several months. By late fall, I was fully entrenched in the application process, and by mid-January of 2016, FSU was in contact with me to complete the updated application requirements.

Throughout my application process the website information for the program evolved. A picture and bio of the program director was posted and to my surprise it was a young, inviting, Black woman with locs in her hair. Her experiences and research aligned with my research interests. She was a member of a Black Greek letter organization like me, and everything seemed to be aligning perfectly. I felt strongly that I would be admitted to the program because of my experiences in the field, my statement of purpose aligned with the director's research agenda, and I met the requirements for admittance. I was elated at the thought of continuing my consulting career while pursuing a doctorate in education policy at FSU. I was also excited about the possibility of having someone with extensive experience in my area of interest mentoring me through my doctoral journey. Moreover, I was genuinely excited to have a Black person leading my learning in higher education for the first time in my academic career. This was change that I could believe in. However, 2016 would mark the end of that change and spark the desire to make America great again.

Admission, Cohort, and Faculty

I was admitted into FSU's online Ed.D. program in April 2016. We began our first semester of classes the summer of 2016. Although the program was online, our cohort was required to meet in person once a year for several days as part of the program requirements. During these meetings we were able to meet each other, engage face to face, catch-up, present and discuss our research, and discuss our matriculation through the program. The June 2016 meeting was our first in-person interaction with one another.

My cohort was the second cohort of this new online program. We were a member school of the Carnegie Project on the Education Doctorate (CPED). There were 26 members in our cohort at the start. I was one of two Black men and one of eight Black students. There were two Latinas, eleven White women, and five White men. One White woman openly identified as gay and another White woman openly identified as Jewish. Are ages ranged from mid-20s to late 50s. I was one of the younger members in our cohort. The majority of the cohort was married and most had kids. I did not fall into either of those categories. Our occupations varied widely. Some were classroom teachers, a couple were principals, slightly more than a handful worked for universities, including three at FSU, and one did not work in the field of education. I was the only student who worked as a consultant or traveled over 90% of the time for work. In all, we had a pretty diverse group.

All of our instructional faculty were White women except for three faculty members-a Middle Eastern male, a Middle Eastern female, and our program director that was a Black woman. In addition to this, one of our White female faculty members openly identified as Jewish. She seemed to be a devout Jew. Consequently, our course work and her availability were influenced by her religious practice.

Something often ignored in education, but becomes exacerbated at the doctoral level, is the personal and inherent bias of educators. Education at the bachelor's and master's level does not provide a great deal of space for students to challenge widely accepted notions. Alternatively, doctoral level work challenges students to contribute new knowledge or fill in knowledge gaps. A major point of excitement for pursuing my doctorate degree was the ability to take a research-based approach to explore my practical experiences. However, I would soon find out that exploring whitewashed narratives about society from racially marginalized perspectives was not well received by gatekeepers of the status quo. Moreover, I began to see who gatekeepers of the status quo were.

Grading Issues

Throughout my doctoral journey, there were several courses where I encountered grading issues. I completed my doctorate degree with a 3.8 grade point average and my lowest grade in any class was a C. The C was in one of the courses where I had to fight for a better grade. Excluding that course, the lowest grade I earned was an A minus.

My first encounter with a grading issue came in my first semester of the program. As part of a discussion board (DB) post, we were prompted to answer the question, "What is the purpose of education?" Our reading for this assignment came from Ornstein et al. (2014, p. 52-130), In the chapter entitled, "The Global Origins of American Education and Pioneers of Teaching and Learning." I met all the criteria to receive full credit. However, the graduate assistant (GA), a White woman in her 40s or 50s, grading the assignment deducted 1/2 point out of 4 for the position I took in my response.

From the reading, I positioned that the purpose of education was to create citizens that would adhere to their intended societal roles. According to Ornstein et al. (2014), "We examined the purpose of education as contributing to cultural continuity or change. Throughout the ancient and medieval periods, education was used to preserve and transmit the culture from one generation to the next" (p. 93). Additionally, the educational philosophies of Spencer, Dewey, and Addams about the purpose of education, listed here respectively, contributed to my position: "Enable human beings to live effectively, economically, and scientifically"; "Contribute to the individual's personal, social, and intellectual growth"; and "Assimilate immigrants into American society while preserving their ethnic cultural heritages" (p. 102). The section on the Enlightenment era's influence on education, the Declaration of Independence, and the Constitution, along with Paulo Freire's liberation pedagogy was the impetus for me to answer the question from the perspective of Black people in America (Ornstein et al., 2014). I added,

Education in America predates the Constitution. When America's founding fathers created the Constitution, they did not do it with the intent of all people being created equally. Yet, education, in all forms, was used to indoctrinate all people into social positions. The practical side of good citizenship is developed most successfully in school, but what type of society is projected on students? If the goal of education is to produce citizens, then are the inequities in education, that largely affect low socio-economic student populations and large populations of Black students, meant to promote citizens the founding fathers had in mind? Equity issues in education are a result of equity issues in society. So, what purpose does education have for students with inequities in education?

The readings communicated a generalization about education's role in the development of American society for all people, while omitting its role in the development of non-White groups in the same society. The abovementioned quotes from the assignment readings may sound great when viewed from the perspective of whiteness. However, when these purposes of education are explored through blackness in these eras, either more questions arise, education looks more like a tool of malevolence, or both. This assignment was my first experience with anti-blackness in higher education as a doctoral student at FSU.

I did not receive full credit for the assignment. When I questioned the graduate assistant about my grade, I was informed that my response made her feel uncomfortable and my position on education as a mechanism to lock people into social roles was inaccurate, and that was not the goal of schools. Since this was one of my first assignments, I did not feel comfortable pushing back any further. A couple of weeks later a similar situation occurred with another DB assignment. After meeting the criteria for full credit, 1 out of 4 points was deducted and I received the following message:

"George,

I appreciate your passionate desire to see a change in the inequity of education in the United States. I agree with you that equity in education has

been a raging problem for many years. You specifically identified African Americans and brought attention to the history of enslavement of Africans by European Americans. In discussing issues of equity in education today, how do you plan to use this historical context to further your research? What is the scholarly relevance of slavery to current issues and will there be valid research to support that? I wholeheartedly agree that the history of African American slavery and degradation in America has had a profound effect on many of the societal constructs, and education specifically, but I am wondering how you will bridge the two together in your research."

I felt the need to be cautious in my response because she said I made her feel uncomfortable with the abovementioned DB post. So, in response, I stated, This would be a great face-to-face conversation. I worry about text being taken out of context while embarking on a relatively sensitive issue. Hopefully there are no issues with tone in my response. I understand how the implications of Black history in America can be a very sensitive topic. So, I will preference my response by saying there is no ill intention meant in my response.

Slavery was one aspect of inhumane practices I highlighted that was used by the dominant group during the early settlement of America. Killing, imprisoning, disenfranchising, discriminating, segregating, and separating non-White groups, especially Black people, from their families and culture were used to create a system that advanced one group over others. If you are not familiar with Critical Race Theory, I suggest checking it out. It could provide some additional insight on the question you posed. For now, I will do my best to provide an ample response.

Critical Race Theory (CRT) pays attention to the idea that race matters (Delgado & Stefancic, 2013; Ladson-Billings & Tate, 1995). It pertains to acknowledging the historical aspects of racism in the educational system and how history has led to the state of persons in the urban landscape of today (Smith, 2005). The historical aspects of racism precede the 20th century and slavery was one component of the system that impeded the advancement of non-Whites in America, especially Black people. The focus is not on slavery, but the systemic oppression imposed upon non-White groups in America. I emphasized Black people in America, because they were the predominant group to fall victim to these oppressive acts, having endured oppression since chattel slavery was introduced to America in the 1600's. Although Civil Rights legislation aimed to make the constitution more accessible to all groups, Rigby & Tredway (2015) contended, "African American and Latino communities face organizational and social structures that systematically differentiate access to goods, services, and opportunities" (p. 4). These oppressive social structures were rooted in the institution of slavery.

From our readings, Ornstein et al. (2014) stated, "Freire asserted that the school's curriculum and instruction can either indoctrinate students to conform to an official version of knowledge, or it can challenge them to develop a critical consciousness that empowers them to engage in self-liberation" (p.127). It is important to understand that inequities in education are rooted in policies and practices that were once openly accepted in the U.S., such as Jim Crow laws. During the Civil Rights era many Americans lead by Black Civil Rights leaders such as Martin Luther King, Jr. choose not to conform to the social norms of the time because it violated their basic human rights. They fought to be liberated. However, evolved systems of oppression continue to deny full access to American liberties for non-White groups, especially Black people.

There was no change in my grade after the exchange with the GA. I eventually raised my concerns to the program director because she was the professor of the course. During one of our check-ins, I shared my concerns with the GA's grading of my assignments. The director heard me out, stayed indifferent, but told me to keep pursing my research interest and to make sure I kept advocating for my grades. Afterwards, she divvied up the grading for our cohort's DB posts between herself and the GA. I was included in her group, and I was no longer penalized for exploring assignments through blackness in the course.

I continued with my research agenda and explored it as much as possible in each course. I cannot prove that my research interest had any influence on my grades, but I did fight for grades more than I think any other student in my cohort did. This included: receiving a lower grade on a major assignment where I clearly meet the criteria for a higher grade to maintain an A in the course; dealing with grades not being updated for weeks then receiving a final grade of B+ right before grades were due to the university while maintaining an A throughout the course; meeting the point criteria for an A in a course, per the syllabus, but being given an A- before advocating for the correct grade; waiting two months for a professor to respond to me about my final assignment to update my final grade; and receiving a D on a final assignment to drop my grade from an A- to a C. In all these cases, I successfully secured the appropriate grade except for the C. The irony in that is I had a 3.95 grade point average going into the semester I received that C. Moreover, the professor of that course was the first university representative I communicated with about my interest in the program. She was the one that said I sound like I would bring a wealth of knowledge to the program. These were just a few examples of my experiences fighting for fair grades.

Noticeable Social Shifts in Attitudes and Behaviors

I kept working as an education consultant right until the data collection phase of my dissertation. As I traveled, I noticed stark shifts in the attitudes of people. Around this time President Obama was nearing the end of his presidency; Colin Kaepernick was kneeling during the national anthem to protest police brutality; and Donald Trump was running for President. White micro-aggressions grew throughout the fall of 2016 to outright racism by the spring of 2018.

For example, on a connecting flight from Chicago to Detroit, I was upgraded to first-class before takeoff. As I was placing my belongings in the

26

overhead luggage bin in first-class, a White male passenger yelled, "Hey just be careful and watch my stuff. Don't mess up my stuff." I told him, "It was all good. I'll look out for it." He went on to say, "Hey, your stuff isn't supposed to be up here. This is for us." I said, "I know that's why I'm moving my stuff here." He said, "No, it's for us, you're supposed to put your stuff back there. This space is for us up here." I responded by saying, "I am us. I'm sitting in first." The gate agent, flight attendant, and my seat mate all shook their head in agreement, and this guy's face immediately turned beet red. He apologized profusely throughout the flight, but the damage was done. Everyone knew what had transpired.

In another example, I was supporting a White female teacher in a school district that was demographically 45%-Latinx, 48%-White, and 2%-Asian and Black students. During Donald Trump's presidential inauguration, the teacher forced crying Latinx students in her fourth-grade class to sit and watch the inauguration or face disciplinary action. Several Latinx students ran out of the classroom crying hysterically. I pulled her to the side to discuss the sensitive nature of this event for these students. I brought attention to the divisive and exclusionary nature of Trumps campaign rhetoric and how it may have personally affected these kids. She kept reiterating this is a part of American history and students need to know it. Later, this same teacher had her students write an essay about the qualities of a good slave master to celebrate the last day of Black History Month.

In my doctoral program these experiences were more subtle but proportional to what I saw across the U.S. During our first face-to-face meeting my cohort was encouraged to develop a method of communication that would work for us to support one another in our journeys. We used a non-school associated app that gave us the ability to chat as a group. By the second face-to-face meeting, the Black students in our cohort recognized the shifts in attitudes and messaging communicated in the group chat by White cohort members. As a result, minoritized cohort members' participation in the group chat became virtually nonexistent. Apparently, we each felt a way about the things White cohort members were comfortable communicating in the group chat. Moreover, it was off-putting and each of us in our own way was not sure we had support if we raised these concerns in the group chat.

Unbeknownst to us collectively, we, as minoritized students, started reaching out to each other individually. In our one-on-ones we discussed commentary we noticed from the group chat that had covert racial undertones. In one of these conversations, I expressed my concerns with the way our White cohort members criticized our program director and how often they did it. The cohort member I was speaking with responded by saying, "Yeah, I deleted the group chat after last semester when I saw it was some bashing going on." In a conversation I had with another minoritized cohort member, the concern was raised that our White counterparts did not give any consideration to our lack of participation in the group chat. In addition, we felt they spoke unprofessionally about our program director, criticizing her abilities and her capacity to lead the program and discussing her personal life. They would complain about anything she did they did not agree with. Whatever they wanted changed or they had a problem with, they would come together in the group chat organize their complaints and then strategically raise issues to our program director and other faculty within the department until things were changed to their liking. They leveraged the cohort members that worked for the university to get inside information and communicate their frustrations to influential people. Yet, they did not do these things in other courses. As other minoritized cohort members and I continued discussing group chat dynamics and our program experiences, we realized some of us were having similar issues with assignments and grading from the same faculty members. Consequently, we decided to create our own group chat for us as Black and Brown students to have space to discuss our experiences and issues.

White Fragility in Practice

According to DiAngelo (2018), White fragility is the wide range of "defensive responses" of White people used to "reinstate white equilibrium, return to racial comfort, and maintain dominance in racial hierarchy" when racial worldviews, positions, or advantages are questioned or challenged. It is a powerful tool of white racial control used to protect white advantage. Some of the emotional responses include anger, fear, and guilt. Some of the behaviors include argumentation, silence, and withdrawal (p. 2). My earlier examples of issues I experienced with grades, travel, and work were examples of white fragility. DiAngelo, a White woman, affirmed the foundations of white fragility are:

- Preference for racial segregation, and a lack of a sense of loss about segregation
- Lack of understanding about what racism is seeing ourselves as individuals, exempt from the forces of racial socialization
- Failure to understand that we bring our group's history with us, that history matters
- Assuming everyone is having or can have our experience
- Lack of racial humility, and unwillingness to listen
- Dismissing what we don't understand
- Lack of authentic interest in the perspectives of people of color
- Wanting to jump over the hard, personal work and get to solutions
- Confusing disagreement with not understanding
- Need to maintain white solidarity, to save face, to look good
- Guilt that paralyzes or allows inaction
- Defensiveness about any suggestion that we are connected to racism
- A focus on intentions over impact (p. 68).

In the examples provided below, my White doctoral cohort members exhibited textbook white fragility in practice. During the spring of 2018 we took a lab course as part of our degree requirements. The instructor for this

28

course was our program director. According to the objectives and description section of the course syllabus, this course was to facilitate students' ability to engender original thinking and research on important educational issues as they relate to issues of human rights and social justice, in local and global contexts. Students were to return to their prior identified "problem of practice" and explore their intuitive theories of action on the topic. In addition, were asked to identify students specific constructions of race, class, and gender with respect to human rights, identify specific theories of justice and oppression, and apply theory and real-time events to deeper understandings of research and practice. Finally, they were to reflect on what it entails to be a researcher and leader in their research context with asocial justice lens.

As we progressed through the readings about race, racism, and power dynamics, the complaints from our White cohort members about our director, the course assignments and readings, and their inability to work on their dissertation in practice prospectuses (DIPP) resonated loudly through our department. Some of the things that were said about the director by our White cohort members were:

- I feel your pain. The organization of these courses, especially the director's, is terrible
- The instructor has to make the call. My guess is the director is too proud to ask for help
- For someone that was hired to direct the program, she has a very vague understanding of the whole dynamic
- Not that I want to keep talking about the director but…
- I wonder if the director would give each of us one week off from DB post. I emailed her about excusing us from a DB
- The director has checked out of this course a long time ago and left it to the TAs to figure out.
- I think we are reading all her sources for her dissertation.
- In all honesty she has surprised me this semester. Not in a positive manner
- She is just a mess right now and she needs to get it together and stop Blaming us like we are a bunch of whiners.
- I tried to convey to her that our chairs want us to be doing DIPP work During these six weeks but I don't think I was successful
- I'm getting the feeling that the faculty might not be enamored of the director
- Has everyone had the phone call/skype with the director? In passing, during our conversation, she told me she separated from her husband and now each is in a different place and each has kept one child

Some of the things that were said about the course by our White cohort members included:

- What a depressing thing to see
- I did not expect this class to be so dense. I thought it would help us advance with our DIPP
- Yeah. A lot of readings and "busy work."
- Worthwhile lenses, but not everyone will use those at this point.
- I did some of the readings for this week. I don't recommend starting with West. I recommend starting with Ladson-Billings or Delgado
- The yes talk by Sir Ken Robinson was riveting! I highly recommend watching it
- It's sad I'm already checked out for this semester. This class seems unrelated to anything I can use to finish my prospectus
- I've always found Cornell West to be interesting and engaging on the tele, but that chapter had me start and stopping. It was thick like the dog on the ranch in the morning
- I mean, this is her area of specialty and she's throwing TONS of stuff at us, which I think is inappropriate for the purpose and context of this course
- I do agree. This course is wholly inappropriate
- What did we decide for the readings for this week, read one and write one? I agree that it would be more effective if we did all those DIPP activities now and the social justice half later

These comments represented a small percentage of comments communicated by our cohort's White students during the first month and a half of the semester. These comments reflected many of the actions and foundations of white fragility expressed by DiAngelo.

During the first week of April 2018, I got a call from our program director. By this time, we were communicating regularly about my DIPP because she was my dissertation chair. However, this call was different. She called to tell me that she would not be returning to FSU after this semester, and she wanted to make sure I defended my DIPP before she left. The following week she sent an email to the rest of our cohort informing them that she would not be returning. The responses in the group chat from our White cohort were prototypical behaviors of white fragility. They sought absolution (DiAngelo, 2018). They sent messages of shock, astonishment, and concern. The ones that worked for the university said everyone was shocked that our director was not asked to return. They talked about sending her flowers and a thank you card. However, a minoritized student said we should advocate for her return. In response, one of the very vocal White cohort members said, "I agree. If you choose to write a letter it should be an individual decision and address your own personal experiences." This was a completely different approach than the unified efforts-a need to maintain White solidarity to look good and save face-used throughout the director's time with the university (DiAngelo, 2018, p.

68). Individuality and discretion were the tactics used to exclude solidarity across racial lines in support for our Black director.

After reading about white fragility for one of our course assignments, I got to see it in practice. It had profound effects on the rest of my schooling. I lost a mentor, an ally, and an advocate. I grew extremely concerned about the ability to conduct my research study because of this event and the experiences I had as a doctoral student. It seemed like whiteness had won, and in a way, I saw our director as a protector of blackness. In my mind she created a safe space and gave permission to openly leverage academia to explore the world through my black lenses without fear, shame, or ridicule. For the first time in my educational career, it was ok to be unapologetically Black. Her dismissal compelled me to feel like I lost all of that. I became extremely concerned about the implications of her departure and what it meant for my dissertation in practice prospectus (DIPP).

My Dissertation

The title of my dissertation was "Hope for Whom? A Critical Race Theory Policy Analysis of Florida's House Bill 7069 Schools of Hope Policy." In my research, I explored the policy's potential to improve poor performance outcomes for economically- disadvantaged Black students attending persistently low-performing schools. My original doctoral committee consisted of our program director, two White men, one with significant research experience with minorities in higher education, and one White woman. As a result of my program director's dismissal, I defended my DIPP to an all-White committee.

My program director/dissertation chair informed me the committee member with experience with the minorities in higher education research agenda would take over her role as my dissertation chair. Two weeks after the program director was gone, I was introduced to a new committee chair. She was a White woman with a different research agenda than mine, and our first interactions were rocky to say the least. Her initial approach was completely opposite of what I had grown accustomed to with my first chair. Initially, I felt my new chair was abrasive and autocratic. We had to have a conversation to clear the air and develop an understanding for each other's style. I successfully defended my DIPP during our summer face-to-face session and began data collection and analysis in the fall.

I appreciated my new chair for her organization, thoroughness, prompt feedback, knowledge of the dissertation format and process, and critiques. However, the process was nothing like I imagined it to be. It was long, lonely, grueling, and isolated. My chair and I did not talk as much as I expected or would have liked. There were occasional check-ins by email. If there was an issue with something that could not be addressed in an email we'd hop on a quick call, but those never went beyond ten minutes or so. Since I did not have a critical race theory (CRT) expert guiding my research, I spent a tremendous amount of time reviewing literature to replace the conversations I thought I would have. The most challenging part was not having methodological examples to reference in addition to not having the CRT support I was expecting. I spent hundreds of hours analyzing data, cross referencing it with literature, pulling additional sources and proving to myself that my findings were valid. I would talk about my findings to anyone I could get to listen to get feedback. As I wrote what I found and discussed it in chapter 5, I wrestled with how to discuss my findings.

Finding my academic voice was difficult. I was looking for a way to convey what I found from my methodological approach because I was looking for a way to make it palatable for an all-White committee. I had to explain how the tenets of CRT demonstrated the policy's potential to improve poor outcomes for economically-disadvantaged Black students attending persistently low-performing schools such as:

- Critique of liberalism- the policy used liberal approaches to address students attending schools consistently rated D or F by ignoring race when 88 of 89 schools had student populations with more than 50% students of color
- Interest convergence- the policy used elementary schools with high populations of economically-disadvantaged Black students to circumvent the state's charter school policy to establish and expand charter schools without school district interference
- Permanence and pervasiveness of racism-empathetic fallacies and essentialism were used by politicians to alter the context of the public problem and develop state statutes that fit their narrative, along with structuring the statutes to reinforce racialize outcomes and racial spaces
- Narratives-the policy did not support economically disadvantage Black students in all persistently low-performing schools according to the interview findings of a large school district with persistently low-performing schools in the state.

I made bold assertions in my findings. I connected state legislators spearheading the policy with the charter school industry through campaign contributions, work relationships, and family ties. I was attending a school in the state capitol and preparing a document that would expose the very politicians that met there to legislate. I was advocating for Black students from disadvantaged backgrounds at the expense of the establishment. I had the audacity to try to present this to the gatekeepers of my degree when my experiences had shown me this type of research was not well received. So, what do I do? I decided to do what I had always done to that point: speak truth directly and support it with sound evidence.

The day of my dissertation defense I was accompanied by one of my close fraternity brothers. There was a late change in the committee. One of the White women on the committee took a new job so she was replaced by an Asian woman. For my defense I was given 10-12 minutes to present my findings, discussion, and recommendations. It had been over a year since I defended my prospectus. So, I felt it was important to revisit the problem of practice, literature, and methodology guiding the study. I started talking about my dissertation with the committee before the official start of the defense to get a feel of how much they knew about my study. Surprisingly, it seemed like everyone was well read up on it and they were very interested in the presentation of my findings. After I defended, I walked out of the conference room without one concern. I knew I had nailed it. My frat brother asked me if I was nervous and I told him not at all. The committee deliberated for around 15 minutes and then my chair called us back to the room. She congratulated me as Dr. Ligon and hugged me. It was one of the greatest moments of my life thus far. She followed up by saying, "We all realize the amount of work you put into your study. It's very clear in your findings. We want to let you know we commend you for a job well done." That meant as much to me as the successful defense. After discussing the next steps with me and taking pictures, the faculty member who was supposed to be my replacement chair pulled me to the side to ask me about what I had planned next. He told me how much he enjoyed reading my dissertation and that I should get it published in a journal. He asked if I mind him sharing it with a couple of colleagues and told me to keep at it with my research agenda. After all I had gone through to get to that point, I felt I truly earned every bit of my degree.

Lessons Learned

I learned progressiveness for Black people in education is governed within the comfort of those with power. In this society the Black leaders of progress generally become casualties for their cause. It was evident in my grading and in the case of our program director. However, it is important to stand within your convictions. As my dissertation defense proved because they will win out in the end.

I also learned that Black people have to live with a double consciousness as Du Bois calls it, or a duality of self as I like to call it (Du Bois, 1967). This was not a new lesson, but a lesson that was further cemented through my experiences. The students of color in my cohort participated in two doctoral programs as exhibited by the two group chats. We were subjugated to the mainstream program dominated by Whiteness. Yet, our collective cognitive dissonances from navigating white spaces combined with our individual experiences and issues with racial undertones lead us to create a space for ourselves. This is a common practice we still see in university student groups, employee resource groups, and historically Black colleges and universities. As long as minoritized people have to enter into White society, there will need to be a place we can retreat to so we can take the polar bear suit off.

Additionally, a Black person's acceptance in White western society is predicated on White peoples' collective comfort of their Blackness or the absence of it. When this comfort is upset, functions of White fragility can manifest in forms so subtle it can be too late when it is realized (DiAngelo, 2018). Thus, it is important for Black people to deepen their understanding of whiteness and White fragility to successfully navigate White spaces.

References

Delgado, R. & Stefancic, J. (2013). *Critical race theory: Thecutting edge* Temple University Press.

DiAngelo, R. J. (2018). *White fragility: Why it's so hard for white people to talk about racism*. Beacon Press.

Du Bois, W. E. B. (1967). *The souls of Black folks: Essays and sketches*. Fawcett.

Ladson-Billings, G., & Tate, W. F., IV. (1995).Toward a critical race theory of education. *Teachers College Record, 97*(1), 47-68.

Ornstein, A. C., Levine, D. U., Gutek, G. L., & Vocke, D. E. (2014). *Foundations of education*. Wadsworth Cengage Learning.

Rigby, J. G. & Tredway, L. (2015). Actions matter: How school leaders enact equity principles. In M. Khalifa, C. Grant & N.W. Arnold (Eds.). *The Handbook of Urban Educational Leadership*. Rowman & Littlefield.

Smith, C. A. (2005). School factors that contribute to the underachievement of students of color and what culturally competent school leaders can do. *Educational Leadership and Administration*: *Teaching and Program Development*, 17, 21-32. Retrieved June 11, 2016 from http://files.eric.ed.gov/fulltext/EJ795072.pdf

CHAPTER TWO

Black & Educated:
Understanding the Experiences of a Black Male Doctoral Student

Vashon Broadnax, Ball State University

Abstract

This two-fold chapter discusses the topic of increasing and preparing Black males who can serve in faculty and senior leadership roles within higher education. The Association of American Colleges and Universities (2019) discovered a 29% rise in students of color enrollment, between the years of 1996 and 2016. This discovery has brought awareness to American higher education that the student population is becoming more diverse; unfortunately, the numbers of faculty and administrators did not show the same growth in diversity. Focusing on Black males, career mobility in higher education, which offers a better livelihood for them and their future generations. Ultimately, there are existing challenges that hinder the ability to diversify doctoral programs that allow Black males to pursue faculty and senior leadership positions. In this chapter, I analyzed the experiences of a Black male navigating a doctoral program and his career development. I look at various pedagogies used in developing Black male doctors allowing them to qualify to serve in faculty and senior leadership roles. Overall, the importance of this manuscript is to look at how institutions of higher education can better develop, retain, and diversify their faculty and senior leadership.

Keywords: Black males, career development, mentoring, doctoral programs

Introduction

I had the opportunity to interview Mike, a Black male doctoral student at a Historically White Institution (HWI), and fellow fraternity brother. One of the reasons that prompted me to interview Mike came after reading of Dr. Carter G. Woodson's (1933) book *Mis-Education of the Negro*. Dr. Woodson's text caused me to have a variety of mixed feelings, because many of the issues discussed in this seminal text still exist in 2020. As I took a deep dive into the literature about Black males in higher education, the discourse that was being presented allowed me to believe that colleges and universities have not had much success in preparing the African American student, particularly the Black male doctoral student.

I was perplexed at what I had read, because I am pursuing a doctoral degree and I share many of the same issues (e.g., isolation, lack of mentorship, financial support, career advancement) discussed in my review of literature. Aware that many of these issues still exist, created concerns about the future for Black males pursuing a doctoral degree at a historically White institution (HWI). Reading other literature about Black male doctoral students that attended HWIs, I found a significant amount of research on best practices supporting this population. Unfortunately, I found very little information about the research being applied in the doctoral spaces.

To better understand the background factors that are connected to the Black male doctoral student and their experiences, requires scholars to review the populations' perspectives and issues (Bentley-Edwards & Chapman-Hilliard, 2015). One of the significant issues affecting this population is the low degree attainment of Black male doctoral students, which emphasizes the need to develop support systems. In 2017, the United States Department of Education (USDOE) discovered that African Americans accounted for 8.8% of all doctoral degree recipients conferred by postsecondary institutions in the United States (USDOE, 2018a). While the African American doctoral student enrollment has risen, it must be noted that this number includes those who have graduated from Historically Black Colleges and Universities (HBCU). Therefore, the actual number of Black doctoral students that graduated from HWIs is lower. It is important to be aware that pursuing a doctoral degree is important for African Americans because professional degrees are a new standard for social capital which leads to middle class status (Johnson-Bailey et al., 2009). From there, increased opportunities in social status is one of many reasons this interview with Mike is important for others to understand the Black doctoral student experience.

I asked Mike several questions and analysis of his responses allowed me to connect to existing research in order clarify the issues. As the author of this text, I feel it is important to tell the story of the Black male doctoral experience and encourage administrators of doctoral programs be aware of this population. Ultimately for my audiences, I intend to bring awareness of the struggles that exist for Black males navigating a doctoral program.

Why Enroll in a Doctoral Program?

I had a chance to sit down and interview Mike about his experiences of being a Black male in a doctoral program. To start our interview, I asked Mike about the driving factors to choosing his current institution. Mike responded by saying,

> "This specific institution is regionally recognized for being an outstanding program in education. As I inquired about the program and spoke with students currently in the program, they spoke highly of how the professors are supportive and well recognized in the field of education. Most importantly, I wanted to learn from the best. [I wanted to get earn a terminal degree so that I would not be denied career opportunities that required certain academic credentials."

Mike unapologetically responded to me by sharing his frustrations,

> "I want to teach at a college, because there are not many
> professors who look like you and I. Oftentimes, it is
> hard to discuss issues affecting my community. Most
> professors I've come in contact with, never lived a day
> in my life, or they have other research or personal
> interests. I did not want to put others in the class at
> unease, with such a sensitive topic. More importantly,
> I want to have a voice at the decision-making table. I've
> found that many decisions for people of color were
> decided by White people."

In understanding his responses, I found out that Mike's career advancement had stalled because he only earned a master's degree. Having only obtained a master's degree, this shortcoming limited Mike from career opportunities, because better paying positions required a terminal degree.

Finding Mentorship

Continuing our interview, I asked Mike about his thoughts on mentorship and what that entailed. Mike explained,
"Finding a mentor at the doctoral level was a little harder. Mainly because most of my current mentors do not have a terminal degree. But when I did meet a person to be my potential mentor, I found out that she was overwhelmed with being a mentor for other students at all levels. Not to mention that she was working extremely hard to get her name out in the academe. I then remembered the saying of how Blacks must work twice as hard to get recognized by Whites."

Mike was pointing out that Black faculty were overworked and ineffective to meet the needs of Black students, let alone Black doctoral students. The American Association of Colleges and Universities (2019) highlighted that 74% of full-time faculty in American higher education are White. This goes to show that finding a mentor that looked like Mike is a question of concern in higher education.

Discussing Race in a White Classroom

I asked Mike to tell me a time when he was part of a discussion about race in the classroom. Mike immediately chuckled and proceed to explain, "Many of my White classmates were clueless about Black issues and would expect me to answer. I remember there was one time when a White classmate of mine discussed that the school he graduated from did not have any racial issues. I found out that the school he graduated from had recently hired a chief diversity officer to manage the hostile racial climate. I did not want to out the kid, but I just shook my head in disbelief."
Mike went on to explain that when the professor discussed theories he became disinterested by saying,

> "I was never much of a theory person, because I knew they were not
> developed to understand my [Black] experiences. How can I relate to
> a theory that is focused on preparing White males? I questioned, where

is the research conducted by authors of color?"

Mike explained to me that he assumed the professor had limited experiences discussing race-related topics and chose not to push the agenda. Mike shared his frustrations of not being able to talk about race-related topics by saying,

> "I paid this tuition to learn from the best. But only to find out that they were not able to teach me what I needed to know to reach my aspirations use "goals." That sort of hurt me because I now feel naïve to believe that this program was well recognized. I had an overwhelming level of uncertainty if I made the right choice in doing this program."

Mike's comment caused me to reflect on DiAngelo's (2011), *White Fragility,* a manuscript that I reviewed. The term "white fragility" coined by DiAngelo, recognized that minimum racial stress becomes unbearable, ultimately causing a wide range of defensive moves in the form of emotions or behaviors. I was able to understand the White perspective, and how some Whites have lived in environments that protected them from race-based stressors (DiAngelo, 2011). Especially in education settings, Whites were only required to have a single multicultural course or cultural competency training, which almost never discussed racism or White privilege.

Advice to Future Black Males Pursuing a Terminal Degree

As I wrapped up Mike's interview, I wanted to get his advice on how to survive my doctoral program. Mike leaned back and thought for a second, then replied by saying,

"Be strong! Remember the poem Invictus by William Ernest Henley. Be strong".

> Mike did not recite the poem, but I was able to remember the poem from when I was being initiated into my fraternity during my undergraduate days.
> Out of the night that covers me
> Black as the pit from pole to pole
> I thank whatever Gods may be
> for my unconquerable soul
> In the fell clutch of circumstance
> I have not winced nor cried aloud
> Under the bludgeoning of chance
> my head is bloody, but unbowed.
> Beyond this place of wrath and tears
> looms but the horror of the shade
> And yet the menace of the years finds
> and shall find, me unafraid
> It matters not how strait the gate
> how charged with punishments the scroll
> I am the master of my fate
> I am the captain of my soul. (Henley, 1875)

This poem by William Ernest Henley essentially reminded me that any road to completing or obtaining a certain object, will not be easy. As a Black male, I am not afforded many opportunities that some of my White counterparts have. Therefore, I have to remind myself that I am the only one who can control my destiny.

Conclusion

As I conclude, I recognize that I am closely connected to Mike's story, because I am maneuvering through a doctoral program as I write this chapter. As a member of this population there have been recurring incidents (e.g., support systems, feelings of isolation, communication, Whiteness) in my doctoral program that have prompted questions. Are all experiences of a Black doctoral students positive? How are the relationships of Black doctoral students with non-Black students and faculty? Are Black doctoral students valued by the institution? There are numerous theoretical frameworks on graduate student development. Unfortunately, many do not account for systemic and institutionalized racism.

In the academe, faculty members may have used several teaching pedagogies to promote active learning in their classrooms (Cook-Sather, 2011). Aware that many teaching pedagogies lack a component on racism, learning preferences, and lived experience of Blacks; continues to cause challenges experienced by those like Mike. The absence of race in teaching pedagogies, brought forth the emergence of research on racism. When discussing the topic of race in higher education, leading scholars such as Ladson-Billings and Delgado-Bernal questioned on whose knowledge the discourse is based and deemed credible (Yosso, 2005). Essentially, there need to be more Black doctors who talk about race in higher education. Because there is an immense lack of research by Black authors, in top-tier research journals.

In spite of the desegregation of HWIs that occurred some sixty years ago, I believe that higher education still has not supporting Black males pursuing a doctoral degree. Seminal literature related to Mike's experience showed that Whites and their good intentions towards educating Blacks was a large undertaking because the focus was to transform Blacks, not develop them (Woodson, 1933). What I took from that statement, is that Black students received an education of lesser quality, in comparison to Whites. The outcome from this inferior education can be witnessed in standardized exam scores. Ford and Helm (2012), affirmed that Blacks had a small influence over standardized tests, in which they were expected to perform as if they were White students.

Thus, literature discussing issues in academia experienced by Black males contributed to the negative stereotypes in higher education. Unfortunately, White liberal faculty, who tried to contribute to the Black community by informing higher education about their plights, only added to the negative beliefs, attitudes, and practices that were created by the dominant

CHAPTER THREE

White Manning

Frederick V. Engram Jr., University of Texas at Arlington

Abstract

As first referenced in a December 2019 article (Engram), I first published the term "white manning" White manning speaks to the inability of white men to recognize when they're taking up unnecessary space (Engram, 2020). White manning takes its roots from whiteness, white supremacy, and white privilege (Engram, 2020). It is meant to be inclusive for white men only, excluding virtually everyone else. White manning allows for white men to perpetuate the problematic cycle of being obtuse to issues pertaining to both communities of color and women. The "value of sameness" speaks to the need for representation for students of color to exist at predominately white institutions (PWIs). The low number of diverse stakeholders on college campuses is due in part to how white manning disallows for the consideration of equitable representation. This chapter is meant to address how white manning and its overuse of space has negative implications for any legitimate diversity, equity, and inclusion efforts at PWIs. For the purpose of this chapter, Black is representative of all members of the African diasporic family. It is not meant to be exclusive of African Americans solely.

Keywords: Blackness, white manning, white privilege, value of sameness, PWIs, HBCUs, racism

Attributes of White Manning

Imagine this: you're seated at a conference table at work the morning after hearing about the death of yet another unarmed Black man or woman. You hear a comment within your earshot that states one of the most insensitive things, *I bet they'd still be alive if they would've simply complied!* The voice then becomes closer and you realize who made the snarky comment. It's Tom, the Assistant Vice President of Enrollment Management and one of your committee co-chairs. You then inform Tom that the comment that he made was a bit insensitive to which he replies, *Lighten up, we all have to die at some point!* Obviously, this is a fictional scenario but it's a scenario that I'm sure many of you who are reading this can relate to or have experienced in some capacity. This is an aggressive version of white manning. This person typically feels that he can say what he pleases and doesn't really think much about any consequences. Why? Because he's a white male at a predominately white institution and best buds with the university president, chairman of the board of trustees, and campus ombudsperson. He, like many of the other campus decision makers, have a baseline understanding of diversity, equity, and inclusion (DEI); the version of DEI that still centers white persons and more exclusively white men. Legitimate experts of DEI work understand that in order for you to create actual change you have to create discomfort. It is also fairly safe to assume that if Tom were a Black man or woman, he would've been fired long ago. The following sections will provide further context for understanding white manning.

White Manning as Dominant Voice

Research confirms that White males in the academy are often considered to be the wisest in the room. This is laden in white supremacy and misogynistic narratives. The white-male effect and alarming incoherence are most certainly attributes of this persona (Barker, 1995; Olofsson & Rashid, 2011; Piller, 2019). Especially when research shows us that this particular group of individuals is often one of the most mediocre in academia (Dutta, 2019; Eaton et al., 2020). Privilege and connections, although unfair, are generally their saving grace (Dutta, 2019; Eaton et al., 2020). Research further indicates that women often receive lower salaries and fewer resources to do equal or more fulfilling work (Guarino & Borden, 2017). Women faculty members often perform more service-related tasks as a way to step in the gap for pre-tenured faculty members (Guarino & Borden, 2017). At many institutions, this service task often falls into the hands of women of color (Guarino & Borden, 2017). The additional optional service often has negative implications in their trajectory toward becoming a full professor at the same rate as their white male counterparts (Guarino & Borden, 2017). In full consideration of academia's opposition to Blackness, the academy stands passively in the background as white manning runs rampant.

Institutional decisions, policies, and procedures are often implemented with the vision of the majority in mind. This absence of legitimate thought continuously perpetuates the normalization of white male mediocrity. The bar is often lowered for the entrance of the dominant class who are then used as a barometer for the entry of everyone else. The not so hidden truth is that the barometer for entry is white maleness, but the password for entry is superior impossibility also known as rigor. The most recent "operation varsity blues" admissions scandal is an example of the aforementioned. William Singer who served as the ringleader of this unethical and white privileged operation presents one of the most dominant forms of white manning. His dominance is more alarming because it deals with the exchanging of goods or currency for space that isn't rightfully their own (Berghel, 2020). His level of emboldened strategic moves was only allowed because of his whiteness. If William were a Black person, he would've been imprisoned for an insurmountable amount of time because a Black person with that level of authority is always a threat to whiteness.

Privilege and Proximity

An indelible characteristic of white manning is its constant proximity to privilege. Like white supremacy, white privilege, and all other white race-driven accesses white manning is not based upon wealth or its distribution of it. There is often the argument from non-wealthy whites that they do not have privilege. White people often fail to realize that the societally-normed privilege of their whiteness gives them the opportunity to ignore anything that questions their unearned space and opportunities (Combs, 2018). What they also fail to realize is that their birth in America alone is, in fact," privilege." As Berghel (2020) discussed about the 2019 "operation varsity blues" admissions scandal, the notion of "quid pro quo" and its availability to whiteness isn't a new thing. It often appears in various forms, mainly as privilege. I recall when I was in the sixth grade and a white male classmate of mine, upset with me because he could not have his way, decided that the use of the n-word was a good idea. The young man did not come from a wealthy family nor did he "appear" to have access to it. However, because of the color of my skin he deemed my existence less than his or inferior. Just as quickly as the violence of that word left his lips my response followed with my fist. The response of my principal was of course one of a punitive nature. My classmate was not punished for his violence that gaslit my violent response. Instead, he was pacified by his privilege and the biased nature of our white female principal while I was made the villain. I was suspended from school and sent home. How is that not privilege? Focusing on the effect instead of the cause is another benefit of white manning.

In consideration of the current climate in higher education, academia, and the two raging pandemics in this country, the volume of white manning is on full blast. The amount of conversations that are being had that center opportunity for discussion and growth is deafening, and the white men are placing themselves in the way. All experts know that they are experts of some things but not experts of all things. Part of the humility of this designation is knowing when to step aside and make space for someone who knows more than you do. However, that is not in the genetic code of white males who manifest white manning. During this time, we have seen more white men jump up and attempt to educate the affected about racism and its byproducts. The level of gaslighting that is occurring is mind boggling. White manning can also be upheld by persons who are not cishet white men, who use their space to prop up mediocre and unvetted white men. This action is typically done via bartering for some level of proximity to his privilege.

The current administration of the United States speaks directly to white manning, proximity, and privilege. Every person who had any level of loyalty or proximity to the current president has benefited from his positioning. He is a classic case of white manning because he fits the full criteria. He is a white male, inexperienced, unvetted, mediocre, cishet, wealthy or presumably in proximity to it, racist, sexist, bigoted, obtuse, and unwilling to yield space even when he is out of his league. The dichotomy for other candidates running for office within his party during 2016 forced them all to decide whether to lean into their morals or desire to be elected (Chaturvedi & Haynes, 2019). Many of them chose their political careers and proximity to the incoming president over true patriotism (Chaturvedi & Haynes, 2019).

Enablers of White Manning

In full consideration of the culpability and full ignorance of white privilege we must also understand the erroneous conscience of it (Block, 2019). Recognizing that ignorance directly causes sin because it lacks the knowledge necessary to deem something sinful (Block, 2019). Over the past few weeks since the murders of George Floyd and Breonna Taylor at the hands of police officers, several members of the president's circle have each spoken out against the notion of systemic racism. Senator John Cornyn of Texas is a great example of someone who vehemently opposes the existence of systemic racism but provides no legitimate understanding of its meaning (Scott, 2020). Instead of yielding that he does not have the bandwidth to speak on the controversial topic, he leans into white manning. An individual has to employ an unfathomable amount of obtuseness to disavow a system that has existed for over four centuries. Similar to white privilege white persons treat white supremacy and systemic racism like a consumer complaint not worthy of further investigation or acknowledgement. It is unnerving to ignore the way that racism in America allows each of the culprits to continue engaging in practices that are harmful for Black people.

Universities also engage in this very same behavior; whether it is intentional or unintentional is debatable. President Jerry L. Falwell, Jr. of Liberty University is another individual who benefits from white manning and his enablers. Liberty University and the Falwells have a long-storied history with racially charged statements and ignoring the voices and complaints of Black students, staff, and faculty (Rankin & Schor, 2020). Falwell's twitter rant which was aimed at discrediting Virginia Governor Ralph Northam, over his responses to the COVID-19 pandemic ricocheted and hit Black Liberty University stakeholders instead (Rankin & Schor, 2020). His racially charged social media outburst in any other instance would cause the offender to be "cancelled" or lose their job. However, he has suffered zero personal losses and his enablers allow him to continue making crass decisions. Employees and students took to social media to denounce his comments and to announce their resignations and transferring to other institutions (Rankin & Schor, 2020). Ranking & Schor (2020) pose that an awakening is occurring at Liberty University. The same reckoning that is currently happening with the rest of the world (Rankin & Schor, 2020). Will Liberty University and institutions with similarly racially tone-deaf thinking patterns survive this awakening and distance themselves from enablers of white manning? Or will they continue to operate as if this way of thinking will not continue to harm marginalized groups, namely Black stakeholders? [Note: Jerry Falwell, Jr. was forced to resign his post August. 2020, and sued Liberty University for defamation in October 2020]

Centering Blackness: What About Us

It has been said that scholars who study race and racism spend more time discussing whiteness than centering Blackness. I disagree and believe that it is quite possible to highlight and bring awareness to how whiteness and its byproducts continue to oppress marginalized groups while also uplifting and centering Black scholarship. Black students have expressed their desire to be in proximity to their community, which is considered the value of sameness (Engram, 2019). This is a discussion that continues to occur at a majority of white campuses (Engram, 2019). Black students continuously discuss harm done to them at the hands of whiteness as they seek to embark upon a higher education (Engram, 2020). Seeking to better yourself in a place that should be considered safe should not send you into a crisis. It should also not be a test of your endurance or ability to battle micro-agressive behaviors before you are welcomed into that space. In a twitter thread created and titled #BlackInTheIvory by doctoral students, Joy Woods and Dr. Sharde Davis intended to create space for Black students, faculty, and staff at majority white institutions. The space was intended to allow the defined group to share in their experiences and find community.

The thread went viral and has now appeared in several media outlets bringing attention to the lived experiences of Black folks in academia. Each person shared their experience under the auspices that our responses would not be used in a random data set. A few days after the viral tweets, a white scholar announced that he had pulled the data and would provide it to any white scholar who wanted to learn about the Black lived experience in academia. The incident provided an opportunity to witness white manning and white scholars who inevitably fail at reading the room. When several scholars, both white and Black, informed the individual of his misstep another white male scholar decided to intervene on his behalf. Another form of white manning, where instead of realizing that there was an obvious violation, he assumed that all of the Black scholars who complained as well as the white co-conspirators were somehow incorrect. The space that was created for Black people in academia and in close proximity to it was still not safe from white manning. White manning is a visceral reaction for whiteness to insert itself in all spaces and it will provide any level of justification for doing so. It is also why liberal whiteness with uninterrupted privilege is a dangerous combination (Jilani, 2019). It should not take an act of congress for Blackness to be left alone. Asking for equitable opportunities for Blackness to persist and to thrive should not be considered a radical idea.

Conclusion

As Black scholars continue to advance our research agendas and navigate what is becoming our new normal, it is fair to assume that it has become more important now than ever before that we dismantle all systems of oppression that kept our Blackness undervalued, underappreciated, underpaid, and over-policed. Black voices are demanding drastic changes to what will shape the course of this country for future generations. As this country, institutions, and organizations begin to reckon with their benefiting from chattel slavery, Jim Crow, and white supremacy it is most important that Black people begin to receive what has been overdue to us for a very long time. As the shift in this country begins to occur we must also remember that we have a great responsibility to create a change that will have a lasting impact. Part of these changes at the academic level should include revisiting and revamping hiring practices, strengthening mentoring, and supporting opportunities, as well as creating space for advocacy without the fear of retaliation. Anti-Black, sexist, and otherwise problematic rhetoric that has been embedded into institutional frameworks also requires disruption. The time to balance the scales of humanity is now.

References

Barker, J. (1995). White Working-Class Men and Women in Academia. *Race, Gender & Class, 3*(1), 65-77.

Berghel, H. (2020). A Critical Look at the 2019 College Admissions Scandal? *Computer- IEEE Computer Society, 53*(1),72-77.

Block, E. S. (2019). White Privilege and the Erroneous Conscience: Rethinking Moral Culpability and Ignorance. *Journal of the Society of Christian Ethics, 39*(2), 357-374.

Chaturvedi, N., & Haynes, C. (June 2019). Polls and Elections: Is Loyalty a Powerful Thing? Republican Senate Campaign Strategy and Trump Coattails in the 2016 election. *Presidential Studies Quarterly, 49*(2), 432-448.

Combs, G. (2018). White Privilege: What's a family therapist to do? *Journal of Marital and Family Therapy, 45*(1),1-15.

Dutta, M. J. (2019). "No, You Did Not Do Me a Favor" The Whiteness Games of Merit. *Departures in Critical Qualitative Research, 8*(4), 50-56.

Eaton, A., Jacobson, R., Saunders, J., & West, K. (2020). How Gender and Race Stereotypes Impact the Advancement of Scholars in STEM: Professors' Biased Evaluations of Physics and Biology Post-Doctoral Candidates. *Sex Roles, 82*(3-40), 127-141.

Engram, F. (2019). *Institutional and Systemic Racism and How it Affects African American Graduate Students Enrolled at a PWI: An Interpretative Phenomenological Analysis.*(Doctoral Dissertation). Northeastern University: ProQuest.

Engram, F. (2019). *Diverse Issues in Higher Education* titled *"The Dangers of Interjection White Narratives in Higher Education Hiring.*

Engram, F. (2020). An Act of Courage: Providing Space for African American

Graduate Students to Express Their Feelings of Disconnectedness. *The Vermont Connection, 41*(4), 18-25.

Engram, F. (2020). White Manning and Lacking Institutional Preparedness Amid Tragedy. *About Campus, 25*(4),1-5.

Guarino, C. M., & Borden, V. M. (2017). Faculty Service Loads and Gender: Are Women Taking Care of the Academic Family? *Research in Higher Education,58*(6), 672-694.

Jilani, Z. (2019, May 20). What Happens When You Educate Liberals About White Privilege? *Greater Good Magazine: Science Based Insights for a Meaningful Life*. Retrieved from https://greatergood.berkeley.edu/article/item/what_happens_when_y ou_educate_liberals_about_white_privilege

Olofsson, A., & Rashid, S. (2011). The White (Male) Effect and Risk Perception: Can Equality Make a Difference? *Risk Analysis, 31*(6), 1016-1032.

Piller, I. (2019). On the conditions of authority in academic publics. *Journal of Sociolinguistics, 23* (5), 521-528.

Schor, E., & Rankin, S. (2020, June 24). *Evangelical Liberty U rattled by its own racial reckoning*. Retrieved from https://apnews.com/40e007fd912b23ec5e82476e3ad4f8c0

Rankin, S., & Schor, E. (2020, June 9). *Jerry Falwell Jr. apologizes for tweetthat included racist photo after black alumni denounce him.* ' Retrieved from: https://www.usatoday.com/story/news/nation/2020/06/09/liberty-universitys-jerry-falwell-jr-sorry-racist-photo-tweet/5325247002/

Scott, E. (2020, June 17). *Sen. John Cornyn's distorted interpretation of 'systemic racism' displayed what a lot of Americans don't get about it.* Washington Post. Retrieved from https://www.washingtonpost.com/politics/2020/06/17/sen-john-cornyns-distorted-interpretation-systemic-racism-displayed-what-lot-americans-dont-get-about-it/

CHAPTER FOUR

We Are Unicorns

Headley White, Bethune-Cookman University

According to the Census Bureau, only 1.8% of Americans over 18 held a Doctorate degree in 2019; of that 1.8 %, only 2.8% (129,000) were Black males. (U.S. Census Bureau, 2020).

After receiving a Ph.D. in Curriculum and Instruction, Social Science Education, I found employment quickly, even in the midst of the beginning of the "great recession." The job was at a small private predominantly white institution (PWI) in a small, rural South Georgia town. It was my first full-time professorship in academia, and I was happy to be employed. However, I was not naïve; I knew there were racial strife and scars in the south. I had to conscientiously watch where and how I treaded. The town still held on to its agrarian past over industrialization; in fact, a main attraction to the area were working plantations that doubled as B&B establishments. And there I was, a Black male who grew up in New York City and Miami with locs that reached my lower back working at a predominately white university in a sleepy southern town.

The college was only 30 minutes from the Florida border, but worlds away in many respects. The town did not quibble about its "separate but equal" institutions. Although there are those in urban areas and northern states who may harbor similar feelings, many hide their beliefs for economic reasons or to promote a façade of acceptance. The town had two distinct school systems: the county school system and the city school system. One was predominantly white, the other predominantly Black, and the two rarely intertwined. This was in the first decade of the 21st century, and it was widely accepted for each high school to hold two proms.

It also became quickly apparent that at small universities you wear many hats. Not only was I a professor, I was also the coordinator of the middle and secondary education program. The majority of students enrolled in my education courses were nontraditional and worked in various fields throughout the United States or served in the army. Due to my years teaching in multicultural classrooms in rural and urban settings, I was accustomed to working with students from diverse ethnic and socioeconomic backgrounds. However, my previous middle and high school teaching experiences were in South Florida and rural North Florida, areas with higher concentrations of minorities. I was comfortable in these settings, but not one that was overwhelmingly white. For many students at the university, I was their first Black instructor at any level, in any setting. At first, the discomfort shone on their faces. Therefore, on the first day of class, I sat among them and waited. One student was clearly frustrated, "Where is this Dr. White person? I have places to go." I was so new to the program that they had not had time to post my photo to the department's website. After several minutes of awkward silence, I got up and introduced myself to collective gasps.

I shared with them my educational background, the purpose of the course, how I intended to prepare them to become qualified instructors and pass the teacher certification exam. There were many micro-aggressive encounters with students throughout my tenue at this university. The most prevalent occurred when using the Socratic method to discuss challenging pedagogy. I would tell them of incidents of seeing bias in the classroom both as a student and educator, they would respond, "I never saw that" or "it's been my experience that..." or they wouldn't believe that effects of segregation still remain. They disguised their challenges as responses to question my intellect and expertise. Having attended both an HBCU and PWI, I understood the not so subtle nuances in both tone and word choice. While it did not ruffle my feathers, I did not expect to witness white college students, mostly adults, exhibit such adolescent behaviors. As the first semester progressed, class interactions improved as cohorts were enrolled in several of my courses. In fact, the campus became an oasis. I avoided traversing the city due to the unsettling, blatant displays of an unwillingness to desegregate.

During my two-year stay, there were two major incidents that remain etched in my memory, and both center on a candidate's itinerary. The first happened when I was asked to pick up a candidate from the airport and take him to a plantation where he would be staying. This was problematic on several levels; the first and most obvious, why, when there are chain hotels, would the chair of the selection committee arrange to have the candidate stay at the plantation. Second, I lived nearly an hour away from the university and I would have had to pass the university to collect him from the airport then pass it again to drop him off at the plantation. I suggested they arrange for a driver or allow him to rent a car. Neither was acceptable to the committee for assorted reasons. At this time, I had a six-month-old son and my wife also worked full-time in a neighboring city. None of the reasons superseded the fact that I simply did not want to go to a plantation, and it bothered me that none of my colleagues could fathom why. I did not see the allure of slavery or the romanticism of antebellum architecture. The plantation is advertised as a quaint respite to relive the past. The working plantation, including slave descendants who call the quarter houses home, also offer cooking classes and a speaking series. The event occurred approximately 15 years removed from "the awakening" that we are now experiencing. Shouldn't the self-projected, liberal whites have understood my refusal? After all, I had shared with them the experiences I encountered when I traveled within a 40-mile radius of the school to observe preservice student interns. Unlike them, I had to call and give the school a "heads up" when I would be on campus to observe students. Having a black person arrive on campus would cause panic; thus, in an effort to mitigate the chances of me being harassed or worse, I made sure to provide a detailed description of my car and myself – a Black man with locs and ask for the name of a contact I could mention were I stopped.

The second faux pas surrounding the candidate's itinerary occurred at the local country club where a number of university vice presidents played. The committee arranged the luncheon and invited faculty; as I had never been there, I was given instructions on what to do. When I arrived, you could hear the proverbial pin drop as I entered. All Arian eyes were on me. I chuckled when I noticed that even the kitchen doors opened and I could see all the black faces looking at me. Soon upon entering, I was asked if perhaps I had inadvertently confused the entrances. Though it was the 21st century, my gut told me otherwise. A colleague yelled, "Dr. White!" and motioned me over. Utensils dropped. It was quite overwhelming, even though I had no delusions that these incidents were behind us. I sat and attempted to make small talk with the candidate, but it was difficult. The luncheon was a haze, the trauma was real.

I knew that I could not remain at the institution much longer. Soon, thereafter, I was afforded an opportunity to work at a state PWI much closer to home and where I earned the doctorate. I was excited. I was once a student there, and I was very familiar with the area, schools and some faculty. Unfortunately, I was wrong. Even though I thoroughly enjoyed the experience, in many ways, issues of students' resistance to having a Black male professor remained pronounced. For instance, I taught "Teaching Diverse Populations" and many students were not overly thrilled that I attempted to ensure that they understood the gravity of their prospective teaching assignments, and that they would most likely work with students that did not look like them or share their cultural norms. The course was designed to demonstrate the importance of diversity and the opportunities that it carries. They were to learn how to grow their cultural competence and value differences. The course touted not only racial and ethnic diversity, but also diversity in ability and sexual preference, as they may have a once closeted student share their identity with them. Over the years, students reported on their evaluations that I dwelt too much on the "diverse part" of the course. Some would complain to other professors or take their concerns to the chair or dean. What I didn't realize until later is that many of my colleagues, who were overwhelmingly white and female, were also passive aggressive in the way they dealt with concerns centered on diverse students. Intentionally or not, these colleagues reinforced destructive behavior that will color their instruction, inflicting more detrimental consequences on an already underprepared and taught population. They were also quite dismissive of prospective teachers of color and quite eager to counsel them out of the program or spread negative evaluations of their performance to others. For example, they would use graduate students to further their own research interests, while not nurturing students' interests. They would also be hesitant to address issues related to racism, cultural competency or microaggressions. Many undergraduate students of color would decide to go elsewhere for advanced degrees. Conversely, faculty's hesitance to address the previously mentioned issues, led to a general malaise amongst minority students. Working teachers enrolled in the graduate program felt that the approaches favored by some professors were either outdated or culturally irrelevant.

Because these very people occupied positions of power in the college, I would try to warn some students that they needed to follow specific steps in order to matriculate through the undergraduate program as smoothly as possible. I found myself doling out some of the same advice that was given to me when I went through the college's Ph.D. program. Make sure that you don't "C" yourself out of the program; receiving a C in a graduate problem is akin to an F in undergrad. Double and triple check any work, research or proposals. Keep some things close to your vest because they might take your work for their own. I often found myself as the lone Black professor being asked to speak for all Black men or Black people. They would imply that the Black male students were from poor or single-family homes, and often confirm each other's bias. Coupled with students' experiences and being caught in the middle, I found myself mentally tired.

It was an interesting situation, and I would find myself in a Black colleague's office debriefing about the problems we encountered with some of the same students and what to do about it. students exhibited the passive aggressive tendencies of my colleagues. As a Black faculty member, I had to consciously make sure that I didn't come across as trying to retaliate, through grading or being condescending. Being a Black instructor at a predominately white college means you have to give the appearance of being in total control and not needing help because subconsciously you know you are being measured by your ability to work within the program. The weight of failure is heavy. They may never hire another minority faculty member or worst hold the new minority faculty to higher, unrealistic standards. Signs of weakness go against the very foundation of education and mentorship. Even though a mentor was assigned, it is very hard to discuss issues they do not, cannot or will not try to comprehend. I have since learned that my Black colleagues and I were not alone. Instructors of color faced similar issues throughout the college and university, which explained the high turnover of minority faculty. I consider myself luckier than most because I had people to talk to and trusted. However, no level of solidarity could withstand the onslaught from faculty and students who were uncomfortable receiving instructions from someone they did not respect.

In any organization, when key personnel leave for advancement, an organizational shift occurs. In my case, it was not for the better. When a key ally of faculty of color left, I found myself increasingly having to answer questions about "aggressive teaching." I was told that I was teaching Martin Luther King, Jr. all of the time, which was not true and would have been evident had I been observed. What I was teaching was cultural competence, and I taught it as an underpinning across all of my courses. Increasingly, I had to defend myself more and more and that became uncomfortable. In addition, the Black colleague I would debrief was being harassed by students because she had an accent. Students claimed they could not understand her. I stood up for her and in doing so made my situation untenable. I was later to learn from a reliable source that there were cadres of students that would get together to sabotage teachers' end of the semester scantron surveys, and if I knew it, I am

52

sure others knew it as well. From the many depictions of white females' passive aggressive nature, I have no doubt that such 'bombing'- [the act of a clique of students either influencing or literally changing teacher surveys or making serial complaints against certain professors] occurred from the majority, white female student population and faculty. Although the pay was commensurate with my skills and the amenities were well apportioned, neither was worth being the Black race's representative or facing increased scrutiny for things my colleagues did without thought or repercussions. Again, I was painfully aware that I could not remain at the institution. Mental health is important, you realize that you have to go where you can make the most impact.

Various academic studies and anecdotal evidence show that Black professors at predominantly white institutions have a relatively high burnout rate. According to a 2017 report from the National Center for Educational Statistics, Black males only account for 3% of full-time academic faculty. They do not remain (American Council on Education), and it takes them almost twice as long to be awarded tenure. Many do not receive promotion or advance to positions of leadership. After seven years, enough was enough. I was fortunate to receive offers from two historically Black universities. While there are always personality clashes and difficult colleagues and students, you find that you do not have the same pressure to qualify and codify your Blackness. You are able to exist on your credentials and are given the opportunity to teach those who look like you, who are willing to learn from your expertise and experience. This is in essence the rationale for the continued existence of HBCUs: Making sure Blacks could and would evolve from the "Normal School" into situations where students, graduates and faculty become experts in varied fields in spite of the racism that necessitated their creation in the first place, and the reason they remain necessary not just for students, but faculty and administrators, too. As we approach the middle of the 21st century, their presence is paramount as they provide an academic respite when Blackballed or Blackmaled in white academia.

References

Cruz-Soto, Thomas A. Jr. "Full disclosure: Examining the experience of male faculty of color at a predominately white institution" (2017). *Theses and Dissertations*. 2380.
https://rdw.rowan.edu/etd/2380

U.S. Census Bureau. (2020). *Educational Attainment in the United States: 2019.* (2020, June 30).Retrieved June 30, 2020 www. Census.gov

Griffin, K.A. (2020). *Redoubling our efforts: How institutions can affect faculty diversity*. American Council on Education. Race and Ethnicity in Higher Education. Retrieved September 27, 2020 from
https://www.equityinhighered.org/resources/ideas-and-insights/redoubling-our-efforts-how-institutions-can-affect-faculty-diversity/

National Center for Education Statistics. Fast Facts: Race and Ethnicity of College Faculty. Retrieved on September 27, 2020 from
https://nces.ed.gov/fastfacts/display.asp?id=61

Blackmaled by Academia

PART TWO

Vantage points of black men trying to thrive in academia while not being allowed to be Black and coping with double consciousness within the context of white silence.

CHAPTER FIVE

Are We Allowed?

DaShawn Dilworth, Institute for Democracy & Higher Education,
Tufts University

4:19 PM   **Background Noise**
*"We selected individuals who we deemed would be a better fit for
our office culture and leadership team dynamic. However, you were a
strong candidate and interviewer."*

This was the response I read the day after summer internship decisions
were supposed to go out for myself and my fellow student affairs graduate
students from a major association. Reading those words in the already
minimalistic email back from the employer, I felt a whirlwind of emotions. I
felt frustrated that they had taken so long to simply reject me, and it was only
after I emailed them that I received a decision. I remember feeling lost, because
that institution and program was my first choice along with receiving
affirmations from my interviewers that I did well. And more than anything, I
felt like an imposter who had finally been "found out." I questioned everything
from how I answered the interview questions to my application materials, and
even questioned my place within my own graduate program. However, the
most important question I didn't think to ask came to me much later: What did
they mean by a "better fit?"

When this question finally surfaced in my mind, all the initial feelings
came rushing back along with a new one: curiosity. It did not take me long to
discover who accepted the internships which, in turn, started to reinforce some
insecurities as well as some criticisms I was having about the field of higher
education and student affairs. The "better fits" for the office were two White
women, which unsurprisingly mirrored the overwhelmingly White and
Woman dominant staff. After discovering this, I started to think about whether
"fit" meant more qualified or simply White. Despite not being surprised by this
hiring outcome, I was still shocked and felt a burden within my chest every
time I reflected on the experience.

Many tears, frustrations, and research articles later, I look back on the
experience, understanding what I experienced was neither an anomaly nor an
isolated incident. As a student affairs practitioner, I now understand and have
the language to explain why student affairs seem to mistreat its practitioners of
Color, specifically Black men. While student affairs as a field may enjoy and
advocate for the ideas of diversity, equity, and justice, those ideas must remain
comfortable for the majorly White profession, which leads to these concepts
being just that: ideas. Words are used in mission statements and words are used

to convince Black staff members that they will be supported because of the espoused value of the institution.

Yet, the entity of higher education and student affairs is obsessed with this concept of a sense of belonging for their students that enter through the doors of their institutions. But what messages are really being intentionally and unintentionally sent about the value of diversity within university settings when most student populations are still predominantly White and there remain issues surrounding the representation of faculty and staff of Color? Specifically, regarding Black men, Pritchard and McChesney (2018) tell us only 5% of student affairs practitioners identify as Black men compared to the 71% who identify as White, with 51% women, 20% men. This is very telling given that nationally, White students only encompass around half of the student population demographics (Pritchard & McChesney, 2018). So where is the disconnect? Reading these statistics, I think of the number of Black men who are told our voices are valued and our perspectives are needed, yet in the same vein we are allowed into higher education spaces at lower rates in comparison to our White peers. And I also think of the lack of support networks to inspire and allow us to progress in the field. Many of us are here to help students of similar experiences to ours, whose voices are silenced and whose access to equitable resources in higher education is continually prevented by the very barriers we hope to dismantle.

From my experience and others, I want to know how many Black men are told of their worth in higher education spaces, yet find themselves facing hiring discrimination, or worse, a lack of support within the very spaces they hope to change. I seek to tell a story of how we are kept from the academy and when we are allowed in, we are policed to obey the White mainstream narrative under a watchful eye. And as graduate students who are told prophetic stories of being able to enact change, yet we face backlash from the very people who claim to support us simply because we are being too vulgar, too raw, or simply too Black. I simply wish to know when are we allowed to be Black men, uncompromising and unapologetic, in these spaces which claim to need us but fail us every day?

9:05 PM   **Do I Fit?**

"Although your qualifications were impressive, we have chosen an individual who more closely fits our needs. We encourage you to review other employment opportunities here at our institution."

One of the invisible yet tangible barriers to certain areas or positions within the field of student affairs is the concept of job fit. Job fit is considered an amorphous and ambiguous term often used within the student affairs hiring process, which can be used to legitimize certain decision-making processes behind closed doors. Reflecting on my own experience in the aforementioned story at the beginning of this chapter, I am amazed at both how bold and vague the connotations of using the word "fit" is as the reason for selecting one candidate while rejecting another.

While it can seem like an isolated incident, "job fit" has been identified as one of the many reasons many new professionals choose to leave a position within their first year in their role (Renn and Hodges, 2007). There are many conclusions that can be drawn from the use of "fit;" yet none of them really answer the question of why someone was rejected for the position. Was it because they were less qualified? Was it because they had less experience? Or was it because they did not align with the office culture, the staff, or the mold already created by the hiring committee of who should be in the position?

While it can be easy to assume this narrative as simply an anecdotal phenomenon referencing a small group of student affairs professionals, it is important to consider two necessary elements that contribute to the broader picture. First, there is very minimal literature established surrounding the topic "job fit" and its multifaceted existence within the field of higher education despite a very high usage in decision-making processes. Within this context, it is also important to note there is a growing body of literature articulating how "job fit" is essentially a myth connected to discrimination, and the construction of white supremacy within the walls of higher education (Reece et al., 2019). From this body of knowledge, scholars acknowledge that both data and experiences of how "job fit" as a concept creates organizational privilege favoring the hiring of White professionals, particularly White men, with the intentional exclusion of professionals of Color and LGBTQIA+ professionals (Browning and Palmer, 2019).

This is directly connected to the second element of the broader picture which is the utilization of the use of Critical Race Theory (CRT) to investigate higher education spaces. Acknowledging race and racism as real constructs allows for a broader understanding of what Black male professionals experience within the sphere of higher education. For example, the experiences I and many other Black men detail about their treatment in higher education cannot simply be anecdotal. Critical Race Theory exists with the tenet of counter-storytelling, which allows for the naming of a reality running counter to the perceived normative reality often held by White and non-Black professionals within the field (Delgado & Stefancic, 2012). With the existence of Twitter hashtags such as #BlackinHesa or #BlackintheIvoryTower, there is a story constructed normalizing the existence of both overt and covert forms of institutionalized racism along with the impact it has on Black student affairs professionals and other professionals within higher education.

This narrative is also important because it showcases the ability of racism to veil the experiences of Black men and women while also providing a story justifying the reason for these racist structures. When there is a dominant narrative created that doesn't align with the narratives of Black professionals, it is often viewed as a problem of the professionals rather than that of the "standard" narrative or the systems at play. This is an element of racism meant to distract people from the focus of inequitable policies and practices to the individuals or groups being the source of the issue (Kendi,

2019). From here, it is also necessary to acknowledge the inherent overlap and compounding nature of oppressive forces centered on someone's identity through the lens of intersectionality (Cho, Crenshaw, & McCall, 2013).

As a Black man, it is important for me to distinguish the ways in which racism affects Black male professionals in higher education because their struggle is uniquely positioned in relation to Black women and Black Trans folk. This is not to say a certain struggle is superior to another, rather giving voice to how racism shapes itself differently to impact different Black identifying individuals. Given the way in which Black men are portrayed in the media, there can be an assumed, underlying bias Black men have to navigate against based on the perception of what people deem Black men to be or do. Black men are violent, often easy to anger, hypersexual, absentee fathers, diversity experts, and so many other fallacies.

With these ever-present narratives, the degree to which Black male professionals are allowed to be authentic and represent their communities often comes at the price of consistent micro-aggressions to behavior policing by colleagues. For example, I remember sitting in a meeting related to my student affairs work and brought up the topic of collaboration with offices that supported our university diversity and inclusion initiatives. I got a pleasant smile during the meeting and was told my idea sounded great. Later, my supervisor came to me mentioning that I had spoken out of turn in the meeting and advised me that I should avoid speaking at those meetings again. I was hurt by this and tried to understand why this was happening while also processing my feelings of frustration as well as annoyance. My supervisor told me later my reaction had come across as aggressive and I would need to do better about checking my emotions while in the office.

This is only one example of countless instances in which Black men are told we are needed, yet consistently sent messages that we do not belong. My experience is one of many for myself, but also in connection to many other Black men in student affairs who have been policed in this manner from being dissuaded from wearing a #BlackLivesMatter t-shirt on casual Fridays to being mistaken as a custodial worker rather than an education professional. Along with the minimized presence of Black men within student affairs and higher education, there is less opportunity for coalition-building amongst Black men which could be seen as intentional. As a result of this, there is more policing and enforcement of the few Black men who are present especially those who hold higher level administrator position. While Black men do represent 8% of the senior leadership positions across higher education, there is very minimal research garnered around their retention in these positions given the track record of Black men leaving senior leadership positions amidst controversy (Pritchard & McCheskey, 2018). Black men are also often placed in stereotypical senior leadership roles, usually as chief diversity officers or in charge of overseeing support services catering to the most marginalized student populations. This begs the question as to whether Black men are viewed as only capable of overseeing areas of diversity directly connected to diversity regardless of their expertise or tenure in the field of higher education. While we may be needed to help further the success of all students, especially Black students, Black men are constantly reminded how expendable we can be within a system ultimately not meant for us.

8:08 PM   **"Can We Get some Space?"**
"Dialtone……………………………………"
"Outlook Inbox (0): No Notifications"

While it can be easy to blame the individuals, the HR department, the student affairs division, or even the institution, the real culprit will always seek to remain hidden. Though it can be seen rather minuscule, the true culprit acting as the right-hand man of systemic white supremacy can be seen as space. Space, meaning the very environment where our institutions, offices, and the resources to accomplish departmental as well as institutional initiatives carries an often-overlooked power within the workplace. Higher education is no different from any other major institution within society in that space can be inherently political (Black et al, 2020; Tull, Saunders, & Hirt, 2009). With resources and physical university space often minimal or rationalized, bureaucracy can emerge in order to maintain a system of allocation of those resources albeit not entirely equitably distributed.

With this background in mind, the "battles for space" can also be connected to money and a perception of importance in the university organizational structure based on the allocation of resources. For instance, Jenkins (2016) makes a connection between the use of social justice and diversity in university mission statements as well as strategic plans, yet offices for diversity, equity, and inclusion receive inadequate funding to operate. And in thinking of this misuse of funds, it is also necessary to consider who often staffs these offices and executes these initiatives. Because of this, there can be a perception of a lack of value attributed to these Black men and women as well as their work given the lack of funding directed to their development.

In thinking of this dichotomy, there is also a necessity to differentiate the experiences of Black men and Black women. Intersectionality becomes an important lens to view the individual experiences of Black men, not as a means of comparison, rather to provide an equitable sense of legitimacy in the Black male narrative (Cho et al., 2013). For instance, it is important to consider the vast impact of Black women's efforts to build coalition and support for one another through the creation of "Sista Circles" (Croom et al., 2017). Because of a need, it is common for Black women to come together in creation of these spaces in order to provide places for authentic conversation and support to build a community of resilience.

Given the small network of Black men within student affairs, similar networks are not as common, and when they are created, they can be hard to maintain due to limited numbers of Black males and policing of their behavior in the academy. Let me be clear, this is NOT to say that Black women and "Sista Circles" do not receive scrutiny from White administrators and also face struggles in maintaining their network. Rather, it is meant to articulate the point that the sheer number of Black women collectively within student affairs places them in a marginally better position to create and work to maintain this coalition. In fact, Black women must still navigate these unsupportive environments in order to protect these "Sista Circles" while also funding and investing time in these spaces for them to continue to thrive often without outside help. In thinking of Black LGBTQI-identifying folks, they also navigate these hazardous environments without much formal or informal supports. While there are Pride or LGBTQ centers present on campuses (albeit underfunded), there are rarely spaces that prioritize the overlap Blackness and sexual orientation/gender identity where professionals can feel supported in both identities. With these experiences in mind, it is also important to acknowledge that the creation of these groups for support, while helpful, is also a response to symptoms of the larger illness of white supremacy and exclusion from higher education.

Given the bureaucracy and historical nature of exclusion within higher education, the case for the lack of representation of and discrimination of Black men is both systemic as well as intentional. No matter how much we are told we are needed or the study of lack of Black men in higher education is highlighted, there are fundamental barriers preventing Black men from entering the institution which needs to be acknowledged in order to create equitable change for the future. This equitable change also cannot simply stop at heterosexual, cis-gendered Black males experience either. The experiences of Black Queer men and Black Trans men must be also be investigated within the struggle of Black men to find space within the field, because they are the most marginalized in the spectrum of Black identifying men. Only through centering the experiences of the most marginalized can we hope to combat racism and white supremacy to claim our space within higher education.

5:25 PM   **Conclusion**

I would like to say that at the end of this chapter like the conclusion of diversity training or a good presentation at NASPA that I have some solutions. I would like to say I have thought of the perfect way to augment the current recruitment and selection process of bringing in Black male professionals to increase our representation. As I sit here listening to the ranging voices of Common, Kendrick Lamar, Jay-Z, and even the old Kanye, I come to a singular thought: I do not have an answer and if I did, would it matter? Plainly, Black men have been shouting for our inclusion in academia as equally as loud as we have been shouting at police to stop killing us. Somehow, it seems that no matter how loud we shout, protest, and demand, the academy simply stays silent while bearing witness to our discrimination and ostracization. We are expected to simply thrive within the confines of higher education under racially-biased rules and a code of professionalism meant to police our actions.

No matter how much research or literature we contribute to the academy, we are useful until we are expendable. Much like the slave who plowed the field in order to sow the cotton seeds in order to line the slave master's jacket and pockets; once the job is completed or our energy to continue is gone, the use for us is no more. So, my solution is this: listen to us. Believe us. Deconstruct your environments and then hire us. Stop policing us. Build us up instead of offering nice platitudes and then disappearing when the real battle is beginning. Pay us for educating your staff on diversity, equity, and antiracism "best" practices.

Treat us as your employees and your colleagues rather than your tokens or your admissions headshots. And know, we are tired but we persist. We persist knowing all that higher education and student affairs stands to gain from our presence. We persist in order to create space and support for those Black male students who have never seen a professor, educator, or person of authority outside of law enforcement who looks like them. Not only that, but we also strive to teach all students how they can advance their understanding of the world in order to make it a better place. Quite simply, I am, like so many before me and so many to follow, a Black man in search of justice within the academy that overlooked my predecessors. And I will not stop because my allegiance is not to the academy rather than everything the academy stands for and what it could be.

References

Black, J. S. (2020). *Organizational Behavior*. Creative Commons Attribution License
v4.0. https://cnx.org/contents/LZQauaxb@5.7:x7Hicyf9@2/Preface

Cho, S., Crenshaw, K., & McCall, L. (2013). Toward a Field of Intersectionality Studies: Theory, Applications, and Praxis. *Signs, 38*(4), 785-810. doi:10.1086/669608

Croom, N.N., Beatty, C.C., Acker, L.D., & Butler, M. (2017). Exploring undergraduate

Black womyn's motivations for engaging in "sister circle" organizations. *NASPA Journal About Women in Higher Education, 10*(2), 216-228.

Delgado, R., & Stefancic, J. (2012). *Critical race theory: An introduction.* (2nd). New York University Press.

Jenkins, T.S. (2016). Committed to diversity? Show me the money. The Chronicle of Higher Education.
https://www.chronicle.com/article/committed-to-diversity-show-me-the-money/

Kendi, I. X. (2019). *How to be an antiracist.* (1st ed.). One World.

Pritchard, A., & McChesney, J. (October 2018). Focus on Student Affairs, 2018: Understanding Key Challenges Using CUPA-HR Data. (Research Report). CUPA-HR. https://www.cupahr.org/surveys/research-briefs/.

Reece, B. J., Tran, V. T., DeVore, E. N., & Porcaro, G. (2019). *Debunking the myth of job fit in higher education and student affairs.* Stylus Publishing, LLC.

Renn, K.A., & Hodges, J. (2007). The first year on the job: Experiences of new professionals in student affairs. *NASPA journal, 44*(2), 367-391.

Tull, A., Hirt, J.B., & Saunders, S.A. (2009). *Becoming socialized in student affairs administration: A guide for new professionals and their supervisors.* Stylus Publishing, LLC.

CHAPTER SIX

Being a Problem Everywhere:
Dodging the White Gaze as a Black Man in Academia

Adeyemi Doss, Indiana State University

Abstract

This essay provides a unique glimpse into my personal experience of being a Black male teaching in a predominantly white institution. I attempt to offer an existential reading of how my existence in this space we call academia becomes a battle with how I am seen within the white gaze. Through a reflective form of writing, I attempt to carve out the existential strain of how I come to experience my being when caught between both the white gaze and America's pathological imagination of the Black masculine body while trying to exist within the ivory tower.

Keywords: white gaze, black body, imagination, existential, invisibility, academia.

Over the past several years, I have witnessed Black men wither away due to the stress of being Black and male in the academy. I have seen their suffering and distress with my own eyes. Their experience is a type of social death, where Black men are forced into a space of loneliness until they become obsolete to the academy and die. Could this phenomenon be the consequence of the fact that Black men pose a problem everywhere they appear? In this reflective essay society that has scripted the Black masculine body in such a way that it becomes a problem everywhere it appears.

The White Gaze in Academia

"I came into this world anxious to uncover the meaning of things, my soul desirous to be at the origin of the world, and here I am an object among other objects.

Frantz Fanon

As a Black man, teaching in a predominately white institution, I find myself immersed in an environment saturated by a gaze[1] that has been trained

---

[1] Note: The concept of the "white gaze" is an expression that we frequently observe in the works of African and African American writers such as Ralph Ellison, W.E.B. Du Bois, Frantz Fanon, Toni Morrison, and James Baldwin, to name a few. These literary artists and scholars force us to examine and deconstruct the notion of the white gaze, which has a

to fix my body as a problem while it becomes restrained within its visual field. The overwhelming feeling of being a problem suddenly becomes an innate response of me being forced to abandon my personhood. It is at this juncture where I start to question whether I should be in academia, or whether I am here because the institution needs to fill its "diversity quota" of racial bodies? Or could this be an intrinsic response of me consciously knowing that I am locked into a state of objecthood, where my body becomes caught in a matrix of fear and lies of my existence in the world?

These questions regarding my existence ultimately become a mental tussle against being seen as the opposite of how I see myself. This frustrating reality expands into psychological barriers to surviving as an academic. Inside the academia, just as outside of it, Black men are forced to battle against untruths regarding their physical presence, which often has them feeling undesired in our society. The battle against lies about one's physical presence is an ontological struggle of escaping the white gaze.   According to Hart (2018), it is under the gaze that "Black people expend massive amounts of energy to do consciously what one ordinarily experiences as an automatic and unconscious movement" (p.18). "I," as a Black man, am bound to become cognizant of how my body exists within the white gaze, which "black people are induced to normalize" (Hart, 2013, p.94). As a racial body in the academy, my body is vulnerable to the same epistemic violence that it encounters outside of it. I am often reminded through side conversations with other black faculty that academia will not protect you as it does other racial and ethnic bodies, because it perceives you as a threat. Through my existing in the academy, I am made to come to the unsettling reality that I only exist outside of the notion of moral concern because my body is not seen through a moral lens.

Understanding the issues that Black men face in the academy and society more broadly requires a critical awareness of how the Black masculine body is fantasized in the white mind and how it is scripted within popular media. It is in the media, where my body is erected as violent, exotic, hypersexual, animalistic, and immature at every juncture of society. These false representations of my body and other Black bodies over a period of time become indoctrinated so deeply within the public imagination that they eventually become authenticated as accurate portraits. Consequently, my body will unavoidably be perceived through the same neurotic lens inside the ivory tower. I am further suggesting that the media shifts into an expansion of the white gaze that often regards my existence as non-human. From the context of my lived experience, the external reality is that my body becomes seized and conserved in white falsehoods, all bound in the belief that Black people and Black men specifically, exist as a problem.

---

history of restricting African Americans' inalienable rights to enjoy the freedom of existing as human beings.

The Fractured Body

"The gaze interferes with the way black people relate to their body parts as they move through space."

William David Hart

Ontologically speaking, the white gaze forces the Black body to become unfamiliar to itself. According to Yancy (2018), "the Black body through the hegemony of the white gaze, undergoes a phenomenological return that leaves it distorted and fixed as a pre-existing essence. The Black body becomes a 'prisoner' of an imago- an elaborate distorted image of the Black, an image whose reality is held together through white bad faith and projection - that is ideologically orchestrated to leave no trace of its social and historical construction" (p.110). What Yancy is suggesting, when the Black body is caught in the white gaze, the body becomes subjected to pathological perspectives that have been conditioned only to see this particular body as a fractured object. The objectification of the Black body within the perception of the white gaze is held together by beliefs that have been built on lies of its existence in the world. In Fanon's (2008) psychoanalysis on how white gaze has the power to fix the body in ways that it interferes with its way of moving about in the world, mainly when the two entities are in close proximity, he states the following:

Locked in this suffocating reification, I appealed to the Other so that his liberating gaze, gliding over my body suddenly smoothed of rough edges, would give me back the lightness of being I thought I had lost, and taking me out of the world put me back in the world. But just as I get to the other slope I stumble, and the Other fixes me with his gaze, his gestures, and attitude, the same way you fix a preparation with a dye (p. 89).

The overt desire of the gaze is to fix the Black body into an undesirable object, restricting the Black body from moving freely around society like other bodies. In resisting the desire of the gaze, I sense a feeling of despair taking over my mind. Despair is entangled with the omnipresent phobia that encases my body, forcing it to be policed by everyone, any and everywhere. For "I" as the object that brings about anxiety in *Others*, I am forced to encounter my existence outside of my body. The white gaze "produces a third-person consciousness in Black people" (Hart, 2018, p.18). There is the *"I"* for self, the *"I"* for the *"Other,"* and then the *"I"* that is imagined by the *"Other."* Consequently, I have to manage all three while attempting to move about in both the academy and the world.

As my body goes through the process of being objectified by the *Other*, I become hyper-conscious of everything that I would typically experience in an unconscious frame of mind. In this process, I am forced to encounter my body as a fractured object or a type of "amputated phantom body" (p.18). I become overly conscious of the stares I give back, the positioning of my body, the placement of my hands, the tone of my voice, and other ordinary motions that every human body goes through; thus, my body becomes foreign to me. I am often compelled to ask myself, could this be the result of being caught in the gaze which interrupts my body schema and how I relate to my limbs, my flesh, and my existence in the world? Or could this be my way of embodying the gaze that carries a vindictive spirit forcing me to objectify myself?

The sensation of being the arcane object, which I often feel through the hesitations of "hellos," "good mornings," to the clutching of handbags, and the nervous tension exhibited through various body positions when my body is present becomes the root of my despair as I walk through this space of certain uncertainty. Each small aggression interrupts my day, and I am abruptly reminded how "the presence of black bodies spoils the *whitopian* dream; an imaginary (utopian) space devoid of black people" (Hart, 2013, p.100).

My awareness is constantly trained on how my body, like the bodies of other Black men and boys in this society, stimulates anxiety within the soul of white America. I start to bring into question whether it is my body or the outer tones of my flesh, that becomes the problem. As a result, I am forced to interrogate the color of my flesh and, more so, how the concept of blackness subsists in an anti-black society. In an anti-black world, where anti-black racism takes the Sartrean form of *bad faith*, both are essentially part of the foundation of white America's attitudes, beliefs, and practices of imagining and believing that people of African descent are inherently inferior and subhuman. Therefore, blackness, black people, and black bodies are wretched, wherever they emerge. The perception of blackness also operates in a metaphysical space that can "encompass both black people and the being of black people" (Hart, 2018, p.31). Those that exist in blackness are subjected to a constant battle of being alienated, forcing one into a state of mental and physical isolation. This struggle becomes the consequence of living in an anti-black world, where you become the "black sheep of the human family," whose aim is not to get snagged in the *Other's* imagination. As Fanon (2008) argues, "In the white world, the man of color encounters difficulties in elaborating his body schema. The image of one's body is solely negating. It's an image in the third person. All around the body reigns an atmosphere of certain uncertainty" (p.90). Not knowing when, where, how, or whether I should exist, becomes part of the difficulties of living in a world where my body is seen through an anti-black lens, that predates the emergence of my existence. My blackness's functionality becomes conditioned in the white mind to not be trusted, to be looked upon as evil, and always to conclude that it is guilty of something. This type of dance with the gaze disturbs how my body is experienced as I move through academia and society as a whole.

In the academy, I can dance around this tragic reality in the academy by playing *The Spook Who Sat by the Door*.[1] As I shift around the Other's

---

[1] Note: *The Spook Who Sat by the Door* is the title of a 1969 fictional text written by Sam Greenlee that later adapted into a film in 1973. The central character, Dan Freeman became the first African American CIA agent. He later quit the CIA to train a black revolutionary organization known as the Cobras, all that he learned in the CIA regarding guerilla warfare

gaze, like the fictional character Dan Freedman, I become an expert in transforming my presence from the imagined predator to the smart Negro. Like Dan Freedman, over time, I become comfortable in my invisibility because I realize that no matter how or where my body is present, the Other sees' criminal, something dreadful, and object that needs policing and if out of place, eliminated.

In academia, it is not the college degrees that decorate my office space that is intimidating, it is my body. My body is a corporeal object that sparks fear in the *Other*. The "great escape" from being feared becomes the way I am forced to experience my existence in academia and the larger world. As a result, I become a fugitive within my own body to avoid the pressure on my being and my way of relating to my existence. To face the reality that my body produces fear in other people creates an ontological world of ambiguity. So, I hesitate on whether I should exist as myself or the thing that the *Other* imagines me to be. In this world, my existence provokes a kind of anxiety that begs me to remove myself or render myself invisible. To render myself invisible, I must transform into what the *Other* has imagined me to be: a problem.

To survive this sense of unwantedness, I must remind myself how my body is scripted within the larger society. In the larger society, I am not just a criminal; I am a sexual predator. Though unspoken in the academy, I confront these social labels as a psychological maze, I must carefully traverse, or else... One awkward glimpse at the *Other* can spark fear. Nevertheless, I must look back. I find looking back liberating to my soul. The process of looking back becomes my way of liberating my body and my movement. The gaze of the *Other* seeks to remove me from the immediate space in which I exist at that moment in time.

Rescuing the Flesh

For Black men in academia, whether you are a student or a professor, academia is a space where you are in constant negotiations with other people's malevolent spirit. The question becomes, should you internalize the *Other's* perception of your existence in society, or resist against it any and every way you can?

Freeing oneself from the gaze is not a matter of physically fleeing from it, although in some instances, that is okay too. It is a matter of metaphysically becoming invisible to what is behind the gaze: the white imagination. It is both a mental and physical practice of doing what it has always done to you; pretend it is not present any and everywhere it appears. Practice this process until it becomes natural. Free your mind from it and push back by dissecting every inch of its soul. It was Du Bois (1903) who asked the unasked question, "how

---

and the gathering of intelligence. What is unique about Dan Freeman was his mastery of overcoming the strife of being a Black man in a predominantly white male organization by using his invisibility to free himself from the anti-black gaze and imagination. In doing so, he was able to control his existence in the world.

does it feel to be a problem" (p. 2)? The only way to not become the problem is to look right back.

Looking back is an act of rescuing your body, your flesh, from a world of uncertainty. It is to retrieve your body from the pseudoscientific discourse that once affirmed that you were not human due to your pigment, broad nose, and knotted hair. Every conscious shift of your body when the *Other* is present, or when you are in the space that is dominated by the physical presence of the *Other*, has been built on lies about your existence. So, one must remember to gaze back. Make your gaze felt by everyone and anyone.

As a Black man in the academy, my black body carries the burdensome past of the struggles of my forefathers and mothers. It is a history of being confiscated and traumatized that does not end at the ivory tower's pearly gates. Everything that this particular body feels stems from the gaze. My body's social DNA is intertwined with the ontological trauma of being seen as non-existent as a human. In my fight to prove that I am human, I lose myself in both the gaze and imagination of the *Other,* and thus continue to fall into a world of despair. In the spirit of James Baldwin (1993), I continue to remind myself that "you can only be destroyed by believing that you are what the white world calls a nigger" (p.4).

References
Baldwin, J. (1963–1993). *The Fire Next Time*. Vintage International.
Du Bois, W.E.B. (1989). *The Souls of Black Folk*. Bantam Dell. (Original work published 1903, A.C. McClurg & Co. 1st ed.)
Fanon, F. (2008). *Black Skin White Mask* (new ed.).Grove Press. (Original work published 1952, R. Philcox, Trans.(1st ed.)
Hart, W. (2013). Dead Black Man, Just Walking. In G. Yancy with Jones, J. (Eds.). *Pursuing Trayvon Martin: Historical Context and Contemporary Manifestations of Racial Dynamics,* (pp. 91–101). Lexington Books.
Hart, W. (2018). Constellations: Capitalism, Antiblackness, Afro-Pessimism, and Black Optimism. *Journal of Theology & Philosophy, 39*(2), 5–33. https://doi.org/https://muse.jhu.edu/article/691691/pdf
Yancy, G. (2008). *Black Bodies, White Gaze: The Continuing Significance of Race*. Rowman & Littlefield Publishing.

CHAPTER SEVEN

Hip-Hop is Dead?
An Essay on the Intersectional Identity of Young Black Professorship

Denzel L. Jones, Antioch University New England

Introduction

"We are advocating that hip-hop is not just a music. It is an attitude. It is an awareness. It is a way to view the world. So, rap music is something we do, but hip-hop is something we live."

KRS-One, 200

Before beginning it is important that I provide a brief introduction. My name is Denzel Jones. I am an assistant professor of a Couple and Family Therapy program and a licensed marriage and family therapist. Before becoming a professor, I earned a B.S. in Psychology, an M.A. in Marriage and Family Therapy, a certificate in Expressive Arts Therapy, and a Ph.D. in Couple and Family Therapy. I have many research interests; however, my primary interest focuses on social and relational processes that impact and influence identity development across time. Oh, fun fact: I absolutely love hip-hop culture!

For many Black youth and young adults living in the United States, hip-hop has held cultural relevance since birth, and one may ground their Black identity within the greater context of hip-hop culture. Since the emergence of hip-hop during the late 1960s and early 1970s (Price, 2006), many people have been influenced by the artistic novelty of hip-hop (i.e., four fundamental elements of hip-hop: MCing, or rapping [oral]; DJing [aural]; b-boying, or breakdancing [physical]; and graffiti art [visual]). Outside of hip-hop spaces, what is often discussed to a lesser degree is how hip-hop has influenced communities by transcending, and including, artistic innovation (e.g., additional elements of hip-hop: fashion, language, entrepreneurialism, and political activism). Each of these elements are essential to hip-hop culture; however, the fifth element, *Knowledge* (or consciousness), is arguably the most crucial. Knowledge, culture, and overstanding (i.e., comprehension of an object or phenomenon with the additional realization of its role within the grander context, how it came to be, and why it serves in the manner it does; (evilelove, 2006) is the infrastructure that bonds the other elements within a sociocultural-political context (Price, 2006). In part, it requires self-knowledge, which is the understanding of oneself and one's own character, capabilities, or motives (Merriam-Webster, n.d.). Thus, knowledge provides a foundation for the hip-hop community to learn about and express their unique individual and group identities. Taking all of this into consideration, one can claim, "I am hip-hop, and hip-hop is me!"

Black Faculty and Identity

A close examination of full-time faculty in college and university settings within the United States introduces an undeniable imbalance of ethnic and racial characteristics. The National Center for Education Statistics (NCES, 2019) shows that in Fall 2017, the majority of full-time faculty in degree-granting higher education institutions were White men (41%) and White women (35%). Comparatively, Black men represented 3% of the full-time faculty population (NCES, 2019). Academia as a whole is born and bred in a predominately White space, consequently fostering White values, narratives, assumptions, perceptions, and expectations. This poses a unique experience for young, Black faculty as others, namely White faculty, have the privilege to actively or passively avoid contemplation of intersectional consolidation of professional and racial identities. Generally, White faculty members' identities are built upon the foundation of a dominant White society. However, for young, Black men in academia the issue of developing an identity takes on additional significance.

Young, Black faculty who fail to explore all possible identities and commit to the self-chosen identity that best fits them (i.e., identity achievement; Marcia, 1966; Marcia, 1980) run the risk of (1) conforming to an "academic-only" identity based on the blind acceptance of expectations and values of others without exploring alternative possibilities (i.e., identity foreclosure; Marcia, 1966; Marcia, 1980) or (2) becoming stuck in a crisis where they explore and/or try possible identities but struggle to commit to identifying in a way that is meaningful for them (i.e., identity moratorium; Marcia, 1966; Marcia, 1980). For young, Black faculty there is increased likelihood of ambivalence as their cultural and professional identities converge. Thus, the purpose of this chapter is to (1) establish hip-hop as a cultural identity, (2) discuss the challenges that young, Black faculty in higher education may face as they attempt intersectional integration of hip-hop and academic identities, and (3) encourage young, Black faculty toward identity exploration and commitment processes.

Hip-Hop as a Culture

One of the greatest challenges for hip-hop proponents is establishing hip-hop as a culture that influences groups of people and individual identities. One of the biggest arguments of hip-hop critics is that hip-hop is not a culture; yet it is a deviant of an already existing dominant culture with contradictory norms and rules (Emdin & Adjapong, 2018). For those who do not understand the significance of hip-hop and its sociocultural-political origins, it is easy to disregard hip-hop as a monstrosity that glorifies and promotes criminal behaviors. I cannot account for how many times I have engaged in the "rap is destroying America" debate. Thus, to open the conversation of establishing hip-hop as a culture that fosters cultural beings, I pose these questions: What is culture? Who decides?

What is (or is not) Culture?

The foundational concepts of culture are far too dense and complex to cover in a single book chapter. Even discussion on a single culture could entail entire programs of studies; utilizing multiple resources and materials dedicated to knowledge and understanding. On a much smaller scale, it is at least important to acknowledge who decides what constitutes as culture. Emdin and Adjapong (2018) note:

What is or isn't culture can only be determined by those who are experiencing it and can only be marginally understood by those who are witnessing it. When one witnesses another person's cultural expressions without participating in the culture itself, it becomes easy to invalidate its worth as a culture. (p. 85)

This statement becomes even more pressing as there is no one clear, definite understanding of what culture is, and hip-hop culture is predominately perceived as an unrefined piece of the dominant culture of American society. Critics of hip-hop and its cultural relevance are those who witness but never experience it. In continuing the conversation, it is important to ask the questions: How and why was hip-hop constructed? Who was it conceived for?

Hip-Hop and Violence

Most hip-hop critics immediately dismiss hip-hop as a positive culture under the guise of a single word: violence. In fact, a Pew Research Center (PRC, 2008) poll notes that roughly 70% of the United States population believes that rap has a negative impact on society. There is a cultural bias against rap and hip-hop that is not present in other expressions of violence in American culture. This stigma of violence such as overindulgence in money, materialism, sex, and drugs and the pursuit of an unashamed, erratic, audacious lifestyle (Price, 2006) is entrenched in and fueled through false media portrayals. Unfortunately, these "sensationalized," media depicted stereotypes are the only accounts of hip-hop culture that many people ever consume. The idea that a perfect culture exists (or does not exist) is debatable. One could argue that hip-hop is a flawed culture and point to instances of violence in rap lyrics; however, the expression of violence, without just cause or an activist agenda, is a minute piece of the culture that becomes exaggerated. "Often spinning the coverage to focus on the violent acts without providing all the facts or full context, the media often presents half-truths and insufficient, biased accounts cloaked as facts" (Price, 2006, p. 79). While there are some facets of rap that can be viewed by some as negative, it is unfair to stereotype the entire art form, the people who produce it, the people who listen to it, and the people who live the culture. Media narrations situate hip-hop as a scapegoat for violent acts that are not perpetrated by or associated with the hip-hop community, and because of this hip-hop movements that could have a positive impact are often overlooked, misrepresented, and appropriated. Hip-hop should not be equated to violence.

Hip-Hop and Activism

Hip-hop is a revolutionary cultural movement birthed as a means of expression for economically disenfranchised, politically abandoned, and socially repressed youth grounded in Black expressive culture.

> As a product of urban neglect and a descendant of the civil rights, Black power, and Black arts movements, Hip Hop arose as a unifying force for young people of all races and ethnicities who had two major things in common: an experience with Black expressive culture (whether through birthright or adaptation) and an experience with the brutal clutches of poverty. (Price, 2006, p. 18)

At its core, hip-hop's intent is to give voice to the underrepresented and over suppressed. Hip-hop emerged as a sociocultural-political platform to draw attention to the inequitable and unjust treatment of a marginalized cultural group, to express one's narrative, and to call for social action. In fact, Grandmaster Flash and the Furious Five released one of the earliest rap songs, The Message (1982); a conscious-rap song that focused on urban social issues. Most notably, The Message moved hip-hop culture toward a social platform while narrating a reality of unsafe and unsanitary living environments, prostitution, drugs, and inadequate education that residents of urban communities are subjected to. This song offers one of the earliest connections between hip-hop and activism. Many hip-hop artists' primary motives are to articulate community despair, honor determination, and offer a critical analysis of the world around them.

Hip-hop has always been grounded in activism, and that activist framework remains solid today. The messages of rap lyrics is not intended to promote violence but tell the experiences of violence. In fact, Price (2006) notes many positive attributes of hip-hop:

> "… including the fact that it presents the real crisis of inter-city living from the inside out, offering an intimate portrayal of the failure of many social service and governmental aid programs and bringing to the forefront the persistent problems of police brutality, racial profiling, and a broken legal system." (p. 61)

It makes sense that many hip-hop critics dwelling in power-latent structures oppose hip-hop's innate nature of calling out oppressive systems and promoting action toward the deconstruction of dominant forces, which can be viewed as violent. Hip-hop is only "ruining our nation" to those building our society through the abuse and maltreatment of marginalized and oppressed groups; principles in which the United States were established upon. You are exactly right; one of hip-hop's many resolves is to cancel the system that has been in place since the birth of the nation that keep minorities down. Hip-hop artists are urban reporters and storytellers who offer raw, uncensored truths. Most hip-hop artists do not encourage violence; they are only reporting narratives of marginalized, oppressed, and underserved communities to caution everyone that violence is still present. Hip-hop's ability to empower; encourage; provide support and entertainment; increase education, social awareness, and hope; and embrace youth and young adults deserves greater attention in media and literature.

The Young, Black Professor

Intersectionality, a term coined by Crenshaw (1989), is defined in many ways. Broadly, intersectionality is a framework for understanding how power collides and interlocks with aspects of a person's social identities (Columbia Law School, 2017) to create multiple forms of inequality… a "prism for understanding certain kinds of problems" (National Association of Independent Schools [NAIS], 2018, 0:33). In this specific context, the intersectional components of an advantaged professional identity (i.e., academic) and a targeted cultural identity (i.e., hip-hop) in predominately White institutions are highlighted. Compared to all other race, gender, and age groups polled in the PRC survey (2008), findings suggest that older White men are far more likely to deem rap and hip-hop as having a negative impact on society whereas young, Black men are most likely to deem rap and hip-hop as having a positive impact on society. This is significant as older White men (least likely to ascribe to hip-hop culture) are the majority faculty in higher education institutions and younger Black men (most likely to ascribe to hip-hop culture) are the minority faculty in higher education institutions.

Academic Culture

For some time, I have felt incongruence between the values of my hip-hop identity and my academic identity, yet I had never come across literature to support these feelings. Thus, I set out in search of literature on standards, norms, and expectations of educators within secondary education. I struggled to find articles in academic journals that addressed academic norms and culture conflict. When reaching out to other professors and scholars across multiple disciplines and universities to locate such literature a common theme emerged: these types of inquiries mostly take place in alternative-academic research and are less likely to be produced through traditional academic channels. Of course, it would be threatening to produce work that could potentially deconstruct the power within traditional academic institutions. Historically, universities have been White male dominated, and the gold-standard professor is "a learned man with no obligations aside from his scholarly and university tasks" (Social Sciences Feminist Network Research Interest Group [SSFN-RIG], 2017, p. 229). Additionally, this image influences what is and what is not valued within higher education, and faculty of color are often held to higher standards and expectations than their White colleagues (Matthew, 2016). With an increased realization of unspoken and invisible standards and expectations of educators, particularly relating to those of color, I decided to turn to tenure and promotion literature as a foundation for understanding how norms are set in research, service, and teaching as values in higher education have been reflected in tenure and promotion criteria. It is critical to acknowledge systemic and institutional racism and the significant barriers it creates for Black faculty obtaining tenure-track positions and earning tenure.

Research and Service

The reward system of higher education stresses traditional research more than community-engaged, service-based scholarship. Additionally, faculty of color typically engage in more community-engaged and service-based activities, sometimes resulting in heavier service burdens (SSFN-RIG, 2017), compared to their White male colleagues. This is likely due to differences in cultural values of White men and people of color. Similar to higher education institutions, tenure and promotion systems are based on individual achievement and principles designed by White men where Black faculty are more likely to engage in work that enhances group achievement and service to others. Scholarship that seeks to hear from the unheard and give people a voice by recognizing the wisdom that exists in communities is often less rewarded than conventional research. Given universities' purpose and mission, it is odd that traditional research (basic knowledge of a phenomenon) is prioritized over applied research and service (practical knowledge used to change or influence phenomenon).

Higher education systems prioritize basic understanding over social action, but hip-hop proponents carry significant advocacy and activism roles. When hip-hop activism merges with Black scholars' passion and desire toward scholar activism, it clashes with a White academic reward structure that glorifies one's ability to successfully "publish and prosper" despite limited significance it may have for generating social change. Ever since I was a student, I felt an internalized narrative of not being good enough and external pressures to do more to become an adequate researcher and scholar. I witnessed my White peers climb the ladder by producing journal article after journal article, and I often wondered what was wrong with me and my ability to produce the same level of work. At this point in my career, I have few manuscripts published in academic journals. This channel of scholarship is not accessible to the public. Additionally, many of my other achievements that are research-informed, community-based, and publicly accessible are often overlooked: co-hosting and producing a podcast, hosting and facilitating community discussion around relevant topics, developing and facilitating community events and trainings, etc. There is an added level of stress, anxiety, and pressure as I take on activities that are more aligned with my hip-hop core that elicit fear responses around missing out on opportunities of professional socialization, development, and advancement.

Teaching

Similar to service and applied scholarship, teaching is also considered less valuable than traditional research in higher education, yet faculty of color are expected to teach an increased course load and have the same research obligations as their White colleagues (SSFN-RIG, 2017). There are also stringent expectations around holding students accountable. There should be structures set in place to hold students accountable, but what is more important is understanding what it means to hold students accountable. Usually when we discuss holding students accountable it comes with a "suck it up" attitude to meet expectations set by the instructor. Examples include no exception late policies, predetermined point reduction for extensions, non-negotiable classroom structures and assignments, and uniformly tailored teaching and instruction processes. There are spoken and unspoken rules around the relevance of unforgiving rigor in higher education. This expectation of rigor and accountability is riddled with individually-focused, cut-throat, Eurocentric ideas of success. Black professors, who predominately hold collectivist cultural values, may struggle navigating this style of rigor in holding students accountable. There appears to be a belief that compassion and flexible teaching equates to lowered expectations of students and encourages less successful students. If a student shows up late to class, I am more inclined to welcome them into the space and set the stage so they show up ready to engage than I am to berate them. If a student misses a class I am more likely to assume life happened and check in to make sure they are well and safe. If students express they are not doing well in our opening class check-in ritual, we as a group use class time to figure out how we can support each other during our time together. While I agree we need to have standards and expectations in place, I argue that we as professors also need to admit our humanity and meet students with their needs instead of pushing unrealistic expectations that make failure inevitable. Being authentic and compassionate as an instructor does not create an unrealistic or unacceptable power imbalance between students and faculty. In fact, I believe it creates an environment where students feel supported and ready to engage.

I recently developed an advanced research class, and expectations of students fall outside of academic norms. There are few written assignments, and the majority of the assignments are applied and focus on public scholarship and community engagement. As students engage in this course, they take on activities that are not often associated with traditional research: producing evidence-based/research-informed infographics, developing a social media presence for professional socialization and microblogging with the general public, and developing a proposal of engaging communities in research and dissemination through open, non-academic channels. I sometimes worry that my academic communities may see this as less rigorous or a waste of time. I feel internalized pressure to teach students advanced statistical analyses and research methods instead of applied research that involves community engagement, advocacy, and activism that is a staple of hip-hop culture and translational research.

Professorial Image

Although not explicitly mentioned in tenure and promotion criteria, there is an expected professorial image associated with professionalism. Far from the days of elbow-patched corduroy blazers and cigar pipes, professors are still expected to dress business formal, business professional, or at the very least, business casual. Hip-hop aficionados consider fashion an essential part of self-expression, allowing a collective cultural identity with individual nuances (Price, 2006). Additionally, in response to stressful situations, encounters, and environments, Black people consider emotional debriefing (i.e., expressing oneself creatively; Utsey et al., 2000) a beneficial Afrocentric coping strategy. Common hip-hop fashion and apparel: Adidas, Nike, Jordan, and other urban street and sportswear do not exactly fit business professional attire. Thus, young, Black faculty are often required to uphold an image that may not be representative of who they are. Black faculty regularly experience micro-invalidations in the academy (Pittman, 2012), and this includes physical appearance. Business professional demands can silence the expression of young, Black faculty and their ability to artistically cope in institutionalized academic environments.

Each day that I wake up one of my first thoughts is "How am I going to dress today?" What this really implies is "How am I 'showing up?'" or "How will I identify today?" Some days I conform toward professional academic attire, some days I am completely unapologetic in hip-hop attire, and more days than not I walk around in a shell of ambivalence and uncertainty. I constantly carry external pressures to conform to professional academic norms and internal pressures of shame and guilt of choosing, or not choosing, to honor myself as a hip-hop being. Although I have never had any overt negative experiences on my appearance as a professor, I carry narratives that I may be perceived as less professional or less credentialed. I was once chastised as a graduate student because I wore a polo shirt with a small name branded emblem to a local high school to meet with students and taught an undergraduate class later that same day. This discriminatory micro-invalidation greatly shapes how my professorial identity continues to evolve. While I agree there must be some standard of professional image that is upheld, there is no room to deviate from norms set in higher education to include diverse cultural identities. Academics stand behind claims that universities and institutions were built to serve the public good; however, we reprimand those who bring public values and culture (read minority expressions) into private academic settings while we show up in public environments with elitist attitudes and presentations (read dominant White expressions). From my own experience, the ambivalence and confusion generated by this dilemma causes daily frustration and turmoil and challenges me to pit professional values against personal and community values.

Recommendations

In closing, it is important to provide specific action items that may be useful to young, Black professors in navigating intersectional identity moratorium on a journey toward identity achievement. Note that these recommendations come from my own personal experiences as an emerging Black professor and include things I have done, am beginning to do, or plan to do to manage and overcome identity moratorium and navigate stressful environments of higher education. If you have other ideas, suggestions, or would like to collaborate on work in this area, please contact me via Twitter (@iAmDenzelJones) or email (djones10@antioch.edu).

Social Support and Black Culture

On the journey toward identity achievement the importance of social support and group identity cannot be overstated. It is vital that young, Black faculty surround themselves with other Black people, both within and outside of academic environments. An additional Afrocentric coping strategy that is important to navigating stressful situations and encounters is collective coping (Utsey et al., 2000). Collective coping is the process of relying on group support and activities when coping with stressful environments that is grounded in African-based value systems that places the group above the individual (Utsey et al., 2000). Further, Gaylord-Harden and Cunningham (2009) conducted a study on the impact of racial discrimination stress on internalizing symptoms and coping strategies among Black youth, and findings suggest that Black youth prefer culturally relevant coping strategies (based in Afrocentric worldviews grounded in historical and cultural traditions; Utsey et al., 2000) over mainstream coping strategies (based in individualistic Eurocentric worldviews; Utsey et al., 2000). This is relevant as we live in an individualistic, Eurocentric society and higher education values and worldviews are situated within these systems; oftentimes placing the individual above the group. The old African proverb "It takes a village to raise a child" is more than just lip service; it is a Black survival tactic and way of life. Black people need Black people, and Black people thrive in communal spaces.

Seek Black Mentorship

There is a decent body of literature on the importance of junior faculty mentorship (e.g., Waddell et al., 2016), and to a lesser degree on mentoring Black students (e.g., Sato et al., 2018). However, there is scarce research on mentoring Black junior faculty, especially Black senior faculty/Black junior faculty mentoring relationships. It is not uncommon that Black faculty do not receive adequate mentorship in academia (Constantine et al., 2008). In full transparency, my primary mentor, who was also my major professor during my doctoral program, is a White woman. She is a phenomenal mentor with a wealth of knowledge, heightened compassion, and a tenacious devotion to deconstructing and challenging academic and institutional systems. I would not trade my mentorship experiences for the world; however, because of differences in our identities, there are some challenges and obstacles that I face that her passion and empathy cannot reach. As a result, I have begun seeking additional mentorship to navigate unique cultural issues within higher education.

There are few Black faculty at my university and due to a solid structure that often stifles liquid networks across programs, I have rarely communicated or interacted with them. One day I was in my office and a Black woman came to my door and introduced herself. She was previously a faculty member at the university and is now the Associate Vice President for Diversity and Inclusion at a local university. More recently I have begun reaching out to her, not necessarily for mentorship at his point, but to expand my professional network to include people that look like me with the hopes of receiving mentorship along the way. Due to the nature of her work, her experiences, and her wealth of knowledge and unique understanding it is important that I allow myself to be teachable and open access that we have to each other. My interest in her is not to discount the senior faculty members within my program, who continue to provide amazing support, or my longtime doctoral mentor; however, there are additional assets that she can provide that others cannot. It is important that young, Black faculty seek out these opportunities to survive in higher education.

Connect with other Black Men in Academia

The research on peer mentorship relationships among Black academics is also sparse (e.g., Minnett et al., 2019). Along with hierarchical mentorship, it is important that Black men in higher education expand their colleague groups to include other Black men for peer mentorship. One group from which I receive support is a group that begun informally within a professional organization of which I am a member. My elder brethren (we refer to each other as "brothers") started a group for the Black men within the organization to provide us a space for connection. One goal of the group is to eliminate the isolation that we experience in academic settings. At every conference we are intentional about constructing time to get together and have dinner. Although some conversations that occur during this time are academically related by nature, the primary purpose of the dinner is for us to come together as one, break bread, and share a sense of brotherhood. Even when the conference is over, we continue to reach out and connect. We share stories, honor and celebrate our successes, encourage one another, and share opportunities for advancement.

One of the brothers and I decided to catch up one-on-one for dinner one night while at a conference. During dinner, we discussed various topics while being our most raw and authentic selves. One topic we discussed, that arose organically, was the job market process. At that point I had been an assistant professor for about a year, and he was just entering the job market. We had a deep conversation about the nuances of being a Black man on the job market. We processed fears, worry, concern, joy, excitement, and all the various emotions that come with being on the job market. I shared advice, tips, and resources from my previous experiences. Once the conference concluded, I made sure to send additional resources and homework to prepare for the next steps in his development. These are the types of relationships that the brothers build with each other. As much as I appreciate everything they provide for me, it is also liberating and empowering to have a space to give back to them as well.

Grow Black Social Networks Outside of Academia

As important as it is to grow Black networks and social support systems within academic environments it is also important to continue to feed similar networks outside of academia. This is honestly an area that I have not been as productive in cultivating; I live in a predominately White area. There are many ways that people can expand their social circles: connect through mutual friends; join or create Facebook groups and other social media platforms; take local classes and attend local events; exchange contact information; host a meet up, party, or event; etc. Considering context, it is important to be intentional about including Black and other people of color as they are often excluded.

An old college friend recently reached out to me, and during our conversation he mentioned that he was thinking about starting a book club for Black men. He invited me to be a leader and a part of turning the idea into a reality. Ironically, I also had thoughts of starting a book club for Black men, but due to my isolation the enthusiasm quickly fizzled. Since we are able to connect, this offers the opportunity for us to be able to support each other through the process. Not only does this opportunity continue to give life to a bond that I have with an old college friend that I admire, it also offers us the opportunity to continue to expand our own networks with other Black men by providing a space to engage with each other and build a positive community. Although I am a Black professor who craves relationships with other Black men in higher education, I am equally excited to have an opportunity to build connections and relationships with other Black men and learn from various walks and diverse experiences.

Self-Compassion

My final recommendation in overcoming identity moratorium is simple in theory, but the application can be challenging; be gentle with yourself. Overt and covert ethnic-racial encounters can sometimes be easy to navigate on an intellectual level, however that does not mean that an internalization process does not exist that can cultivate feelings of increased tension, anxiety, guilt, shame, etc. It is important to continue to practice self-compassion and forgiveness. Whether in teaching, research, service, or professionalism, it is acceptable to not have all of the answers. Some days I think I have it all figured out, and other days I have no idea what I am doing. If this is your experience and process, you are not insufficient or defective. Challenges faced while developing your identity is not a reflection of you or your abilities, but a side effect of engaging in environments constructed by people who do not look like you for people who do not live like you. Be sure to celebrate moments of achievement and prosperity and honor moments of uncertainty and ambiguity. In honoring negative feelings and emotions, acknowledge that they are the result of systemic oppression within higher education and continue to recognize your value and worth as a young, Black professor.

Conclusion

I have provided my personal experiences, obstacles, and challenges with identity moratorium on my path to identity achievement as a young, Black professor with a hip-hop lifestyle. As higher education is a White dominated environment, I imagine that other Black faculty may face similar hardships of intersectional professional and outside cultural identity development. This may be increasingly challenging for young, Black male faculty ascribing to a hip-hop culture where beliefs, values, and worldviews do not align with the culture of academia and higher education. Developing an achieved identity is critical to the overall well-being and success of Black men in academia, and as systemic influences are multi-lateral, our institutions and outside communities will also grow to flourish as we support, encourage, and value Black men and the significance of their unique cultural experiences in academia.

References

Columbia Law School. (2017, June 8). *Kimberlé Crenshaw on intersectionality, more than two decades later.* https://www.law.columbia.edu/news/archive/kimberle-crenshaw-intersectionality-more-two-decades-later

Constantine, M. G., Smith, L., Redington, R. M., & Owens, D. (2008). Racial microaggressions against Black counseling and counseling psychology faculty: A central challenge in the multicultural counseling movement. *Journal of Counseling & Development, 86*(3). 348-355.

Emdin, C. & Adjapong, E. (2018). (Eds.).*#HipHopEd: The compilation on hip-hop education.*Brill Sense.evilelove (2006). Overstand. In *Urban dictionary.* https://www.urbandictionary.com/define.php?term=over stand

Grandmaster Flash and the Furious Five. (1982). The message [Song]. On *The message* [Album]. Sugar Hill Records.

Crenshaw, K. (1989). Demarginalizing the intersection of race and sex: A black feminist critique of antidiscrimination doctrine, feminist theory and antiracist politics. *University of Chicago Legal forum, 1989*(1), 139-167.

Gaylord-Harden, N. K., & Cunningham, J. A.(2009). The impact of racial discrimination and coping strategies on internalizing symptoms in African American youth. *Journal of Youth and Adolescence*, *38*(4), 532-543.

KRS-One. (2001). Hip hop knowledge [Song]. On *The sneak attack* [Album]. Koch Records. Marcia, J. E. (1966). Development and validation of ego identity status. *Journal Personality and Social Psychology*, *3*(5), 551-558.

Marcia, J. E. (1980). Identity in adolescence. In J. Adelson (Ed.), *Handbook of adolescent psychology* (pp. 159-187), Wiley & Sons.

Matthew, P. A. (Ed.). (2016). *Written/unwritten: Diversity and the hidden truths of tenure*. UNC Press Books.

Merriam-Webster. (n.d.). Self-knowledge. In *Merriam-Webster.com dictionary*. https://www.merriamwebster.com/dictionary/self-knowledge

Minnett, J. L., James-Gallaway, A. D., & Owens, D. R. (2019). Help a sista out: Black women doctoral students' use of peer mentorship as an act of resistance. *Mid-Western Educational Researcher*, *31*(2), 210-238.

National Association of Independent Schools. (2018, June 22). Kimberlé Crenshaw: What is intersectionality? [Video]. YouTube. https://www.youtube.com/watch?v=ViDtnfQ9FHc

National Center for Education Statistics. (2019, May). *Characteristics of postsecondary faculty*. https://nces.ed.gov/programs/coe/indicator_csc.asp

Pew Research Center. (2008, February 5). *Rate rap low*. https://www.pewresearch.org/fact-tank/2008/02/05/rate-rap-low/

Pittman, C. T. (2012). Racial micro-aggressions: The narratives of African American faculty at a predominantly White university. *The Journal of Negro Education*, *81*(1), 82-92.

Price, E. G. (2006). *Hip hop culture*. ABC-CLIO, Inc.

Sato, T., Eckert, K., & Turner, S. L. (2018). Perceptions of Black student athletes about academic mentorship at a predominantly White institution in higher education. *The Urban Review*, *50*(4), 559-583.

Social Sciences Feminist Network Research Interest Group. (2017). The burden of invisible work in academia: Social inequalities and time use in five university departments. *Humboldt Journal of Social Relations*, *39*, 228-245.

Utsey, S. O., Adams, E. P., & Bolden, M. (2000). Development and initial validation of the Africultural Coping Systems Inventory. *Journal of Black Psychology*, *26*(2), 194-215.

Waddell, J., Martin, J., Schwind, J. K., & Lapum,
J. L. (2016). A faculty-based mentorship circle: Positioning
new faculty for success. *Canadian Journal of Higher
Education*, *46*(4), 60-75.

CHAPTER EIGHT

Welcome to the Terrordome:
My Oppression in a Doctoral Program that Fights Oppression

Myron C. Duff, Jr.
Indiana University Purdue University Indianapolis

Right around the time my youngest son turned 8 years old, I realized that if I was going to further my career in higher education, I needed to pursue a doctorate degree. As I was already in my mid-40's at the time, I wanted the most convenient route to this goal. Therefore, I began to seek out doctoral programs with an emphasis in higher education. I found two that I felt were ideal for my busy life which included marriage, a full-time job, and 3 very active sons. I applied to, was accepted, and excited about having the option to choose between two different schools, but my mentor suggested that I apply to doctoral programs with more rigorous academic reputations. Considering this wise advice, I decided to apply to two doctoral programs institutions in my home state with stronger academic reputations. My original intention was to address the necessity of andragogy for African American males drawing attention to the teaching methods used in institutions of higher education. This idea was initiated by Paulo Freire's (2000) writings and my years of working with adult learners. Consequently, recent circumstances have forced me to reflect on my year and a half of making my way through the Indiana University Urban Education Studies (UES) doctoral program.

Upon my application, I had no desire to become a faculty member. My original intention was to climb the administrative ladder of higher education. Yes, I would teach the occasional class, but my aspirations remained rooted in becoming a high-ranking college administrator. However, my time in the Urban Education Studies program has completely changed my career goals. After becoming entrenched in the course readings and being highly impacted by critical scholars such as Michelle Alexander, David B. Track, Paulo Freire, Russell Skiba, Lori Patton Davis, Shaun Harper, Richard Valencia, Roxanne Dunbar-Ortiz, Robin Hughes, Richard Delgado, and Gloria Ladson Billings, my career trajectory changed. In their bravery to stand against the status quo and challenge dominant ways of thinking that are firmly established in the thread of American culture as the ***right way***, I have chosen to become a scholar, researcher, and advocate for social justice and stand against inequity. Ultimately, I felt that I could have the most impact on the minds and lives of others as a college professor.

I applied to and was denied admission into two doctoral programs that were considered prestigious before applying to the UES program because of my low GRE scores. Disappointed, I was elated that someone took a chance on me and was willing to look at my credentials from a holistic perspective as opposed to rejecting me because I did not score well on an entrance exam.

Everything about the UES program has lived up to my expectations and more. One of the first things that I learned was the chasm between my writing at the onset of starting the program and the scholarly writing needed to complete a doctoral program of study. I immediately recognized this after my first paper was returned. I was embarrassed by the "red marks" I received but was appreciative for the feedback and opportunity to rewrite the paper. Having another chance made me feel as though I did not have to have it all figured out before I arrived, which was the case in most of my prior academic experiences. This program was communicating the message of, "I will teach you what you need to know to succeed". As Guinier (2015) quotes Jim McDermott, a former University Park Campus School (UPCS) English teacher, "it's writing to learn," rather than writing to show learning" (p. 53) a mindset that was crucial in my journey through doctoral study.

Another aspect of the program that was positively impacted my experience in the UES program were the opportunities the department made available to doctoral students. For example, funds were set aside for doctoral students to attend, present, and learn at various conferences further aiding our development as scholars. This was a great way to further bond with faculty and doctoral students in our program as well as meet other doctoral students across the country. In addition, we were all invited to participate in the interview sessions of potential faculty members. The various styles of the candidates' presentations, research interests, and expertise helped me when I defended my dissertation and interviewed for faculty position. Additionally, observing the faculty's questions and responses to the candidates reinforced the necessity of being prepared and well-informed.

In addition to these opportunities, I was one of two doctoral students from our cohort selected as a doctoral scholar for the Southern Regional Education Board (SREB). Through SREB, Doctoral Scholars of color are provided multiple layers of support. This includes financial assistance for academic costs, funding for research, and career counseling. The program is also offering a job postings site and providing a scholar directory. In the fall of each year, SREB hosts the Institute for Teaching and Mentoring Program providing seminars, job search and networking opportunities, and other tools to aid in the professional success of Ph.D. scholars. According to their website, "The goal of the Institute is to provide a safe environment for doctoral scholars to share insights and survival tips for success in graduate work, build community among themselves, enrich their research and teaching strategies, and give scholars the skills that will serve them in the profession of their choice." Although the office of Diversity, Equity, and Inclusion at my institution covered our registration, travel, and lodging for three annual conferences, it was nice to know that our program coordinator was also invited to participate and serve as our mentor.

Meeting scholars of color from doctoral programs across the country was invigorating, encouraging, and in many ways enlightening. Our group sat in on thought provoking sessions, met highly intelligent individuals, and was exposed to intriguing strategies designed specifically for doctoral students of color pursuing doctoral degrees. These tactics were essential to us as it is well known that people of color start with disadvantages our White counterparts could never imagine. The conference was beneficial, and I looked forward to returning as a scholar every year.

Add to this, one of the faculty members in our department who is also the editor of a prestigious education journal, graciously extended to the doctoral students in our program an opportunity to serve as student reviewer. A student reviewer was paired with a faculty member where they would meet to be mentored in the process of reviewing of manuscripts for a peer-reviewed journal. My development as a scholar was further enhanced by serving as a student review for this journal as I learn what reviewers expected when manuscripts were submitted. It also showed me the ways to cultivate an academic style of writing. This, among other remarkable attributes to the UES program including a cohort model to build a strong student community, high expectations and support from faculty, and a commitment to admitting students from marginalized populations into the program continued to confirm that applying to the program was the correct academic decision.

Despite these overwhelmingly positive attributes regarding the doctoral program, there were a few areas that I believe could it fortify to better establish itself on the front lines of research and training doctoral students to stand against social injustice. Before these reflections are shared, it must be understood that what is shared in this writing was not designed to complain, nitpick, or villainize anyone or the program. Instead, these perspectives came from a place of concern and compassion for the spirit of the future program and the students who are and will be attending. These ideas, therefore, are based on the very readings we were assigned, the critical lens that the program taught us to think through, the implications for scholarly research, and my own personal experience as a doctoral student.

Interestingly, I did not to think too heavily about these "gaps" in my doctoral program until I read and we as a class discussed Fanon's work. One statement that stood out for me in his book was, "The colonized subject is constantly on his guard: Confused by the myriad signs of the colonized world he never knows whether he is out of line" (Fanon, 1961, p. 4). The quote symbolized how I began to realize my own wretchedness even in our program that staunchly clung to research and taught about social justice. Surprisingly, Fanon's teachings helped me realize that we were a colonized group when I began to observe some of the realities of our program. We were slaves who happen to have "good slave owners." They (the school's faculty and administration) did not whip us, they did not sell us or our chillens' off, they fed us well, they even taught us how to read, but in all, we were still colonized. We were still the wretched; the oppressed. Said in another way, we were confused about the entire doctoral process from the paperwork, to the academic style of writing, to dissertation committees. In some ways were told to "figure it out" and in others, we were given convoluted messages assuming that our interpretation information was accurate. Indeed, were at the mercy of the School of Education. This must be and will be address in this document.

Colonization

Considering these matters, I strongly believe that one way we as doctoral students were colonized was by having only one professor who taught most of the core classes in the program. Given that the program was interdisciplinary, there were other professors from other departments within the School of Education who aided in the instruction of the program, but their vested interests were in their respective disciplines, not the Urban Education Studies program. Hence, the primary voice that we heard throughout our department originated from one individual who also happened to be the program's coordinator. Suffice it to say, this reality is not to necessarily criticize his voice. Instead, I am suggesting that there needed to be another perspective whose primary responsibilities also included teaching, mentoring, and managing the program. Guinier (2015) quotes the director of the Jacob Hiatt Center for Urban Education at Clark University in Worcester, Massachusetts stating, "How teachers learn together will have a big impact on students' learning Del Prete says. The goal is to build a professional culture devoted to working with struggling students" (p. 59). Hiatt's thoughts spoke to the how my doctoral program could have benefitted from a more collaborative effort among colleagues who challenged, supported, and encouraged one another.

In my master's program, there were two faculty members who partnered in its leadership. It was clear that they played off one another's strengths. Their different perspectives and styles of teaching enriched our experience as students, and we longed for this variety of expression in our doctoral studies. Delgado Bernal & Villalpando further support this perspective with this quote:

Higher education in the United State is founded on a Eurocentric epistemological perspective based on white privilege and "American democratic" ideals of meritocracy, objectivity, and individuality. The epistemological perspective presumes that there is only one way of knowing and understanding the world and it is the natural way of interpreting truth, knowing knowledge, and reality. (p. 171)

Whereas we were pleased with how the program coordinator was exposing us to the theories and practices of Urban Education and providing the tools to effectively navigate a doctoral program of study, there was a desperate need for balance with at least one more full-time faculty person. Having only one faculty member who is White and male, despite his sincere commitment to social justice, was not a healthy representation of the students in the program. There was a desperate need for more faculty, more Black faculty (Bridges, 2011, Patton, Harper, and Harris, 2015), more Black male faculty (Palmer & Gasman, 2008), and women faculty because if "we do not create a mass-based movement which offers feminist education to everyone, females and males, feminist theory and practice will always be undermined by the negative information produced in most mainstream media" (hooks, 2015, p. 24). Thus, a doctoral program that touts social justice and thumbs its nose down at racial injustice cannot remain a one-man show. This structure further contributes to the colonization of critical research and students in an institution that is already systemically racist. This constitutes a great oxymoron.

The second and final aspect of the colonized state of the students in my doctoral program has to do with the volume of reading. As I stated earlier, we were exposed to great critical thinkers of our time. However, while I was awed at the vast treasures of knowledge and wisdom that we explored, the amount of reading required a system that better allows us to process the information. Often, there have been times when we came to class after reading these great works by renowned authors only to leave disappointed because a deep, thorough discussion was not allowed in the classroom. Fanon (1963) would call this colonialism. Paulo Freire (2000) would call this form of oppression banking education. Banking education "minimize[s] or annul[s] the students' creative power and to stimulate their credulity serves the interests of the oppressors, who care neither to have the world revealed not to see it transformed" (p. 73). In other words, banking education continued to be a part of our academic experience in our doctoral program core courses. The instructor was all knowing, all wise, and we are but empty vessels anxiously awaiting him to impart his expertise into our uninhabited minds.

Indeed, this was a sad indictment of our program and one that must be quickly rectified if any doctoral program wants to establish an environment of co-learners and co-constructors of knowledge. If the instructor has determined that the students in the program should be exposed to renowned scholars, then there should be adequate time in the classroom where the students can explore the discussion, even if the instructor is uncomfortable with or not as knowledgeable about the subject matter. According to Freire (2000), when:
The teacher presents himself to his students as their necessary opposite; by considering their ignorance absolute, he justifies his own existence. The students, alienated like the slave in the Hegelian dialectic, accept their ignorance as justifying the teacher's existence - but unlike the slave, they never discover that they educate the teacher. Freire (2000) p. 72.

If instructors wish to create a space of co-learning requires a resistance to banking education. As a Black man, I was often frustrated with reading many pages of books and articles and then left with no space to process my thoughts. I was being exposed to new ideas that spoke to my unique experience and I would come to class excited to discuss the things I read. Unfortunately, I left class frustrated because there was no opportunity to express my reactions to the readings or hear the perspectives of my classmates. To that end, if the instructor desires students to experience a deep understanding of the literature, I suggest that classroom be the primary location for discussion of the reading to take place. Creating time to process the information is crucial for mutual learning may continue to take place. Like my classmates, I had taken the time to read the assigned readings. Prescribing high volumes of reading and rushing on without the opportunity to process in the classroom setting is an oppressive practice that undermines the learning environment. In short, this was a very oppressive way to conduct a progressive, critically thinking, and socially sensitive doctoral program.

In closing, I would like to reiterate my point of reasoning for sharing this information. It was not my intention to criticize the program, but to accentuate its positive attributes as a whole as well as bring attention to some areas that could help enhance its effectiveness for critical research, the School's current students, administration, faculty, campus, and potential applicants. In light of this I do hope that the response from those who have an opportunity to read will not take an approach of White fragility which, as is described by Robin DiAngelo as "a state in which even a minimum amount of racial stress become intolerable, triggering a range of defensive moves" (p. 57). Instead, it is my hope that the administration and faculty of many doctoral programs strongly considers what I have shared true intention of addressing these changes. In doing so, I would like to encourage you to include doctoral students in the decision-making process. Their perspectives and opinions are valuable with insights about their experience in doctoral study that help to include the quality of program for future students. Further, it is my hope that the reaction of faculty and administrators invokes a strong sense of pride realizing that its students are so committed to social justice that they are willing to apply its tenets to the examination of their own internal racism and to their academic program whose very foundation is based on fighting against social inequities.

References

Bridges, E. M. (2011) Racial identity development and psychological coping strategies of undergraduate and graduate African American males. *Journal of African American Males in Education, 2*(2), 150-167.

Delgado Bernal, D. & Villalpando, O. (2015). An apartheid of knowledge in academia: The struggle over the "legitimate" faculty knowledge of faculty of color. *Equity & Excellence in Education, 35*(2), 169 -180.

DiAngelo, R. (2011). White fragility. *International Journal of Critical Pedagogy, 3*(3), 54-70.

Fanon, F. (2004). *The wretched of the earth.* Grove Press.

Freire, P. (2000). *Pedagogy of the oppressed.* Continuum.

Guinier, L. (2015) *Tyranny of meritocracy: Democratizing higher education in America.* Beacon Press.

hooks, b. (2015). *Feminism is for everybody: Passionate politics.* Routledge.

Palmer, R., Gasman, M. (2008). "It takes a village to raise a child: "The role of social capital promoting academic success for African American men at a Black college. *Journal of College Student Development, 49*(1), 70.

Patton, L. D., Harper, S. R., & Harris, J. C. (2015).*Using critical race theory to (re)interpret widely studied topics in U.S. higher education.* In A. M. Martinez-Aleman, E. M. Bensimon, & Pusser (Eds.), *Critical approaches to the study of higher education.* Johns Hopkins University Press.

Blackmaled by Academia

PART THREE

Perspectives on mutual support, mentoring, and the positive role modeling by Black men to overcome the historically-perpetuated mis-education by academia of young black men and in K-12 schooling.

CHAPTER NINE

I Mean You No Harm:
Implicit Bias and Black Males in Higher Education

Alan Acosta, Clark University

Abstract

Throughout the history of the higher education profession, the success of Black male students has been identified as a critical issue and overarching concern for institutions and administrators (Harper & Quaye, 2015; Hotchkins & Dancy, 2015; Kim & Hargrove, 2013; Palmer et al., 2014; Smith, 2015). Numerous barriers to Black male success in higher education have been identified in the literature, including academic preparation; enrollment; access to resources that support persistence, including economic, medical, residential, mental health, and other basic needs; and access to various forms of cultural wealth and capital that support Black male achievement (Harper & Harris, 2010; Harper & Wood, 2016; Mishra, 2020; Palmer et al., 2014; Scott et al., 2013; Warren, 2017).

One underexplored barrier to Black male success in higher education is the impact of implicit bias. Black males on college campuses experience many forms of discriminatory treatment, particularly at Predominantly and Historically White Institutions (Harper & Quaye, 2015). Numerous scholars have discussed the impact of both overt acts as well as smaller acts of discrimination, often referred to as microaggressions; however, there is a dearth of literature on the impact implicit biases have on the experiences and success of Black males in higher education. This chapter addresses this gap in the literature. Further, this chapter defines implicit bias, discusses how Black males are impacted by implicit bias, and shows how higher education administrators can address implicit bias regarding Black males in higher education. This is explored in the context of the author's experience.

What is Implicit Bias?

Scholars across a variety of disciplines have had difficulty in identifying and agreeing upon one universally accepted description and definition of implicit bias. While research about the concept of implicit bias is grounded in the field of psychology, particularly social psychology, literature on implicit bias is most robust in the fields of juvenile justice and criminal justice (Applebaum, 2019; Rynders, 2019). There are a few common aspects of the different descriptions of implicit bias. Many scholars believe implicit bias stems from stereotypes or other negative mental connections based on a person's understanding of or affiliation with some kind of group, including social identities such as race, gender, ability status, gender identity, or sexual orientation (Payne et al., 2017; Rynders, 2019). Additionally, most explanations of implicit bias frame it as unconscious, subconscious, or unintentional (Applebaum, 2019; Mitchell, 2018; Payne et al., 2017; Rynders, 2019; Selmi, 2018). Often, the mental connections or associations that form stereotypes which lead to implicit bias are based on someone's inclusion in a social identity group and is directed towards individuals that comprise historically marginalized, targeted, or discriminated-against groups (Applebaum, 2019). It has even been suggested the mental connections or associations that create implicit bias "may be the involuntary product of living in a culture with a history of discrimination and inequality" (Mitchell, 2018, p. 43).

Beyond these commonalities, scholars differ on what additional elements constitute implicit bias and how implicit bias works, both in the human mind and in actual behavior. One idea is that people engage in behavior that demonstrates implicit bias when they have a lot of demands on their time and mental capacity. If an individual has many decisions to make, particularly if those are of great importance or carry significant weight, or if the decision-maker is managing a lot of high-pressure situations or incidents in a compact time period, implicit bias is more likely to occur. The rationale most given for why this happens under these conditions is that the person making these decisions relies on mental shortcuts in their decision-making process (Mitchell, 2018; Rynders, 2019). Rynders (2019) notes administrators within the education system often are required to function in these types of situations.

Other dynamic scholars, particularly in social psychology, have analyzed are the conditions and environments in which implicit bias is most likely to happen. Most research related to implicit bias in the field of psychology centers around the Implicit Association Test (IAT; Greenwald et al., 1998). The IAT uses a series of computer exercises to measure the mental connections and associations individuals have related to different groups. The psychological literature that focuses on the test mostly centers on its effectiveness in correctly measuring people's bias, with many arguments to be made for and against IAT's utility and accuracy (Daumeyer et al., 2017; Gawronski & Bodenhausen, 2017; Payne et al., 2017). Payne et al. (2017) argue against the idea implicit bias is the result of ingrained attitudes residing inside of people and that people act upon the stereotypes they have associated with different groups of people. Rather, they assert in their Bias of Crowds model that implicit bias appears more often within the context of specific situations and that, as a social phenomenon, it passes through people's minds, fluctuating in strength, duration, and occurrence based upon a given time and context. Gawronski and Bodenhausen (2017) critique the Bias of Crowds model by contending implicit bias is the result of both factors related to the person and factors related to a given situation, and all of these factors involve the impact of pre-existing mental associations and given stimuli that activate the brain's processes. These scholars present an alternative view to the commonly understood perception of implicit bias, one that eschews unknown, uncontrollable attitudes resulting in actions for a more dissected, cerebral process resulting in the exhibition of behaviors.

Within the legal literature, scholars have had a more difficult time wrestling with the concept of implicit bias because proving at most legal standards of proof that someone acted in an unlawful manner based upon unconscious, underlying attitudes, warranting a punitive response is extremely difficult (Mitchell, 2018; Rynders, 2019). As a result, legal scholars argue over on the appropriateness and legality of setting legal standards or instituting criminal sentences based on implicit biases (Mitchell, 2018; Rynders, 2019). Another aspect discussed in the literature that is important in understanding implicit bias is its bifurcated nature. Several scholars note most people think of implicit bias on an individual level; that is, specific individual acts of discrimination based on implicit biases. However, many people often overlook that implicit biases and the discriminatory behaviors they engender are also the result of structurally oppressive forces that facilitate an environment conducive to the creation of implicitly biased attitudes (Applebaum, 2019; Rynders, 2019; Saul, 2018). These scholars argue that understanding how implicit biases work on both the individual and structural level is imperative for creating mechanisms that work towards change (Applebaum, 2019; Saul, 2018).

It should be noted there were several limitations with the research discussed in this chapter. First was that all of the reviewed literature was quantitative in design or some form of legal or conceptual analysis of the concept of implicit bias. While understanding implicit bias using these frames is important, no scholars chose to engage in qualitative research to understand implicit bias. Further, most scholars concentrated their quantitative research on participants completing the IAT, opting to dissect the test and how people responded to it as opposed to focusing on the people who have engaged in or been the target of implicitly biased behavior. Additionally, no scholars chose to take a critical approach to understanding implicit bias, as critical research would better uplift the stories and experiences of marginalized people and disrupt oppressive systems (Stefancic & Delgado, 2012). Also, scholars overwhelmingly emphasized their approach as striving to be as objective as possible in understanding a distinctly subjective topic, with some scholars noting the paradox of struggling to dispassionately examine an emotionally charged topic. The difficulty in finding these other forms of research about implicit bias highlights the potentially problematic frame most scholars are using in attempting to understand this phenomenon. It also magnifies the glaring deficiency in the literature in identifying and centering the lived experiences of historically marginalized populations directly impacted by implicit bias.

This chapter defines implicit bias as the unconscious mental connections and associations, attitudes, and stereotypes of others based on social identities that are involuntarily activated in a person's mind and unintentionally guide their decision-making processes. This definition was chosen as it is the best definition given the available literature on implicit bias.

Within the scope of this book, this definition relates specifically to Black males in higher education.

The Impact of Implicit Bias

The literature is overwhelmingly clear incidents where implicit bias occurs has a negative impact on the targeted individuals. Studies indicate implicit bias results in negative outcomes, particularly for communities of color and Native American and Indigenous communities, resulting in poor legal service, health concerns, and educational deficits (Rynders, 2019).

Within higher education, implicit bias has a host of negative impacts on students, particularly those from historically marginalized groups. Applebaum (2019) states, "Implicit biases and microaggressions undoubtedly contribute to a hostile campus climate for students from marginalized groups" (p. 131). Actions that are a result of implicit bias often lead students to feelings of helplessness, isolation, and diminish students' sense of belonging, which can inhibit the persistence and graduation of historically marginalized students, including Black males (Harper & Quaye, 2015).

While not much research studies implicit bias and its impact on Black males specifically within higher education, there is information that addresses the negative consequences of implicit bias towards Black males within the K-12 educational system. As Rynders (2019) discusses, Black males comprise 8% of the total public school students, but account for 25% of out of school suspensions. Further, Black students were more likely than White students to have some form of a disciplinary violation and were disproportionately more likely to be removed from a classroom due to disciplinary reasons. This inequitable treatment of Black males based on implicit bias in the K-12 system is undoubtedly a factor that leads to the disproportionate rate at which Black males drop out of schooling and contributes to the "school to prison pipeline" that has hampered Black male success in American society. Too often, Black males are betrayed by the American educational system preventing them from even reaching postsecondary educational opportunities. Addressing the implicit bias that prevents Black males from enrolling in and graduating from postsecondary institutions not only has numerous benefits for Black males, but for U.S. society as a whole. Black males that graduate from postsecondary institutions can increase their racial group's overall socioeconomic status, improve the nation's economy, and lower a number of significant societal costs, which include health care or the need for emergency services (St. John, 2003).

Suggestions for Higher Education Administrators

There are a number of suggestions for higher education administrators to address implicit bias in their work, particularly when working with Black males on campus. As noted previously, scholars suggest tackling implicit bias from both an individual and structural level to address the root causes of implicit bias issues (Applebaum, 2019; Saul, 2018). One of the most common interventions used to combat implicit bias is training (Payne et al., 2017). Implicit bias training is increasingly being used by companies, law enforcement agencies, and educational institutions to raise awareness of people's implicit biases and also provide tangible ways to work through them (Selmi, 2018).

When creating and incorporating an implicit bias training program, scholars suggest the training not simply be an explanation of what implicit bias is and stop there. This caution is given because studies indicate if people are simply made aware of their implicit biases and taught that all people have implicit biases and there is nothing they can do to control them, then the trainings can actually make people more comfortable about their biases and prevent substantive change. Trainings which only define implicit bias can also reinforce the systems of oppression they are designed to dismantle (Applebaum, 2019; Rynders, 2019). Researchers also encourage that implicit bias training address both individual and structural acts of implicit bias and discrimination, which can include training on microaggressions and explicit discrimination. This approach helps educate participants on the nature of implicit bias and situates it within larger hierarchies of discrimination as it relates to race, sex, gender, and other social identities (Applebaum, 2019; Saul, 2018).

It is suggested effective trainings give participants at least one tangible, concrete action they can take and complete after the training is over, even if it is a simple, straightforward action, such as having a conversation about implicit bias or discrimination with friends, families, or colleagues. Doing so encourages participants to apply some of what they have learned and provides an opportunity for them to practice skills they have received (Saul, 2018). These trainings also need to focus on implicit biases regarding Black males, the stereotypes that often form these biases, how Black males experience microaggressions, and how to create more equitable systems for Black males on campus.

Beyond offering trainings, institutions can provide structured opportunities for Black males to interact with students, faculty, and staff from different racial identities, as that allows for cross-cultural learning and the potential breaking of stereotypes. Additionally, institutions can create systems that review hiring decisions or other discretionary decision-making processes to ensure fairness and equity has been achieved. Institutions can also create recognition programs for staff members that have created positive, equitable, inclusive environments specifically for Black males. Any of these opportunities can address both individual and structural implicit bias (Rynders, 2019).

Administrators who do not identify as Black males need to recognize and prioritize a commitment to ensuring Black male success on college campuses. This means advocating for Black males within their scope of control, whether it be for funding, physical space for meetings on campus, providing considerations for potential impacts of proposed policies, and taking the initiative to learn about the experience of Black males. Non-Black male administrators must also proactively spend time listening to and being in community with Black males, both on campus and outside of the institutional community; examples include attending events that are highly attended by Black males or facilitating and participating in community service projects with Black males when possible. This kind of relationship building will give administrators an understanding of and appreciation for the Black male experience (Rynders, 2019), which will make it easier for them to identify opportunities to combat implicit bias and advance Black male success on campus.

Applebaum (2019) gives words of wisdom to higher education professionals who want to create a better institutional environment for all students, including Black males: Institutions must be willing to honestly examine how they are complicit in the campus climate they claim to want to remedy. The responsibility for campus climate begins with a commitment from the institution to proactively prioritize social justice issues. The tone and directions of university administrators through their actions and words shape campus climate and must not model a will to ignorance. When administrators only respond to campus climate issues in an ad hoc manner or because of public pressure resulting from bad national or local press, genuine change will be elusive (pp. 139-140).

Higher education institutions are comprised of people. Focusing on building capacity and changing the attitudes of people is essential in making substantive change which benefits Black males in higher education. It is often difficult for higher education professionals to engage in individual reflection on the behaviors or assumptions they have that contribute to the creation and maintenance of their own implicit biases. It is also challenging for higher education administrators to identify the institutional policies and structures they create and employ that unintentionally foster implicit bias on campus. Implementing a campus climate survey or having external reviewers conduct interviews or focus groups with important campus populations, particularly Black males on campus, and provide a summary of their findings to key institutional decision makers can assist higher education professionals in identifying and addressing any implicit bias "blind spots" they have created at their institution.

Case Study

To help frame what implicit bias is and how it affects Black males in higher education, as well as ideas on how to incorporate individual and structural change, the following case study is used as a guiding reference, taken from the author's experience, which occurred in the author's professional setting. Literature shows case studies are an effective method for learning how to successfully understand and employ theoretical concepts in practical situations within the appropriate context, making the information more "real-world" applicable and enhancing the learning process (Prado et al., 2020; Rand, 2003).

Years ago, one of the functional units within the author's scope of supervision was the campus student conduct office, and the office adjudicated a case involving a Black male student. The incident involved the student with whom the office interacted and the student's Black male friend, who was affiliated with a different institution and identified by police as a possible drug trafficker. The police noted as part of their surveillance the unaffiliated male spent significant amounts of time at the student's residence, and there were several instances over the course of a few weeks that individuals who did not reside on the property would visit the student's residence, presumably to purchase illegal drugs. The police eventually raided the student's residence; neither male was on the premises at that time.

Inside the student's residence, the police found a duffel bag with the student's name stitched on the outside and a firearm inside the bag; no drugs were found at the student's location, but drugs and other evidence consistent with drug trafficking were later found at the unaffiliated male's residence. When questioned by the police, the student denied any involvement in any drug trafficking activity or any drug trafficking occurring at his residence; however, the police proceeded to arrest and charge the student with intent to sell illegal drugs.

Per institutional practice, the student was temporarily separated from the institution pending the outcome of his student conduct case. The student's conduct case was heard by one of the White male student conduct staff members, and all student conduct cases used a preponderance of the evidence or "more likely than not" standard of proof. The hearing officer found the student responsible for distributing illegal drugs. He made this determination based on the bag with the student's name stitched on it, with a firearm contained inside, found in his residence, and the amount of interaction the student had with the unaffiliated male within the student's residence. The hearing officer reasoned it was more likely than not this information indicated the student knew of and was involved in drug trafficking with the unaffiliated male. The hearing officer noted the student had a previous violation of the institution's drug policy on his conduct record, and as a result of the prior record and egregiousness of the finding, sanctioned the student to a suspension from the institution.

The student appealed the decision of the hearing officer, and the author served as the appellate officer for the student conduct case. The author facilitated an appellate meeting with the student to hear his perspective regarding the incident. As he did with the police and at his conduct hearing, the student emphatically denied any involvement in the allegations, stating the unaffiliated male was a lifelong friend who visited him often because they would hang out and study. The student said he had loaned the customized bag, which had his name on it due to receiving the bag in high school as part of his participation on a sports team, to the unaffiliated male several months prior to the incident and was unaware of its contents. He reaffirmed he had no knowledge of his friend's involvement in drug activity and that there were never any drugs in his residence. He also shared the reason he had a prior record was due to the police showing up at his previous residence where his girlfriend had marijuana and he decided to take responsibility for the illegal drugs on her behalf.

In reviewing the information, the student provided during the appellate meeting and in the author's review of the audio of the hearing, all indications were that the hearing officer's decision was influenced by implicit bias towards Black males. All of the information used by the hearing officer to reach a decision was based on circumstantial evidence at best, and the student gave reasonable, logical explanations to all of the hearing officer's questions and concerns. Further, it took almost six months to schedule this student conduct hearing, and during the hearing, the student emotionally expressed annoyance with the length of time it took to schedule the hearing. Additionally, the student demonstrated his anger with the treatment he received from the police throughout the situation, and he directed a profanity at the officer providing an oral statement.

The author sensed that based on how the student presented during the hearing, with his raised voice and demonstrations of various frustrations, the White hearing officer likely viewed the student as agitated, playing into the mental connection and stereotype of an "angry Black male." Further, as the appellate officer, in listening to the hearing audio and reading the White hearing officer's decision letter, the language used did not articulate a clear basis for a finding of responsibility. While there may have been some concerns with the student's story, the author detected the hearing officer let their preconceived attitudes about Black males and the stereotype of angry Black males to influence his decision and favor a finding of responsibility, despite no strong foundation for that finding. The author determined the student deserved the benefit of the doubt in this case, a benefit the student, as a Black man, likely had not received from people in authority throughout his life. The author also recognized the sanctions were of a severity that they could prevent the student from graduating, thus potentially negatively altering the course of the student's life. The author decided to reverse the hearing decision: the finding of responsibility and all associated sanctions were vacated.

After the author reversed the decision, the author was concerned about how his relationship with the White hearing officer would be impacted by the decision. The author chose to facilitate a conversation with the staff member and discuss the decision, describing the author's concerns with the decision and how implicit bias could have played a role in the White hearing officer's finding. Somewhat surprisingly, the White hearing officer expressed appreciation and understanding about the decision made and articulated a commitment in wanting to learn from the situation and use that knowledge to inform future decision making. The author was also able to successfully advocate to campus partners for the student to get the needed institutional assistance to return to classes. The author recognized his position within the institution afforded him much more agency and flexibility in intervening in this situation than most other higher education professionals have when presented with a similar instance of implicit bias. Using the institutional mechanisms to

100

appropriately benefit the student was an obligation the author recognized and upon which he acted. The author understands he was fortunate there was no personal or professional cost or negative impacts in making this intervention. Had there been a professional or personal cost, the author recognizes this situation could have ended differently. Higher education professionals must assess the personal and professional risks associated with fighting implicit bias and decide for themselves if the cost is one they are willing to bear.

The author was supported by his supervisor in using the lessons learned from this situation to incorporate change which would minimize implicit bias in future conduct decisions. Individually, the student in this situation was supported in re-enrolling at the institution and eventually graduated, which likely would not have happened had the appellate officer not overturned the hearing officer's decision. Also, the White hearing officer attended several inclusion workshops to increase his awareness and understanding of different racial identities, including Black males. Structurally, the *Student Conduct Code* was updated and revised to require any student conduct decision where a separation was being imposed to be reviewed by the Dean of Students and their designee, in which they could affirm or modify the separation.

This case study demonstrates how a non-Black male staff member identified and intervened on an incident of implicit bias within his locus of control. He also subsequently implemented corrective measures individually and structurally as a means of addressing and minimizing incidents of implicit bias in the future. Higher education professionals faced with similar situations at their institutions can incorporate some of the lessons discussed.

Conclusion

Implicit bias is a detrimental dynamic on college campuses that can be an impediment to Black males' success. It is imperative for institutions to identify all individual and structural mechanisms that must be addressed and implement proactive measures to create a more welcoming environment for Black males on college campuses. Higher education administrators who do not identify as Black males must demonstrate a commitment to battling implicit bias towards Black males. Professionals must also continue to learn about and be in community with Black males, which can help expand their knowledge and identify ways to be a resource and support. By fighting implicit bias, college campuses can make the higher education experience better for Black males, increasing their likelihood for success and graduation.

References

Applebaum, B. (2019). Remediating campus climate: Implicit bias training is not enough. *Studies in Philosophy & Education, 38*(2). 129-141.

Daumeyer, N.M., Rucker, J.M., & Richeson, J. A. (2017). Thinking structurally about implicit bias: Some peril, lots of promise. *Psychological Inquiry, 28*(4). 258-261.

Gawronski, B., & Bodenhausen, G. V. (2017). Beyond
persons and situations: An interactionist approach to
understanding implicit bias. *Psychological Inquiry, 28(4)*.
268-272.

Greenwald, A.G., McGhee, D. E., & Schwartz, J.L.K.
(1998). Measuring individual differences in Implicit
cognition: The Implicit Association Test. *Journal of
Personality and Social Psychology, 74*, 1464–1480.

Harper, S. R., & Harris III, F. (Eds.). (2010). *College men
and masculinities: Theory, research, and
implications for practice*. Jossey-Bass.

Harper, S. R., & Quaye, S. J. (Eds.). (2015). *Student
engagement in higher education: Theoretical perspectives
and practical approaches for diverse populations* (2ⁿᵈ ed.).
Routledge.

Harper, S. R., & Wood, J. L. (Eds.). (2016). *Advancing
Black male student success from preschool through
Ph.D*. Stylus.

Hotchkins, B.K., & Dancy, T.E. (2015). Rethinking
excellence: Black male success and academic
values in higher education. *Spectrum: A Journal on Black
Men, 4*(1), 73-98.

Kim, E., & Hargrove, D. T. (2013). Deficient or resilient: A
critical review of Black male academic success and
persistence in higher education. *The Journal of
Negro Education, 82*(3), 300-311.

Mishra, S. (February 2020). Social networks, social capital,
social support, and academic success in higher education: A
systematic review with a special focus on "underrepresented"
students. *Educational Research Review, 29*.
https://reader.elsevier.com/reader/sd/pii/S1747938X1830304X?token=67
64ABA04127A11E2BF837470C49EC95BD3A350D10C222B2098BD6
AF93C2DE11E4AFFE08986CAE6B6E3F9AC507D906D4

Mitchell, G. (2018). An implicit bias primer. *Virginia
Journal of Social Policy & the Law, 25*(1), 27-57.

Palmer, R.T., Wood, J.L., Dancy, T.E., & Strayhorn, T.
L. (2014). Black male collegians: Increasing access,
retention, and persistence in higher education.
ASHE Higher Education Report 40(3). 1-60.

Payne, B.K., Vuletich, H.A., & Lundberg, K.B. (2017). The
bias of crowds: How implicit bias bridges personal
and systemic prejudice. *Psychological Inquiry,
28*(4), 233-248.

Prado, A.M., Arce, R., Lopez, L.E., García, J., &
Pearson, A. (2020). Simulations versus case studies: \
Effectively teaching the premises of sustainable

development in the classroom. *Journal of Business Ethics,*
161(2), 303-327.

Rand, J. W. (2003). Understanding why good lawyers go bad: Using case studies
in teaching cognitive bias in
legal decision-making. *Clinical Law Review, 9*(2), 731-782.

Rynders, S. (2019). Battling implicit bias in the IDEA to
advocate for African American students with disabilities. *Touro
Law Review, 35*(1), 461-480.

Saul, J. (2018). (How) should we tell implicit bias stories? *Disputatio:
International Journal of Philosophy,10*(50), 217-244.

Scott, J. A., Taylor, K. T., & Palmer, R. T. (2013).Challenges to
success in higher education: An examination of educational
challenges from the voices of college-bound Black males. *The
Journal of Negro Education, 82*(3). 288-299.

Selmi, M. (2018). The paradox of implicit bias and a plea for a new
narrative. *Arizona State Law Journal, 50*(1), 193-245.

Smith, D. G. (2015). *Diversity's promise for Higher education: Making it
work* (2^nd^ed.). The Johns Hopkins University Press.

St. John, E. P. (2003). *Refinancing the college dream: Access, equal
opportunity, and justice for taxpayers.* The Johns Hopkins
University Press.

Stefancic, J., & Delgado, R. (2012). *Critical race theory: An introduction*
(2nd ed.). New York University Press.

Warren, C. A. (2017). *Urban preparation: Young Black men moving from
Chicago's south side to success in higher education.*
Harvard Education Press.

CHAPTER TEN

A Black, Queer Man's Dialogue with Himself
About His Experiences in Academia

Steffen Glenn Gillom, Antioch University New England

Positionality

I am a 30-year-old Black, bi-racial, queer Ph.D. student at a predominately white institution (PWI) in New England. I have attended PWI (both large and small) for the entirety of my academic career with every setting looking different but feeling the same as if I'm in some matrix, forced to navigate one paradoxical situation after the other, to be a fly on the wall rarely speaking but always seen. To exist as a Black, queer, and male in academia is to be invited to several spaces to realize you are genuinely welcome in none of them. Too flamboyant to be a "man," too queer to be "Black," and too Black to be queer. At times, the hypervisibility produced an out of body experience that I liken to the development of a "spidey" or "sixth" sense. I walk into a room, and time slows down, and the tingling sensation in my fingers start, and I know, I am technically welcome but probably *not wanted* here. While I am sure that I am not unique and that there are scores of Black, queer men who have similar experiences across the country, I know that very few of us are blessed with the opportunity and platform to speak to these phenomena from a place of authenticity. Since this chapter is a rare opportunity, I believe it's best to structure this work unconventionally. So, I have crafted a rich and descriptive dialogue between my Black and queer identities (or egos as I like to say) that is guided by a series of questions aimed at teasing out significant moments, feelings, emotions, frustrations, and thoughts. My hope is to provide a "peek behind the curtain" that may resonate with readers and allow them to reflect on and maybe even relate to my experiences. I think it's is also important to mention that Gloria Watkin's spirited interview with her famed writing voice bell hooks in her book *Teaching to Transgress* (1994) directly inspired how I structured this chapter.

The Dialogue

Black ego: *In what ways did your queer identity impact the beginning of your college experience?*

Queer ego: Though I consider myself fairly well-read, I've really never come across any text that specifically speaks to what it is like for a queer man as they first transition into the university, though I do recall searching for such material at the time. Like many other Black sexually diverse beings I know, I experienced bullying in the form of teasing and even physical attacks that started in elementary and carried on through high school. Those experiences created anxiety, hyper-vigilance, anger, and sadness in me that I longed to escape. I remember feeling extreme naiveté, driven by my hope that our college experience would be different and less traumatic. Those collective traumas seemed to be at war with a strong desire to put me "out there" to be in community with our collegiate peers. I remember gaining the courage to finally speak in class after remaining relatively silent for the first week. I also recall how many of our male classmates looked at us as they listened to our voice, realizing that queerness might be housed in our Black body. I believe that this realization caused many of them to treat us differently, which caused me some distress. However, in a way, I wanted to be seen, to rip the band-aid off, so that my queer perspectives could partake in the history that we were making together, and I wanted you to make friends too; I knew it would be hard to do both. So, I pulled back, only resurfacing occasionally for the rest of the semester. I know that it might not have helped much since they still snickered when we talked and mocked how we said things from time to time. Still, I want you to know that I tried. Thinking back, I am still upset at the professor for never noticing and never stepping in to protect us. I think she could have *made a difference.*

Black ego: Yeah, I remember that time like it was yesterday. I recall that just for a moment, I was angry at you too. I thought, why couldn't you speak with a less flamboyant tone, why couldn't you have tried to sound "straighter." I really wanted to be friends with those other men, especially the Black ones, and I felt like you got in the way. It did hurt me to be excluded from that group of guys, and it hurt me even more that I was so upset at you since you've always been there for me; you are a part of me. Then again, I did compromise. I used our Blackness to bond with Black women and even some straight Black men who would engage with us, making the best I could of every one-on-one conversation or small group activity to culturally connect, and that really helped.

Queer ego: Yes, it did. However, you still never mentioned how you felt about that professor who never intervened, which led me to wonder *if you ever felt supported by those in our previous or even current academic institutions?*

Black ego: This is a complicated but albeit important question. The term "supported" can and does mean many things to me. I would say that I was somewhat supported as a budding Black intellectual but not as a complex Black individual, that part felt merely tolerated. Actually, your question reminds of an article by Dancy et al., (2018) who speaks directly to this experience in their piece *Historically White Universities and Plantation Politic: Anti-Blackness and Higher Education in the Black Lives Matter Era.* They brilliantly conceptualize that PWI's view the Black body and mind as the property of the institution, positing that we are used to caretake, labor, and uplift our colleagues while also being forced to contend with a slew of anti-Black behavior perpetuated by years of racist institutional memory. The black male-identified folks seem expected to entertain or serve (i.e., the college athlete) but not to *think.* While their article does not speak directly to the queer experience, as a Black man, I commonly feel expected to be entertaining, accessible, extra-nice, and funny at all times.

Queer ego: That article may not have spoken directly to the queer experience, but I deeply resonate with what you say. I feel hyper-connected to "divine feminine energy," which seems to draw our white peers and colleague to us. Sometimes I wonder if the intersection of my queerness and your Blackness creates a type of "*fem- Black-maleness*" that alters the way our white peers intermingle with us? ***Maybe that has helped us?***

Black ego: Maybe it has in that they enjoy hearing "our unique perspective," but, in all reality, what have those interactions ever led to besides the exploitation of our intellectual currency? Name one white professor that has been pre-emptive in fostering our personal, academic, or professional growth? I don't believe that any have.

Queer ego: That's a good point, and it makes me wonder, ***has there ever been academic mentorship or specific community that has fostered our growth?***

Black Ego: Yes, there were some, but only one of them was a professor, and she also ran the diversity center, the tall Black woman. She seemed to instantly notice us, asking us questions, setting us up with an advisor, and seeking out a genuine friendship with us. Looking back, I would call her a confidant and mentor.

Queer ego: That's ironic because we had several Black male professors, and none of them ever did that, they were always so stand-offish.

Black ego: Right. Do you remember what happened that one time we tried to reach out?

Queer ego: Of course, I do, how could I forget it? He was a reasonably young Black professor and poet with whom we both wanted to build a relationship. I remember we stopped by his office several times that semester, "just to say hi," hoping to be noticed. I knew he was straight, but he also seemed so lovely, so smart, and so "woke" that I assumed that he would never take attempts at our attempts at connection out of context. We always tried to make conversation with him, mentioning projects that we could work on together to which he often replied, "that sounds like a great idea, and I'll be sure to let you know when I get started on that," but he *never* did, and eventually we quit asking. Sometime later, I learned that he participated in projects with several of our Black male colleagues that were straight. Until today, I've never actually said this out-loud but, I don't think he felt very comfortable working with sexually diverse people.

Black ego: I think you are right, and I found it perplexing because he always called on us in class and complimented us for our steadfast work ethic. I believe that it was around this time that I started to realize that while our Blackness bought us tickets to the cookout, our queerness meant that we could only ever sit at the women's table. Anyway, on that note, ***how would you describe our relationship with the queer community, was it just as nuanced?***

Queer ego: Oh, yes, it was also very nuanced. I believe that being both Black and queer altered that way that they received us. Do you remember our

106

first group project in our master's program, when another queer guy, who was white, "called me out" for my "bad attitude" because I disagreed with his vision for our group project? I could feel him "sizing us up" from the minute we met, verbally excusing his discourteous behavior as a "type-A workstyle" and his rude comments as part of his "alpha" personality type. He made sure to follow-up every suggestion that I made with a sassy remark, eye roll, or deep-breath of displeasure. The other group members, who were white women, also witnessed his behavior, and it seemed to make them uncomfortable, though they did nothing to intervene, and one even seemed to slightly enjoy his antics. Growing tired of feeling disrespected, I calmly but firmly said, "if you keep acting in this disrespectful manner, then we will have a problem." I later found out that he told several other classmates that I threatened him. There were other times where I was warmly received by white queer men in peer-group spaces, only to be later shunned when I brought up the issue of race or reacted unenthusiastically to their sexual advances. These interactions sometimes left me feeling like they were more interested in "fighting or fucking us" than "standing with us" as siblings in the queer community. So, in short, I've made very few white and queer "good Judy's" over the years. Nevertheless, I still stand with the queer community and advocate for our collective empowerment.

How do you think navigating these relationships, structures, and stressors impacted our mental health?

Black ego: To be a Black person attempting to navigate relationships and structures within the PWI is to be in a constant state of anxiety and inauthenticity that impact our mental health. I feel forced continuously into conversations about "*safety*" where I am expected to "show up" as my "full and authentic self," even though, more times than I can count, I've wanted to yell: "How can I feel safe in a space where no one Black has any power? How can I feel safe in a place where the folks in power seem blind to every micro-aggression and structural oppression? How do I feel safe in a place where I have to teach more than I learn about the concept of racial and social justice? This system does nothing to protect me while profiting from my attendance and labor, so no, I don't feel safe. Now, run me my degree!"

However, I would never publicly say that as I believe that sort of "radical honestly" would be cataclysmic to our academic career. Like several of the other Black folks I know, I simply "play along to get along."

Queer ego: I feel the exact same way. **How to overcome these challenges?**

Black ego: We get grittier, we get louder, and we get more strategic as we aim to increase our structural power. We walk into the room together, arm in arm, and *own* it. We become unapologetically Black and queer and rebuke the messages that "they" told us about who we are - because we are beautifully and artfully made - and after we make it, we reach back and lift up the other Black queer bodies, creating a positive feedback loop that empowers and engrains us into this system and we do it healthily.

Queer ego: That sounds like a plan. I am ready. *I love you.*

Black ego: *I love you* too.

Discussion

The above interchange depicts a conflict-dance between two of my most salient identities that were both informative and therapeutic to explore. While there are many theoretical approaches I could take when crafting this analysis that best speaks to the conversation above, I believe that minority stress theory (Meyer, 2015) fits best. Minority Stressors (Meyer, 2015) are unique or additional types of stress that those who belong to a specific group (i.e., Blacks, Muslims, LBGTQ) face due to their marginalized status, such as ostracization, xenophobia, and homophobia; this theory allows me to directly name the unique stressors faced by Black queer men, allowing for straightforward discussion.

The pressure to intentionally form one's own community, participate academically, and withstand the economic and social loads that often come with being a college student created a unique recipe of overwhelming stressors for me. These minority stressors (Balsam et at., 2011; Blockett, 2017) impacted my mental and physical health.

The conversation between my Black and queer egos is laced with a slew of unique minority stressors, such as instances of anti-queerness and anti-Blackness (Blockett, 2017). Real-time illustrations from the dialogue include cases of me being mocked by my, mostly Black, male classmates for my "effeminate" sounding voice and a tense interaction with my white gay male colleague after he harshly snapped in a "sista-girl-type" tone that felt inappropriate and, in a way, anti-Black. Other types of minority stressors present within the dialogue include instances of isolationism, bullying, ostracization, and internalized homophobia. For example, my queer ego spoke about the withdrawal of their feistiness so that we could better blend in with the crowd, and my Black ego discussed attempting to halt the presentation of their authentic opinions in fear of academic and professional exclusion. Both of these incidents expose isolationist behavior that detects deep-rooted patterns of internalized homophobia and anti-Blackness that came to pass as I attempted to avoid being "found out" or "left out" by various groups.

The constant pressure to academically thrive while dealing with the plethora of minority stressors also created trauma responses in the form of emotional dysregulation, hypervigilance, and inappropriate guilt (Protocol, 2014). My queer ego experienced difficulty regulating their emotional response to being teased and isolated, noting extreme feelings of "anger and sadness" that they longed to escape. This prolonged suffering and exclusion seemed caused by a strong sense of hypervigilance that led to the unhealthy comparison of opportunities granted to those with more structural privilege than myself, such as me noticing that the professor whom I attempted to bond with had taken on several straight male mentees while craftily skirting around my requests for mentorship. That situation, and others like it, left me perplexed and riddled with a weird sense of guilt as I played back every interaction that the professor and I had in my mind, scanning for anything that I might have said or done that led to my rejection.

If I'm sincere, part of me did not want his mentorship any more than he wanted to give it. I now realize that I sought him out because he seemed to be the more "open-minded" and empathetic than the other Black heterosexual professors, making him closer aligned to the mindset espoused by many of the queer Black and brown academics, which is what I was ultimately looking for. What I really wanted was access to intentional community and scholars who were vested in my personal and professional growth on a granular level, which took me many years to find. The absence of Black queer intellectual contribution also meant there were little to no curriculum, programming, or scholarly spaces dedicated explicitly to Black sexual minorities. This nonexistence created a specific type of labor for me that is hard to articulate, although (Blockett, 2017) does so eloquently, pointing out that Black queer men often struggle to form "kinship connections" within the context of the white heteromerized PWI's where only white LGBT spaces exist. I add to that statement, "Black heterosexual spaces too." Nevertheless, as evidenced in my dialogue, not all outcomes of this trauma and labor have been adverse. My Black ego talked directly to the holistic sense of self that was forged in the fires of discrimination, theorizing that after years of trying, they realized that their only choice was to walk "hand in hand" with my queer ego. My Black ego also mentioned the development of "grit" or the ability to persevere in unsatisfactory conditions (Merriam-Webster, 2020). Both parts of me could survive alone, but they *thrived* together, gaining the ability to walk into the room authentically, unapologetically, and prepared to contribute. These moments of lucidity helped me realize that the isolation that stifled also give me time to grow, that the anti-gay micro-aggressions enabled me to develop a thick skin that could withstand criticism, and that the lack of institutional support made it mandatory that I find my own voice. It is also essential for me to note and appreciate the contributions that women (both cis and gender nonconforming) had on my development with my Black ego, noting that the only professor to proactively consider mentoring me was a Black woman.

Although not explicitly mentioned in the dialogue, women of all racial backgrounds and ages, such as my long-time writing tutor, academic advisor, peers, and professional colleagues, rooted for and tangibly supported my educational journey. These women advocated for me, continually reframing anti-queer remarks hurled at me and pushing for the inclusion of my thoughts in mostly heterosis spaces. Women made me a seat for me at their table, and I am glad to be there, and in turn, I use whatever male privilege or platform I have to carry forward their collective advancement.

Implications and Conclusion

Through sharing my inner thoughts, I aimed to (1) highlight the unique experiences of Black queer men in higher education, (2) identify and consider the impact of minority stressors on Black queer men and their identity development, (3) highlight the emotional labor that it takes for Black queer men to simply *exist* in academia (4) and to provide suggestions towards the creation of a more inclusive environment for Black queer men in higher education. I hope that the anecdotes and analysis in this chapter encourage all who read it to critically contemplate and reframe their interactions with their Black queer male colleagues. For those of you who wish to take a more proactive role, I invite you to consider using what structural power you possess to enact one or more of the following accommodations: The establishment of safe space, such as affinity groups. (2) The implementation of bi-weekly check-ins or advising appointments. (3) The intentional development of a community of allies that specifically contend with and support members of the Black queer community. (4) The intentional advocacy and outreach to Black queer students, staff, and faculty. (5) The proactive support for and uplifting of the scholarship of Black queer men. (6) The creation of Black queer intellectual societies and think-tanks. (7) The invitation of Black queer guest speakers and activists to your institution. (8) The establishment of an institutional policy that directly uplifts Black queer people. (9) The creation of mentorship networks and career pipelines and (10) the integration of Black queer scholarly research and literature into your curricula.

Implementation of one or more of the above-suggested accommodations into the framework of your institution helps expand your Queer Black male colleagues' position within academia, thus granting them more freedom to authentically express themselves and you the opportunity to bond with them in a genuine, meaningful way. If you consider yourself an ally to our community, then I expect you use your sphere of influence to do something.

References

Balsam, K.F., Molina, Y., Beadnell, B., Simoni, J., & Walters, K. (2011). Measuring multiple minority stress: The LGBT People of Color Microaggressions Scale. *Cultural Diversity and Ethnic Minority Psychology*, *17*(2), 163-174.

Scroggs, B., Durtschi, J., Busk, M., Goodcase, E., & Jones, D.L. (2020) Within-minority group discomfort in lesbian, gay, and bisexual emerging adults of color: Implications for group identification and well-being. *Journal of Gay & Lesbian Mental Health* *24*(2), 155-172 DOI: 10.1080/19359705.2019.1703869

Blockett, R. A. (2017). 'I think it's very much placed on us': Black queer men laboring to forge community at a predominantly White and (hetero) cisnormative research institution. *International Journal of Qualitative Studies in Education*, *30*(8), 800-816.

Chaudoir, S.R., Wang, K., & Pachankis, J.E.(2017). What reduces sexual Minority stress? A review of the intervention "toolkit." *Journal of Social Issues*, *73*(3), 586-617.

English, D., Rendina, H.J., & Parsons, J.T. (2018). The effects of intersecting stigma: A longitudinal examination of minority stress, mental health, and substance use among Black, Latino, and Multiracial Gay and Bisexual men. *Psychology of Violence, 8*(6), 669 - 679. https://doi.org/10.1037/vio0000218

Merrium-Webster.com. "Grit." Retrieved July 14, 2020 from: https://www.merriam-webster.com/dictionary/grit

hooks, b. (2014). *Teaching to transgress*. Routledge.

Johnson, E. (2005). *"Quare" studies, or (almost)everything I know about queer studies I learned from my grandmother* (pp. 124-160). doi:10.1215/9780822387220-008

Means, D. R. (2017). "Quaring" spirituality: The spiritual counter stories and spaces of Black gay and bisexual male college students. *Journal of College Student Development, 58*(2), 229-246.

Meyer, I. (1995). Minority stress and mental health in gay men. *Journal of Health and Social Behavior, 36*(1), 38-56.

Meyer, I. H. (2015). Resilience in the study of minority stress and health of sexual and gender minorities. *Psychology of Sexual Orientation and Gender Diversity, 2*(3), 209-213.

Rober, P. (1999). The therapist's inner conversation in family therapy practice: Some ideas about the self of the therapist, Therapeutic impasse, and the process of reflection. *Family Process, 38*(2), 209-228.

Story, K. A. (2017). Fear of a Black femme: The existential conundrum of embodying a Blackfemme identity while being a professor of Black, queer, and feminist studies. *Journal of Lesbian Studies, 21*(4), 407-419.

Substance Abuse and Mental Health Services Administration (2014). *A treatment improvement protocol: Trauma-informed care in behavioral health services*. U.S. Department of Health and Human Services. https://ncjtc-static.fvtc.edu/resources/RS00006428.pdf

CHAPTER ELEVEN

Blackgaymaled by Academia

Lawrence Bryant, Kennesaw State University

Introduction

This contribution seeks to illuminate my experiences in academia. My journey is filled with great successes, memorable milestones, and many disappointments. From life-threatening personal struggles to successfully walking down the aisle of a southern university with a PhD, my journey has been a story of transformation, commitment, and gratitude. This journey has afforded me the opportunity to realize my childhood dream of becoming a professor, leader and mentor for other Black men and women seeking the academic experience. My journey is riddled with experiences of brazen racism, disrespect, and discrimination. Not only because I am a strong Black man, but because I am also a Black gay man. One of the greatest life lessons from these experiences is that, in spite of the obstacles, I have learned to remain vigilant and steadfast in my determination to fulfill my life's purpose. That is to be a beacon of hope for other Black men, so that they can achieve their lifelong dreams in academia. Moreover, my mentors and PhD committee in graduate school helped me realize that the many experiences that I had and am still having are meant not only for my success, but for the success of others. Being a Black male in academia is oftentimes challenging; however, adding sexual orientation to the mix can be a double-edged sword. This became very apparent to me as a tenured tract professor with research interests that did not align with the values and beliefs of departmental administrators and other faculty. Although I was denied tenure based on bias and malfeasance, my spirit will never be broken, because I believe the best is yet to come.

Academic Bio Sketch

It all started on July 13, 1953 in a sprawling urban city called Philadelphia (Philly), affectionately known as "The City of Brotherly Love." That was the day I was born. Cheesesteaks, hoagies, water ice, and yes – soul music was all the rage back then. We had the Delfonics, the Spinners, the Stylistics, the Intruders, and yes Patty Delmonico, the fabulous Miss Patty Labelle. I loved them all. Mom and dad said that when I arrived, they were the happiest people in the world, until their deaths, those feelings never changed; we were a caring and tight-knit family. Although by many standards we would be considered poor, that never phased me. We were exposed to many cultural and social experiences, including, the world's fair, Willow Grove Amusement Park, block parties, and family reunions. These events garnered true pride in me for my community and family. Most of my childhood was happy, joyous, and carefree; except for one thing: I was sexually, emotionally, and physically attracted to the same sex, and I knew this as early as eight years old. This realization would shape many of my childhood and adult experiences, both socially and academically.

The Way We Were

Much of my childhood learning was shaped by the formative educational institutions I attended: elementary, middle, and high school. In an effort to achieve mandated integration, we were bussed to an all-White middle school. It was during this time that racism and discrimination in the school setting became real for me. Many White parents were livid that their children had to attend school with Blacks; but despite that, I gained many new White friends during this period and cherished their friendship. These formative schools helped shape my values, morals, and standards. These principles were further nurtured by my experiences in higher education, including, undergraduate, graduate, and my doctoral studies. In a spirit of humility, I am proud to have received my AAS in Respiratory Therapy, a BSW in Social Work, an MPH in Public Health, and a PhD in Adult Education, Administration and Policy.

This higher education trajectory set the stage for my becoming a tenure track professor at one of the largest state universities in the country. Additionally, I also served in teaching positions in various other institutions of higher learning. These experiences totally exemplify the chapter topic "Blackgaymaled By Academia" in both positive and negative ways. This chapter explores my journey through academia as an unapologetically proud Black gay man; this includes the good, the bad, and the unforgivable. My sexual orientation helped shape my world view in both my educational and personal experiences.

It seemed everybody in my neighborhood knew I was different, sure, I played the traditional childhood games (except basketball), but I was also interested in other things - like making money, so I ventured into things like going to the store for many of my female neighbors, going to the Acme Supermarket to carry groceries for old ladies, and stints at various other jobs. What was most impactful during this period was my paper route. For many years, I delivered the Philadelphia Tribune throughout my community; this was the city's premier Black newspaper. Not only did I deliver the paper, I also incessantly read this paper, which gave me a sense of pride and awareness about Black culture, especially the entertainment section.

These are some of the things that helped shape my thought process in terms of Blackness and Black pride. Although my friends knew I was different, sometimes they let me know this by calling me unflattering names and bulling me, but for the most part, they still accepted me for exactly who I was, that is, everyone except my father and grandparents, this would be a long arduous process. Although my father was a caring, virtuous and loving man, and my grandparents very religious, they did not understand this part

113

of my life, after all it was the 60s - that's just the way it was!

I'm Coming Out
(But I didn't Want the World to Know)

I remember this day as if it were yesterday. I am sitting in class at my high school and I hear my name over the loudspeaker "Lawrence Bryant, come to the principal's office immediately." Fear gripped me as I left class and headed to his office. I hadn't been cutting class, my grades were good, and I had good attendance, what could this man want with me? As I nervously walked into his office, I found out. There sat my father, this 6'2" towering figure, crying his heart out. As our eyes met, no words were exchanged, just an empty stare. The principal then led me to my counselor's office, where she proceeded to tell me that because of suspicion, my father had gone through my drawer and found some letters. These were not just any letters; they were very descriptive, romantic, and explicit, love letters, not from a girl, but from a man. My counselor then proceeded to tell me that my father thought I had homosexual tendencies and was extremely upset, he told her that he wanted me to be home by 6:00 that evening to discuss this matter further.

As I walked into the house at exactly 6:00 PM, I was shocked at the scene that was unfolding. In the living room sitting in a circle, were my dad, my mom, my grandmother, and an aunt. In the distance, I could hear my grandfather, who was a Pentecostal minister, praying to God for my immediate deliverance. In the middle of the circle was a chair, just for me. I sat down while my family (mostly my grandmother) hurled insults and innuendos at me because of my sexual preference (she called me a freak). This hurt me to my core and resulted in us not speaking for many years. Ultimately, we became the best of friends and she began to accept my sexuality. I would have never dreamed that my coming out to my family would have unfolded the way it did.

Sexual Healing

After my grandparents left and it was just me and my father, he abruptly asked me to strip naked to assess whether some male deformity was the cause of my homosexuality. After finding me normal, he seemed relieved. Finally, my father said to me that he loved me and if this was the lifestyle I wanted to live, that he would accept it; but he warned me not to do anything to embarrass the family. Although relieved to hear this from him, the emotional damage had been done, both in a negative and positive way. Although this experience was traumatic, it resulted in me making a personal proclamation, that if my father could except my sexuality then it didn't matter about anyone else. Nevertheless, at the ripe age of 16, I decided to leave home and move into my own apartment. I could no longer stand the silent tension in my house. I would use education and personal development to help fill that gaping hole in my gut, that thing that says I'm not good enough just as I am. I needed something to show the world and my family that I was more than some freak. Academia would be my deliverer - I needed sexuality healing.

We Moving On Up
"The Academic Ladder"

I was highly motivated and driven to go to college and pay my own way. Fortunately, throughout high school, I maintained a fulltime job as an orderly in a university hospital operating room. During this tenure, I began to observe respiratory therapists. I watched their every move, loved the fact they wore a shirt and tie, a white lab coat, and presented themselves in a very professional manner. Moreover, they were highly skilled and specialized in heart and lung diseases. After graduating high school, I made the wise decision to enroll in a community college respiratory therapy program, this was where my academic journey began, the year was 1972. The program was challenging and time consuming, especially since I was still working fulltime at the hospital. Although the work was difficult, I welcomed the challenge; I was truly "moving on up." That urge to make my family proud of me was the driving force. However, as the only Black male in the class, I faced racism and discrimination from both the White students and instructors.

I felt like the director of the program hated my guts and in no uncertain terms let me know. I must admit, for the first year I barely passed my classes, and was threatened that if I didn't do better, I would be kicked out of the program, no advising, no encouragement, just do better or get out! My saving grace came in the form of a political science class that I took as an elective. The instructor in this course was Black, this made a significant impact on me because none of my other professors were Black. Although this man looked every bit the "Nutty Professor," he was intelligent, articulate, had a commanding presence, and he listened intently to what I had to say. It was in that academic space that seeds were sown for me to also become a professor. This was extremely important because up until this point I had not personally known a Black professor, let alone having one as my teacher. Although my White professors played a pivotal role in my academic experience, this professor instilled a sense of hope that I also could one day become a professor.

I knew the only way to achieve the goals that I dreamed of was to buckle down and get serious about my course work. It was then that I started getting better grades. This shocked the director, who was ready to kick me out of the program, more importantly, it shocked me. However, this determination, fortitude, and commitment followed me throughout my entire academic voyage, after that experience, I got nothing but As and Bs, which bolstered my self-esteem and self-efficacy. On May 15, 1975 this Black gay man from Philly graduated from a community college with an associate's degree in Respiratory Therapy, the first person to do so in my family. My journey would continue in this field for 45 years and include both clinical and academic experiences. However, I would have to challenge countless episodes of Bigotry and discrimination.

To Be Young Gifted and Black
Challenging Bigotry in Respiratory Therapy

I had the dubious distinction of being the first in my family to graduate from college. This achievement inspired others to follow suit. Little did I know that this part of my journey would thrust me into the clutches of racism and discrimination. I had been working as an orderly for about five years, when I graduated; so, it was only natural that I would apply for a respiratory therapy position at my hospital after graduation. However, much to my chagrin, I was told that a degree from a community college was inferior, given that the hospital had its own respiratory therapy program and considered it superior to any other. I proceeded to march right down to the Equal Employment Opportunity Commission (EEOC) office and filed a discrimination complaint. I never thought that it would have such far reaching consequences. Meanwhile, I applied for and got a position at another hospital. It took about a year for my case to be resolved. Nonetheless, revenge was swift and sweet.

My complaint resulted in the director being fired, the department hiring multiple persons of color, and me being offered a fulltime staff position, which I accepted. This position resulted in one of my greatest learning experiences as a respiratory therapist. During this time, I also passed the National Board for Respiratory Therapy Registry exam, after five attempts, I also relocated to Los Angeles California in 1979. It was at this juncture that respiratory therapy and my academic professional life merged.

One thing that became apparent early on was just how in demand respiratory therapists were. I have always been able to find a job, and when I arrived in LA, I had already secured a position at a large metropolitan hospital. Many large teaching hospitals have collaborative relationships with area schools and colleges of respiratory therapy. In this relationship staff therapists are responsible for educating and evaluating student clinical abilities, knowledge, and skills. Many therapists prefer not to have students, since this compounds their daily responsibilities. However, I loved and excelled at teaching, such that, my department director appointed me, along with another young White therapist, as clinical instructors for all respiratory therapy students rotating through our department. Ironically, these students were from an area community college, the same kind of institution that I had graduated from. As clinical instructors, we functioned as a conduit between the college and the hospital. It was during this time that I learned the intricacies of evaluating students on their clinical performances and determining their suitability for become respiratory therapists.

My knowledge and skills as a respiratory therapist would be under constant scrutiny and question by some students regarding my knowledge and capabilities, most of these students were White, and not used to A Black man telling them what to do. However, this scrutiny and disrespect was not displayed to my White counterpart. What was most challenging was when I had to make the determination that some students were not capable of translating the classroom experience into the clinical arena. I learned very quickly that I had to be ten times better and more knowledgeable than my peers. For example, students constantly challenged my knowledge and skills related to respiratory therapy, oftentimes going to my White counterpart behind my back questioning my knowledge and skills. At first, I began to doubt myself and my abilities. However, I realized that my yearly evaluations from my supervisors were impeccable and acknowledged that I was one of their best therapists. The fact that it took me multiple times to pass my boards was a blessing in disguise, because I knew respiratory therapy like the back of my hand. This helped me totally embrace my truth of being "young, gifted, and Black." That being said this kind of racism and discrimination follow me throughout my entire professional career as I climbed the academic ladder. However, this experience resulted in a renewed sense of purpose.

Ain't No Mountain High Enough

This new sense of purpose resulted in me going back to school after 25 years. I decided to seek an undergraduate degree, not in respiratory therapy, but in social work. Given what I had gone through, I wanted my life to exemplify service. It was during this time that the HIV/AIDS epidemic was raging in my community and killing many of my close friends. It seemed like I was going to a funeral every day. In many instances, Black gay men were treated like scum by many in society, some of this contempt came from their own families. For example, some Black churches refused to funeralize Black gay men, even if they were members of their church, significant others were oftentimes not permitted to see their partners in the hospital on their death bed, and many families disowned their children when they found out that they caught the virus from living a gay lifestyle. To add insult to injury, the White gay community was just as racist toward Black gay men as the general society, especially when it came to dissemination of federal and state resources for HIV/AIDS prevention, treatment, and education. Back in the early eighties, much of the funding and resources for HIV/AIDS went to White gay organizations; however, many of these organizations did not include Black gay men in their outreach. Subsequently by the nineties the face of HIV/AIDS changed to Black gay men in terms of new cases. (Airhihenbuwa et al., 2006) It was during this time that my personal life also took a dark turn into substance abuse, however, through the help and support of a 12-step program, I am now clean 28 years.

Through this backdrop, I committed my life to research and education around HIV/AIDS and sexuality among Black men. Of course, my undergrad program welcomed and was on the front lines of this war. My professors encouraged my research trajectory, and some faculty even looked like me. I particularly remember an amazing Black female instructor from my group dynamics course; she was intelligent, unapologetically pro-Black, and confronted the racist ideologies of my White classmates. She demanded and got total respect from everyone in the class. I wanted the same for myself. There is a great freedom in being authentic and not biting one's tongue when it comes to confronting racism and White privilege in academic spaces. I knew deep inside that I possessed that same vociferousness, vehemence, and tenacity.

Upon completing my undergrad studies, I moved to Atlanta, after a couple of years of settling in, I decided to go back to school for my master's in public health. Although I wanted to go to an HBCU, none in my hometown would accept me. I found myself at an elite, ivy league, mostly White, private university. How I managed to get into this expensive academic space was nothing short of a miracle. It just so happened that during the application process, a Black professor was in the role of interim chair of the school of public health; in fact, he was one of only two professors of color in the entire public health program. During my interview to assess my suitability for the program, I was determined to take a risk and be as transparent as I could. I shared about overcoming many personal struggles, and how the HIV/AIDS epidemic was raging in the Black community, and my commitment to doing research in this arena. He listened intensely, finally saying:

Mr. Bryant, it is so refreshing to find someone who literally has the very experiences that we in public health teach about. There is not one professor in this entire department that has been through what you have, therefore, you have a powerful gift for not only public health, but also the world. I am going to personally walk your application over to registration to admit you into our program. (R. Braithwaite, personal communication, March 20, 2001)

Hence my graduate journey began. By this time, I knew exactly what impact I wanted to have on the world, every writing assignment, every research endeavor, and every conference, to the extent that I could, was related to HIV/AIDS and to a lesser extent sexuality.

By this juncture in my academic journey, I got used to being the only Black male in most of my classes, and I only had one Black instructor during my entire time at this institution. This was the same instructor that admitted me to the program. There were more Black female students in the program, and they along with me felt that the university and department should hire more Black professors who are in decision making positions to better reflect the increasing Black student body. (Naylor et al., 2015) Thus, we created the Black Student Union, which is still in existence today. We demanded and got more Black professors, we promoted policies that took into considerations the interest and needs of Black students and the Black community overall. This also resulted in the department being less exploitive of Black communities where they did research, as it turns out, we were advocating for a research methodology called Community-based Participatory Research (CbPR). Formative research by Israel, et. al. (2008) highlights the tenants of CbPR. She posits the following, CbPR: TENANTS

118

- ➢ Recognizes community as a unit of identity
- ➢ Builds on strengths and resources within the community
- ➢ Promotes co-learning and capacity building among all partners
- ➢ Involves a long-term process and commitment
- ➢ Emphasizes local relevance of public health problem and ecological perspectives that recognize and attend to the multiple determinants of health and disease
- ➢ Disseminates findings and knowledge gained to all partners and involves all partners in the dissemination process
- ➢ Involves systems development through a cyclical and iterative process
- ➢ Integrates and achieves a balance between research and action for the mutual benefit of all partners. (p. 18) .

These principles have guided my scholarship and research endeavors throughout my career, in fact, I will not engage in research that is not inclusive of the communities where I am doing research. Oftentimes White researchers would hire Black research assistants to go into these communities to do research and not include members in decisions that impacted them (Lahnston, 1973). Sometimes the research results would be biased in favor of racist and patriarchal standards, ideologies and perceptions. This was not challenged by the community, because the results were often not shared with these individuals. Our coalition sought to make the research process more participatory in nature, we advocated for research that respected and was inclusive of the communities being researched. I recently joined the Black Student Union as A Board Member, only to find out that many of the issues from 20 years ago are still being experienced by students.

The greatest gift from this experience in graduate school, was the autonomy to do the type of research I love, this was reflected in the title of my master theses: "The Black Church and Black Gay Men in the Era of HIV'AIDS"; this would be the beginning of my research publications and the inspiration for continuing to obtain my doctorate. I truly felt that there was no mountain high enough!

To Dream the Impossible Dream
My Doctoral Journey

I would never have dreamed during my darkest hour that one day I would be entering into a doctoral program, because who would have known that all of the pain and agony that I experienced in my personal life would come full circle so that those experiences would give me the inspiration to achieve higher heights and more importantly, the opportunity to allow my journey to help others, especially my Black brothers and sisters. I must admit for the most part, my doctoral journey was an exceptional and fulfilling experience. I continued to do research around homophobia and racism. I developed a special bond with three Black professors, two of which were in my department and the other outside.

Throughout my doctoral journey, I developed a special bond with these professors, this was important because it gave me the opportunity to discuss my research interest and dissertation topic, for which all three fully embraced and encouraged me to "Go for it." I developed a special bond with my female professor, she was one of the most powerful persons I had ever met. Her research focus was on Black Women's studies, and much of what she taught about oppression, included Black gay men. In addition, she frequently discussed racism within the department, paralleling much of my own experiences. I was fortunate to have all three of these professors on my dissertation committee. As I entered the dissertation phase of my journey, I tried to select my committee members very carefully, my decision to include these Black professors was simple – I trusted them. Lastly, because my topic dealt with Black gay men, I felt I had to have an expert on this topic on my committee, so I chose the only gay male in the department doing research in this area, he was White.

The dissertation journey was a vigorous undertaking, especially since I was still working fulltime. My committee members were very supportive, encouraging, yet demanding. Notwithstanding, the final stage of my dissertation would prove to be one of the most stressful experiences I have ever encountered. The day was March 21, 2008, my dissertation defense, I was nervous, anxious, yet confident. I knew I had done my best and my committee seemed to feel that I was ready; yet as I sat outside the room waiting to be called in, uneasiness came over me. As the defense proceeded, I just knew that I was on the home stretch; I was able to successfully defend my methodology, my pedagogical approach, and my research significance. Each committee member had reviewed my final draft beforehand, and made minimal suggestions for change, all except my White gay committee member.

He proceeded to tell me that while the content and research approach was great, he had a problem with some of my grammar and formatting. He further commented that he could not approve the dissertation without major grammatical corrections. When he handed me my copy of his review, almost the entire document was marked in red ink. Not only was I devastated, I was angry. He had reviewed my dissertation multiple times and never once commented on any grammatical issues. Little did I know that behind the scenes there had been brutal racial tensions between this individual and my other committee members, I was the fall guy. Fortunately, my Black committee members literally came to my defense, especially my chair.

The first thing that everyone agreed upon was to reconvene the defense in one week, all agreed to rearrange their schedules to accommodate this effort. Secondly, my chair invited me over his home over the weekend to address the concerns of this committee member. I am forever indebted to him for offering to do this, we worked tirelessly to address every single issue. The next week we reconvened and the remarks from each committee member were stellar, all noted the magnificent contribution that my dissertation made to the field of

120

adult education. As a result of the support and the unwavering commitment that my chair gave me, I promised to deliver the same to those that come under my tutelage. I would have a chance to do just that in the next phase of my academic journey. When I walked down the aisle and accepted my doctoral degree, my lifelong dream had come true.

A Ball of Confusion
Blackgaymaled by the Academy

After graduating with my PhD, the stars seemed to line up in my favor. I was offered a fulltime tenure position at a large southern state university. Moreover, the position was in a school of respiratory therapy. This program offered an undergraduate and graduate degree in respiratory therapy and claimed to be one of the nation's top programs. It took many of my colleagues' years to get this kind of position. What I knew early on, was that I was hired solely because I am Black and had a PhD, this was a rarity in respiratory therapy circles. Many of the Black, mostly female students had been complaining for years that there were no faculty of color in the program. But I knew that I brought much more than color to the table. I had many years of experience as a respiratory care practitioner, was very knowledgeable of the field of respiratory care, and had past experience teaching community college students in the clinical setting. (Abdul-Raheem, 2016)

As a tenured track professor there were lots of expectations. Although I was in the school of respiratory therapy, we were under the department of health sciences and the college of nursing. Our department chair was a White female with an EdD, we also had four very conservative White male faculty, all had their master's when I was hired. To round off our department, we had a faculty member from Turkey, who also had her PhD. From the beginning, the culture was very toxic. My White male counterparts were very conservative and exemplified the good old boy mentality. My feeling is that they were extremely jealous that I was Black, on a tenure track, and had a doctoral degree, they indirectly let me know early on that my sexual orientation was problematic. Black support staff and our administrative assistant warned me that I was in for a bumpy ride in my efforts to achieving tenure. They said that the White males in the department would do everything in their power to derail my tenure.

During the first two years, I felt totally supported by my chair in my scholarship and research endeavors, the problem was that there was no support mechanism in place in the department to nurture tenure track faculty in respiratory therapy, because up to that point there had not been a tenured respiratory therapist in the university's history. Basically, they provided me with a set of nursing tenure guidelines and had me fend for myself. Up until this point, my research and interest were in HIV/AIDS. However, this trajectory did not sit well with department administrators, even though respiratory therapists are on the frontline in caring for these patients, since many exhibit co-morbidities with severe pneumonia. Much to my displeasure, my chair recommended that I go into tobacco control, so I relented. Since my father was a smoker and had passed away from lung cancer, I thought this would be something I could do to honor him; however, I felt that I was compromising to satisfy their ideologies.

Nevertheless, I took off carrying the tobacco torch. Two things became very clear to me; firstly, I had to publish, or perish; the second thing was that I needed to embark on a research trajectory that brought substantial dollars into the institution. Fortunately, I was able to bring in tobacco related research funding from the state and from several other funders. This was the most funding brought into the department up to that point. Subsequently, many articles resulted from this research. Up until this point, my chair was very supportive of my research, we even published together. After about my third year, departmental winds changed. My chair was promoted to associate dean of academic affairs, and one of my conservative White males in the department became chair. I was shocked, since none of these positions required a search for the most qualified person, also, neither of these individuals had significant publications or research funding. Although I had a PhD, was published, and had brought in funding to the department, I wasn't even considered for the position of chair. This was all a ball of confusion; nevertheless, I kept my eye on my tenure journey.

The Torture of Tenure
Plain Old "Bad Luck"

The process of tenure and promotion became an arduous maze of conflict, discord, and outright mayhem. Starting with the new faculty chair, whose highest degree was a master's. Our first altercation came during my third-year faculty review. In all of my professional career, I have never experienced such acrimony and disrespect. My previous faculty reviews were good, so I was quite angered that this person basically gave me an unfair and totally biased evaluation. He said that several students were not pleased with my teaching methods; therefore, he recommended that in the future they make their concerns known in my reviews, knowing well that good student reviews are required for tenure. The meeting went further south, when I told him exactly what I thought of the review and his obvious bias. As time progressed, our relationship became more strained; not only did he taint my character to the other White male faculty members, he proceeded to consistently badmouth me to our new dean. The school had just hired this individual to lead our college, by the time I formally met her, she already had preconceived ideas of who I was.

The working environment became so toxic and so emotionally draining, that I sought psychological counseling. I also sought help from our new diversity officer who worked out of the provost office. It was obvious to me that she had little to no power to do anything about what was happening in our department. By this time, I continued to publish, do research, and developed relationships with fellow colleagues. My work in tobacco was

122

becoming well known, such that I was invited to Shanghai, China to do several presentations on tobacco prevention and HIV/AIDS. When I returned to the university, not one person acknowledged or asked about my trip, I just shrugged it off. I had just one year left to go for my tenure review.

It was on a Saturday afternoon, I was just relaxing at home when I went to retrieve my mail, among the mail was a formal looking letter from the university. I opened it and almost had a heart attack; I couldn't believe what I was reading. It was from the dean's office saying that my contract would not be renewed the following year, and that this decision was recommended by my department director. The reason given was that my research trajectory was unacceptable. This was perplexing to me since the dean had not even read any of my materials, or even discussed any of my research interest. I was equally puzzled as to why my director would say this when I had previously received a positive third year review. Moreover, my director and I had been in recent discussions about possible research collaboration (Helgesson & Sjogren 2019). Nevertheless, when I returned to work the following week, my director rushed into my office, frantic, nervous, and out of breath, he said that he had also received a copy of the letter and tried to intercept it before it reached me but had been unsuccessful.

My director was extremely apologetic, noting that he had not said the things the dean mentioned in the letter, he further noted, that he was not at all in agreement with the dean's decision, this sentiment was also shared by my department chair. However, it is my contention those months of behind the scenes of character assassination to the dean by both the director and the program chair added to what was obviously her decision. Ironically, the dean had not so much as had a conversation with me regarding this matter. However, behind the scenes the dean herself was in a firestorm, her policies, lack of leadership, maltreatment of faculty and inability to move the college forward, drew the ire of the entire college, and the provost office. It was at this point that I consulted with a lawyer, who in no uncertain terms told me it would not be worth my time or money to pursue this. He told me that if I sued the dean and university, that not only would this be extremely costly, but that the dean would probably destroy my academic career.

Following this uproar, I was asked by my chair to head an effort to gather information from nursing and other faculty staff on grievances and concerns with the dean's leadership. I made sure that I gathered as much information as I could from the nursing faculty. Subsequently, this was the beginning of the end for her, after I left the institution, I heard that she was unceremoniously fired and escorted from the university premises by security. Unfortunately, many faculties of color have had similar experiences as I did. For example, findings from a qualitative study by Turner and Graverhotz (2017) make the following poignant statement:

The reality is that unless you have support networks around and above you that are going to protect you, and often those are not in place, what will end up happening is: 1) you are going to deplete yourself; 2) a narrative will start to form about you—whether it is accurate or not—and that's going to lead to 3) your marginalization and your removal from the system before you are there long enough to bring in other people, create change, and do some good. You have to be there long enough to establish yourself, really establish yourself, as a thinking, thoughtful person, because that benefit of doubt isn't given to you as it is to your other coworkers. (p. 219)

Fortunately, I had respiratory therapy clinical practice to fall back on, and at this point I went back into practice to regroup and decide on next steps. These experiences further validate recent work done by Turner & Graverhotz (2017), they note that "The lack of other Black men in the professional ranks and the disparate treatment they received made them question both the institution's commitment to diversity and themselves" (p. 212).

I Got A New Attitude

Although bruised and battered after the above experiences, I was not defeated; however, I was not sure I wanted to continue in the cutthroat environment of the academy. Meanwhile, I was presented with an opportunity to work for the state department of public health, there I led a team in developing a statewide strategic plan in response to the emerging threat of the opioid epidemic. This research was different than what I had been doing, but certainly in line with my personal goals and ambitions. This trajectory allowed me to do research in HIV/AIDS, sexuality, and substance use disorders, which encompassed much of my life experiences, both personal and professional. Unexpectedly, while at the state department of public health, an opportunity presented itself for me to work as a part-time assistant professor at another state university, no tenure expectations, no scholarship responsibilities, just teaching. I thought this would be great, I left the state and embarked on another academic journey.

Although I had no expectations at this university, I could not help but be drawn into scholarship and research (seems it's in my DNA). I wrote a grant and was funded to do substance use disorder research among minorities as an extension of the work I did for the state, I also found myself developing a curriculum for substance use disorders and teaching this course to our public health students. I became the go-to -faculty for presentations on this subject, guest lecturing, and doing local and national presentations. After about a year, an announcement was posted for a tenure track position, and with some trepidation I applied. When the search committee failed to even grant me an interview, I was incensed, especially since the individuals who were interviewed were basically new graduates, with few publications and little research. Given my experience at the previous state university, however, I wasn't totally surprised at this flagrant omission. By this time, I had learned to pick my battles and considered that this omission was their loss. I am in a good place now and have my own LLC, my company activities include, substance use disorders, HIV/AIDS, and health and wellness related to Black gay men. I also now teach online and love the autonomy this offers. So, in the words of Miss Patty Labelle, this academic journey has given me "A New Attitude."

Final Thoughts

As a child growing up in Philly my mother always gave me old axioms to live by, that is: "If you are given lemons, make lemonade" this saying certainly captures my sentiment in terms of my academic journey. Firstly, I realize I am not a victim here, but a champion of resilience, courage, and faith. As I have gotten older, I have learned to live by another truism "What God has for me is for me." This was a lesson learned the hard way, I no longer cry over spilled milk. As mentioned earlier, my journey represented the good and bad. Through the brazen racism, discrimination, and disrespect, were many bright and poignant moments. Had I not been in those academic institutions, both as a student and a professor, I would never have appreciated the personal fortitude it took to go from a life steeped in addiction, to the highest levels of academic bliss. Had it not been for my academic journey, I never would have had the chance to go to China to share my research and knowledge, certainly, having published over twenty peer reviewed articles would not have been possible, or a research trajectory that allows my personal and professional experiences to coalesce. I now am able to transmit my abilities, knowledge, and skills to a new generation of Black men and women, both straight and gay.

My mantra is that "Life is 10% what happens to us and 90% the attitude we take." Today, I am not bitter, have forgiven all those that have trespassed against me, and am in a good place. No more tenure track expeditions, no more expectations that academia is a means to an end. As I complete writing that chapter, I have just celebrated my 67th birthday, I am partly retired now. Having obtained a part-time position as an online dissertation mentor and instructor in both addiction and public health, this path is appropriate in the era of Covid-19. In my estimation, things in academia have not changed much, even in the era of the Black Lives Matter Movement. The academy has a long way to go to be truly inclusive. What's most important in life is not the accolades and letters behind my name, but the dash in the middle of my lifeline. In the powerful words of poet Maya Angela "I wouldn't take nothing for my journey now." Although I was Blackgaymaled by Academia, I am pressing on toward the mark of a higher calling and "I ain't gonna let nobody turn me around."

References

Abdul-Raheem, J. (2016). Faculty Diversity and Tenure in Higher Education. *Journal of Cultural Diversity, 23*(2), 53–56.

Airhihenbuwa, C. O., & Liburd, L. (2006). Eliminating health disparities in the African American population: The interface of culture, gender, and power. *Health Education & Behavior, 33*(4), 488-501.

Helgesson, K. S., & Sjögren, E. (2019). No finish line: How formalization of academic assessment can undermine clarity and increase secrecy. *Gender, Work & Organization, 26*(4), 558.

Israel, B. A., Cashman, S. B., Adeky, S., Allen III, J.A., Corburn, J.,

Montaño, J., & Eng, E. (2008). The power and the promise: Working with communities to analyze data, interpret findings, and get to outcomes. *American Journal of Public Health*, *98*(8), 1407-1417.

Naylor, L. A., Wyatt-Nichol, H., & Brown, S. (2015). Inequality: Underrepresentation of African American Males in U.S. Higher Education. *Journal of Public Affairs Education, 21*(4), 523–538. https://doiorg.ezp.waldenulibrary.org/10.1080/15236803.2015.12002218

Turner, C., & Grauerholz, L. (2017). Introducing the invisible man: Black male professionals in higher education. *Humboldt Journal of Social Relations*, *39*, 212-227.

Israel, B. A., Schulz, A. J., Parker, E. A., Becker, A. B., Allen, A. J., Guzman, J. R., & Wallerstein, N. (2008). Community-based participatory research for health: From process to outcomes. *Critical issues in developing and following community-based participatory research principles*, 47-66.

CHAPTER TWELVE

Safely Uncomfortable
A Framework for Advocating for Diversity & Inclusion Work

Anthony L. Heaven, The University of Mississippi

When your presence is political, and your body is meant only to be consumed, never worthy of intellectual contribution, how do you push a diversity and equity agenda? When you are the first or the second Black, or the only in a room, when their presence magnifies your presence, what should you do? Wake up every morning, look yourself in the eye, you can be a tempered radical, disrupt the status quo from the inside. Once they know you, they feel their knowledge of you erases your race, then you can use your connection to reveal the challenges you face. This framework and the approach are not without repercussion, constantly fighting with yourself causing an emotional concussion. Torn between feeling complicit with the system, and being a change agent, know that you are not a traitor to your people, you are an undercover agent.

As a child I was groomed to play by "their" rules; their rules being the rules of a society dominated by White supremacy. The consistent underlying message was that if I acted a certain way, the likelihood of me "having trouble" with White folks would be decreased. Take your hands out of your pockets, do not let your pants sag, disarm people with your kindness; these were some of the messages that echoed through the corridors of my childhood. This ideology led me to feeling conflicted but inspired. Within myself I questioned, "Why should I have to make them feel comfortable when the issue is their perception of me and not the reality of me?" Emerging as a young adult, I realized that my ability to navigate the rules of White supremacy gave me access to spaces where I could promote change. It was not until graduate school that I identified that my approach was rooted in a Tempered Radical framework. I am tempered enough to be accepted by the system, but radical enough to challenge it from within. I walk a tightrope, always striving for change but rarely in a manner that creates dread or panic within White folks. My goal is to make them safely uncomfortable.

I walk into a room, my Blackness softened by a suit and eloquent diction; understanding that some people view me through a lens that makes them think my Black experience is fiction. I look around the room and I am the only person of color I see. I ask them, "If I wasn't here would you all miss me?" Then I immediately respond, of course you would, because I am the only Black person in this entire sea {of Whiteness}. I temper the sting with a charismatic smile, but I have highlighted the reality -- that we need more diversity right now.

The poem above is inspired by a real-life experience I had at an office potluck. Though I had presented on and talked about diversity, the reality that our office was ivory White had finally been stamped into their psyches by my "joke."

The joke, tempered by my smile, made them feel uncomfortable but not affronted. According to Meyerson (2003), tempered radicals set themselves apart by successfully navigating a middle ground. They recognize modest and doable choices in between, such as "choosing their battles, creating pockets of learning, and making way for small wins" (p. 6). The concept of making people safely uncomfortable hinges on the notion that people in positions of power should be made to feel uncomfortable but not intentionally threatened. By balancing the seriousness of the lack of diversity with humor/lightheartedness, I have been able to lean into my racial identity in a manner that does not alienate or outwardly threaten White people, my White people. They are "my" White people because they are the ones in close physical and emotional proximity to me; they are the White people that my experiences can reach.

For me, tempered radicalism has been about creating community and then leveraging the communal experience to promote change. It has enabled me to invite people into the fold of my life, and then expose them to the reality of how destructive White supremacy can be. They get a front row seat to the plight of my people, filtered through shades that make the intensity of the struggle palatable for them. This form of activism requires a belief in change, but an understanding that viable and sustainable change comes more subtly versus through means that are more radical. Tempered radicals, essentially, critique radical change and the status quo simultaneously (Kirton et al., 2007). There is a focus on professional ascension and challenging the system strategically while maintaining an ambivalent attitude. Meyerson and Scully (1995) illustrated this by saying, "We find ourselves in the awkward position of trying to master the norms of our profession in order to advance and maintain a foothold inside important institutions, but also trying to resist and change the profession's imperative and focus" (p. 587). Tempered Radicalism requires embracing a duality of understanding professional ethos and culturally-driven personal values.

Some of my friends are experts at the practice of being tempered, so much so that people call them the golden children within their respective spaces in academia. Their approach, charisma, and conviction allow them to be situated in spaces where they can advocate and promote systemic sustainable change. When incidents arise, they have to be the ones to speak up and educate their White peers, because if they are not educators, who will work to change the perspectives of folks who are inundated with unfettered Whiteness? They are able to connect with folks in a meaningful way, and then they challenge the status quo in a manner that makes them uncomfortable, but not threatened. One of my friends would say, "When they feel threatened, they may lash out or shut down." That is why I recognize the importance of using humor and building community while advocating for the dismantling of practices and structures that promote racial oppression.

For me, some of the greatest allies to my brand of Tempered Radicalism have been socially conscious White women {and sometimes White men}. I acknowledge that to move the needle, there have been moments when I needed a couple of people in agreement to help promote

128

diversity/equity/inclusion and advocate for my overall success. Having them to speak power to the ideas that I espouse, especially in spaces where I do not have access, gives White leaders' permission to invite these ideas into their conversations and consider that they may have validity. The fact that we need the support of socially conscious White folks to push a concept is another example of White supremacy, but it is also an example of how working in the system can allow us to infiltrate and promote change. I have seen White allies promote a cultural shift by standing up for people of color, advocating for the change of policies, etc. To know the power of White allies is not selling out or compromising, it is simply using the privilege of those around us to propel the movement. We have seen privileged be used throughout history to achieve progress in the treatment of those marginalized in society.

There is a dark side to Tempered Radicalism. The duality of it can create internal violence as one may be torn between leaning into radicalism while still maintaining a professional ethos that assuages the masses. In the era of trying to convince society that Black lives matter, Tempered Radicalism can feel inadequate and like a form of placation. We have to show up in White-washed and Eurocentric spaces and are forced to perform even when Black bodies are being murdered. The thought that expressing ourselves radically and unapologetically is plagued by the belief that our activism will alienate us within academia. Personally, I have had moments when I spoke out about certain issues and then certain people seemed to distance themselves from me in fear of the retribution they might face. They may be on board with you pushing for change and equality, but when they perceive you as advocating too strongly, they may back away to avoid being labelled a "radical." I have witnessed comments like, "We never realized you were so radical", and "We are not ready to make those type of drastic changes, be hurled into the atmosphere. Justifications of, "at least we have taken a step forward," become a resting place for colleagues who want to pacify change agents. Though some of us experience this internal chaos, we still persevere and leverage the climate to promote DEI in our spaces. We speak up about the issues we face within higher education, and then we provide suggestions for how to correct these issues. We work tirelessly because even though some of us present as moderates, on the inside we are hiding radical change in tempered container.

I see you little brother, little sister, trying to maintain your composure, orchestrating change like a composer. I see you smiling, pulling them into community; focused on changing their hearts through patience, education, discreet resistance and commonality. Maintaining a calm tone when the pressure makes you want to scream. My people are dying, but I refuse to go to work and make a scene. Always grappling, wondering if you said and did enough. Challenging the status quo slowly, even when you don't see change you try to never give up. The tension between who you are, and who you have to be; the duality drives you insane, but you know that making them safely uncomfortable, is your version of taking a knee. I know you feel torn and subjected to emotional violence; know that we love and need you, please never be silent. Your work speaks volumes, changing systems that we once didn't have access to. Your Tempered Radicalism is a picket sign, your form of activism changes lives too.

Why do we do this work? Why is our narrative vital? The narrative of a tempered radical showcases that there is diversity within activism. Additionally, it also reminds us that the radical and tempered radical approaches are both vital to achieving change within a reluctant society. Usually, some systems will change through radical action (police brutality), and some will shift through a tempered approach (diversification of higher education leadership). Regardless of where you are situated on the radicalism spectrum, as long as your work is authentic, centered in integrity, and well-informed then your work contributes to change. Together we realize that whether you are radical or tempered, you will face some form of institutional violence. Through our shared goals and experiences, Black activists utilizing a variety of methods can validate and heal each other. Our narratives have the same end goal, even though the strategies and perspectives may be crafted differently. We must remember that two different approaches do not have to be at war with each other.

We are not very different, you know. Both clothed in Black skin, pain hidden within, hearts connected by experiences, we are cultural kin. You wield your desire for change like a sword, and I wield mine like a pen. You carve out plans for change and I write them in permanent ink, our various approaches cause folks to think. Our rhetoric may vary, but our goals are the same, we want liberation for our people, freedom from tyranny's reign. We are not at odds with each other, we are working in tandem. From radical to tempered, our impact will be strategic, never random. We are hope, we are change, we are activism, our approaches are different, but our goals are the same.

References

Kirton, G., Greene, A.-M., & Dean, D. (2007).British diversity professionals as change agents - radicals, tempered radicals or liberal reformers? International Journal of Human Resource Management, 18(11), 1979–1994. https://doi org.umiss.idm.oclc.org/10.1080/0958519070163 8226

Meyerson, D. (2003). Tempered radicals: How everyday leaders inspire change at work: Harvard Business School Press.

Meyerson, D. E., & Scully, M. A. (1995). Crossroads tempered radicalism and the politics of ambivalence and change. *Organization Science*, *6*(5), 585-600.

Blackmaled by Academia

Part Four

Tales by Black males of resilience, strength, persistence, and strategies that address the mischaracterizing, fear-mongering, shell games, and injustice perpetuated within institutionalized racist structures, and how strong 'negroes' overcome internalized oppression with intelligence, self-love, self-respect, and savvy navigation within these repulsive systems.

CHAPTER THIRTEEN

Game Recognize Game

John Anderson, Ball State University

Introduction

Too often Black men flock to college upon graduating high school because we have been conditioned to believe that it is how we "make something of ourselves and be somebody". It is a mainstream societal script we typically follow that was not written by or for us, and one that many of us are ill-prepared for. We don't recognize the game. I contend that success in college has less to do with academic coursework preparation, and more to do with savvy navigation and persistence. College is a context (game) that Black men must fully learn and come to understand how it functions so that we can succeed more frequently and succeed in ways that demonstrate our knowledge of the context, its strengths, weaknesses, opportunities, and threats.

The word, recognize, often used in a phrase ("game recognize game", or "you betta recognize") in Black culture is frequently understood as an admonishment to acknowledge and/or to respect the game (i.e. context, individual, skill-set, talent, etc.). As a kid growing up in the San Francisco Bay Area, "game recognize game" is a phrase that I first heard from the local rapper "JT the Bigga Figga". The gist of this phrase, as I understood it, was to bring my game in a way that commands the respect of the other actors in the game. It carried the idea that I personally have a keen knowledge of the game sufficiently enough to acquire the respect of the other actors in the game. Many readers can conceive of being recognized by people, but not necessarily a context. When an individual or group of individuals are recognized in a context, it implies they have participated in ways that they have conquered the objectives, awards, promotions, and recognitions that are unique to that context. In the context of academia, it can be anything from graduation for students, promotion/tenure for faculty, and implementation of one's ideas into the curriculum, to name a few.

This chapter is a nonfiction narrative of my journey in higher education, both as a Black male collegiate student and a Black male college faculty member. The chapter will describe my experiences in higher education, which began in the Fall of 1996. As a California high school graduate, I refused to take the SAT exam due to feelings of internalized oppression, I opted to begin my collegiate journey at a local community college. Currently, I am completing my Doctorate in education (EdD) while serving as a college faculty member at a research university in Indiana. This chapter will encourage readers to understand the necessity to recognize:

- How the higher education game functions.
- Why self-determination is essential to avoid intellectual colonization.
- The difference between allies and mentors in higher education.
- The usefulness of an entrepreneurial mindset in higher education.
- Leveraging every relevant resource at the college/university to complete one's program of study.
- The importance of networking with purpose.

My journey in higher education is filled with meaningful experiences that will offer strategies, encouragement, and hope that can be useful to the success of Black men in the academy.

Entering the Game

I entered college, a Black male who had a lot of early trauma from my experiences in education. By the sixth grade, I was herded into special education. This particular special education program was what the school district called the "Special Day Class". It meant riding the short yellow bus to the other side of town to attend school, rather than the school up the hill from my house. I still remember how much of an ally my short yellow bus driver was to me. I would ask him to wait and allow my friends to pass, so they would not see me get off the short yellow bus in the mornings. I would also ask him to meet me down the street so that I could get on the bus to go home to avoid the end of day school crowds. This experience seared a stigma onto my consciousness that thankfully manifested in my drive to shake the inner sense of feeling 'dumb and stupid.' I have carried this in my sub - and conscious memory since then.

By the time I was a junior in high school, I knew that I wanted to attend my local community college because I did not want to take the SAT and possibly get a test score that reinforced the 'dumb and stupid' stigma I carried. I also knew that I wanted an associate arts degree in psychology specifically. In the Fall of 1996, I began my studies at Skyline College in San Bruno, California. During that time California Proposition 209 was on the ballot, which was essentially a measure to abolish affirmative action in college admissions, and educational support programs for racially minoritized students in California state funded colleges and universities. This initiative was being asserted by Wardell (Ward) Anthony Connerly (Carey, 2020). At the time, I entered college, this ballot initiative was playing out in the social backdrop of my lived experience. I chose not to enroll in the African American Success Through Excellence and Persistence (ASTEP) program at Skyline College, a Black learning community on campus that existed to connect Black students to Black professors, and other Black students. My thought was, "I didn't want to use any crutches for my academic success." I realized that an aspect of my struggle in my early experience in higher education was because I succumbed to one of the subtle narratives around Proposition 209. The notion that programs geared to aid and support minoritized students are a type of crutch used and is the only reason minoritized students have any success in higher education. I understand now that this experience was an expression of what sociologist W.E.B. DuBois called "Double Consciousness," he described in his book *"The Souls of Black Folk"* this way, "It is a peculiar sensation, this double-consciousness, this sense of always looking at one's self through the eyes of others, of measuring one's soul by the tape of a world that looks on in amused contempt and pity" (p. 3, 1903). Similarly, Charles H. Cooley (1902) conceptualized as "The Looking Glass Self" wherein he posits that one's self-image comes from a process of self-reflection that is informed by how they think others perceive them. One's perception of how they think others perceive them, comes from their daily social encounters in society.

I also understand that my experience back then was an expression of internalized oppression, whereby one unconsciously believes the dominant stereotypes and/or negative social narratives about the racial-cultural group to which they identify and belong. I ended up on a probationary dismissal for poor academic performance. I entered college and got swallowed up because I did not know how to navigate the game. I also did not understand the value of accessing and leveraging the culturally specific resources like ASTEP.

I returned about two years later and was readmitted by an ASTEP academic counselor. I enrolled in the ASTEP learning community where I had affirming Black cultural learning experiences. I excelled in my classes, worked with faculty, and received mentorship that resulted in life-long friendships. My participation and experience in the ASTEP learning community at Skyline College showed me how powerful, culturally specific learning communities in the academy can facilitate student success, encourage one's motivation to learn, increase student retention, and student persistence.

The Academy: A Game Envisioned in Whiteness

Colleges and universities in America were not envisioned with Blacks as the ideal student. Our collegiate experience has a storied history rooted in resistance to the Eurocentric/White hegemonic underpinnings of higher education in America. Generally, education for Blacks has and continues to be a perpetual act of resistance in our enduring quest for liberation. The first African "Black" souls on American shores arrived enslaved and perceived as chattel, prohibited from formal learning to sustain their subjugation. In the PBS documentary film *Tell Them We Are Rising* (Nelson, Williams, Seidlitz, & Smith, 2017), Kimberly Crenshaw, executive director of the African American Policy Forum asserted:

A slaveholder could do virtually anything to his slave. He could work his slave to death, He could rape his slave. He could sell his slave. It's my property, the argument was, so I can do whatever I want to with my property, except one thing I can't do with my property. I can't teach my property. I can't teach my slave how to read or write. An educated Black population could not be an enslaved population.

In the collective cultural memory of African Americans education has always been tied to freedom. Our education was/is, in some form or another, tied to the larger purpose of improving our lived experience in a country built on the denial of our humanity. Our education necessitates that we are prepared to successfully engage and win against the diverse expressions of institutionalized racial oppression in America. The academy in America is a mere microcosm of the larger racial realities in this country. Therefore, when we make the choice to enter the academy, particularly those campuses that are understood to be predominantly or historically White institutions; we should assume that we are entering into mentally, emotionally, and spiritually hostile environments, which necessitates that we actively seek out safe spaces that permit us to thrive.

Kujichagulia (Self-Determination)

The second of the seven core values of Dr. Maulana Karenga's Kawaida philosophy is Kujichagulia, which means self-determination. Karenga's Kawaida philosophy argues that, "we must prefigure the good we want and struggle for it" (Karenga, 2010, p. 263). Self-determination as described by Karenga, has to do with defining ourselves, naming ourselves, creating for ourselves, and speaking for ourselves (Karenga, 2008).

When I entered college, I knew that I wanted an associate arts degree in psychology. I remember an advising counselor asking me why because in his view there was not much that I could do with just an Associate's degree. My own thinking was that rather than just earning enough credits to transfer to a four-year school, I wanted to have an actual degree as evidence of having completed a program of study. If we don't know and define our "why" for attending college we waste time, money, and more importantly we leave ourselves vulnerable to someone else taking the liberty to define our experience. In extreme cases, not owning or defining our purpose for being in the academy opens us to be victims of a cultural environment designed to colonize Black minds to White-Eurocentric hegemonic values, goals, attitudes, and perspectives. Davidson(1970) masterfully describes the process of colonization of Black graduate students in the academy below:

The practice of cultural imposition leads Black graduate students to see how totally their careers are determined by White academic standards and develop a sense of abject powerlessness in the department which allegedly is trying to help them advance as young professionals. The colonizer's standards determine the quality and acceptability of his work; they determine when he is "ready" to be evaluated for his M.A., when he is prepared for his Ph.D. orals, and whether his topic for a dissertation is even worthwhile. At every level, the colonizer's standards are used to determine whether he will continue, drop out or be forced out. Although these standards and procedural rules are also applied to whites, they have for the Black students the force of assimilating agents which must be accepted, or he dies as a student. For Blacks these standards are bleaching or whitening agents which are perceived as virtually antithetical to one's self and one's experience. There is again here a subtle shift of forces which acts merely on the principles of the White graduate student, but which attempts to descend to the very roots of Black identity and utterly remake it. Both the blindness and the insensitivity to the existence of alternative constructions of American life are typical of academic tradition. (p. 203-204)

In my own graduate school experience, self-determination was essential, not only as a Black male graduate student, but also as an adult learner. When I began graduate school for my master's program, I was thirty-six years old, married, with four children, and adjunct faculty at a local community college. Most of those in my cohort were young twenty-somethings who had just completed their undergraduate degrees. I inwardly pledged that while I was in my master's program that my wife would not be a single mother raising our children. There were times that I determined that I would earn a B in a course so that my responsibilities as a husband and father would not be neglected. In my opinion, it would have been ridiculous to earn a master's degree and lose my marriage and family. Some of the professors in my department resented my approach, but the onus was exclusively on me to define and know my "why" for being in the graduate program.

There is a difference between mentors and allies

All mentors are allies, but allies are not mentors. During my master's program, I learned that there were professors who were willing to assist me with needs and/or challenges that I had, but the interactions that we had were transactional, meaning that after I got the help that I needed, it was over. These individuals are what I call allies because they were willing to help me and had the means to do so. However, there is no long-term relationship with allies, once they assisted me with whatever support I was asking, or in some instances that they recognized I needed, the task was done. Allies are giving people who sincerely desire for students to succeed, but there is no relationship that develops. Mentors on the other hand, are those individuals that you meet in the academy with whom you develop and have a relationship with. Mentors labor with you and give you sustained support toward your success in the game. Both the student and the mentor recognize a chemistry and kinship of interest, goals, and in many cases lived experiences, which serves as the foundation for the long-term mentoring relationship.

During my master's program, I was blessed to have two mentors. My first mentor I met in the third month of my first year of graduate school. I was a non-traditional graduate student and the oldest student in my graduate cohort. I felt out of place, and my course of study was unfolding not to be what I had anticipated. During this time, my mentor was hosting and facilitating community discussions on and off campus through her racial healing initiative. I received many of her campus email blasts, but on this day, I decided to reach out to her. She invited me to an impromptu meeting, during her lunch hour, and I shared my challenges with her as a first-year graduate student. After an hour and a half meeting with her, she encouraged me to remain in my sociology graduate program, challenged me to add a second major in Adult & Community Education, pointed me in the direction of a graduate assistantship, and challenged me again to present at an on-campus student-faculty conference. I am humbled to say that I successfully completed everything she encouraged me to do. Our chemistry and kinship were instant and even after graduating she pushed and encouraged me to enroll and pursue my Doctorate in education. Her nurturing mentorship and recognition of my potential caused me to excel in the academy.

My second mentor came to me in my second year of graduate school from the department of sociology, the graduate program that I was originally accepted into. At the start of my second year of graduate school, I learned that she was assigned to me for the academic year. There was instant chemistry and kinship, she is a master educator, and we were matched because of my experience and desire to grow as an educator. She expressed genuine interest wanting to know about who I was, what my interest were, and where I was trying to go with my career goals. Throughout the academic year we met regularly either bi-weekly or a once a month. She assisted me with strategic thinking concerning my career, provided guidance as my program of study was finishing up, and she always genuinely inquired about my physical and mental health because she knew that I was a non-traditional graduate student. My mentor in my sociology program also taught the course where I designed a Black Sociology course. She recognized my ability as an educator and arranged for me to come back after graduation to teach the course. In the Spring of 2017, I came back to teach the course, it was a great success, and now I am a faculty member in the department.

It is important to know the difference between allies and mentors, so that we do not engage allies as we would a mentor; likewise, so that we don't relate to our mentors like we would an ally. Students in higher education must understand nuances like this so that they navigate the game efficiently.

Cultivate an Entrepreneurial Mindset in the Academy

Students in the academy are generally groomed to complete their program of study to go to work for someone else. College campuses are equipped with career centers, which host job fairs that bring government, and corporate employers, as well as local mid-sized businesses who are looking to hire soon to be graduates from the academy. As a Black male student, I have found this to be highly problematic because the expectation of "going to get a degree so that I can get a good job" does not factor in systemic racism in America's job market. In fact, back in 2008, my family and I moved from our home back in the San Francisco Bay Area to the East Central Indiana area. It was not until I moved to Indiana that I realized that I could not be in this part of the country without a bachelor's degree, even though I had equivalent to a bachelor's degree in credits between my associate's degree and my certificate in Biblical Studies from Bible college. After about a month and a half after I moved to Indiana, I enrolled in a private Christian university, which accepted all of my credits. I essentially took ten courses online to establish residency at the university and earned the degree in just under eleven months with an April 2009 graduation. By August 2009, I was hired as adjunct faculty at a local community college. With an earned bachelor's degree, and my years of work experience from back home in San Francisco, I was able to teach college success courses, and select courses in the criminal justice department. After about five and half years of teaching, I realized that I would never be hired without a master's degree, so I applied and was accepted to a graduate sociology program. When I realized that I needed to return for a graduate degree, I reached out to one of my former professors and mentor from Skyline College in the ASTEP program. She advised me and helped me to recognize the I could teach criminal justice courses with a master's degree sociology, but that I could not teach sociology with a master's in criminal justice. I chose to earn a master's degree in sociology because it allows me to teach courses across many social science disciplines. When you know how the game works you decide and move with greater precision and efficiency.

When I decided to return to school to earn a master's degree, I eventually recognized the futility of earning a degree in an attempt to be given a better job by an employer. During my program, I began designing a framework for my own consulting practice. I recognized that my training in sociology and adult education was adding skills that I could market to businesses, organizations, and individuals on fee for service basis. I inquired about what it meant to develop independent business contracts, 1099 tax forms, and what an appropriate fee schedule would be for my skills and expertise. It was important for me to design my job and business so that I could have the freedom to do the work and create income streams that would put me in the driver's seat concerning my career. The career center at my university could not help me with this because it was never designed to assist students with designing and building their own business, contract consulting practice, or just creating a robust freelance income stream.

As a thirty-six-year-old non-traditional graduate student, the question that I was trying to answer was not, "What do I want to be when I grow up?" I was more concerned with the question of, "How do I design my work life going forward?" I needed to answer this question in a way that addressed my personal need for money, meaning, and variety, Wapnick (2017). Wapnick (2017), describes three domains that need to be met for individuals to the extent appropriate and unique to them. First is money, it refers to what one's financial goals are based on their financial needs and lifestyle preference. Second is meaning, which has to do with work activity that brings the individual maximum fulfillment. Finally, variety has to do with engaging in work activity that addresses one's diversified interest and skillsets. The career center at my university was ill-equip to support me as a Black male who needed to think entrepreneurially, and as a non-traditional student looking to reinvent himself.

I had to be intentional about securing my own resources to prepare to work on terms that I designed once I graduated.

Teaching in the Academy

Having taught the last eleven years in higher education, I recognize the lack of Black male faculty in this game. Before I entered the academy as a faculty member, I already had career success in the field of recreation, and in human services. It was not until the move to Indiana, that the opportunity presented itself to teach college. My career path prior to coming to the academy, makes it such that my approach to teaching is different from those who have been groomed to be college faculty. I teach with the hope to equip and empower students to discover their purpose, reach their highest potential, and to create positive change in themselves and their surroundings. I make every effort to teach in a way that assumes that students' presence in the classroom is motivated by a variety of personal and professional goals. In many instances, specific stressors in life are the impetus for seeking post-secondary education, learning thus becomes a *means to an end, not an end in itself.*

As early as I can remember, I have had the best experiences with teachers who were 'unconventional' and not rigid in their teaching approach. The conventional approach to teaching in higher education is characterized by the student having a passive learning experience. It is where the instructor is the expert and is the primary source from where the knowledge is conveyed. It is not uncommon that students in the conventional college classroom find themselves having a learning experience that is highly individualistic, competitive, and overly focused on memorizing content versus gaining a deep and meaningful understanding of the course content. The college instructors that I considered unconventional were the ones who facilitated learning spaces where I could participate in co-constructing knowledge and learning. The unconventional instructors gave me ongoing feedback and coaching, which encouraged me to master the content to reach the objectives of the course, versus merely receiving a score or grade. These experiences shaped my own teaching approach.

I believe that each student comes to the classroom with a unique set of educational and life experiences that influence how they interpret information, understand content, and achieve the goals for the course. Students come to the university with various levels of academic preparation. I embrace the responsibility to facilitate a learning environment that delivers the objectives of my course, while at the same time nurturing the development of every student toward generally being stronger. An example of my commitment to building stronger college students is when students are responsible for completing a major writing assignment, I have developed proof-reading review rubrics that must be completed by a college tutor or instructor in the college writing lab. Building this into the course gives students exposure to a college resource, which can support their success for any course at the institution. Students need to be encouraged to become aware of the resources their tuition

140

pays for. There appears to be a general assumption that students will just naturally seek out these resources. However, as a faculty member there is a way to craft assignments that require them to use and discover the institution's resources. In turn, this contributes to their overall development as a college student. These approaches and strategies to teaching in higher education have not yet become the norm. It is why they can be understood as unconventional.

As a faculty member, I feel obligated to help students learn the game of higher education. I think it can be equally as dangerous to encourage Black men to enter the academy and be unaware of how to navigate the context. We admonish our children to stay away from the street game, but enthusiastically encourage them to enter the academy "so they can be somebody." The academy, particularly predominantly White institutions, with its racist cultural underpinnings can potentially be equally as damaging to Black men. We must understand the academy as a game that requires savvy navigation and persistence.

References

Carey, K. (2020, August 21). A detailed look at the downside of California's ban on affirmative action. *The New York Times.* https://www.nytimes.com/2020/08/21/ups hot/00up-affirmative-action-california-study.html

Cooley, C. H. (1902). Looking-glass self. *The production of reality: Essays and reading on social interaction, 6,* 126-128.

Davidson, D. (1970). The furious passage of the Black graduate student. *Berkeley Journal of Sociology,* 192-211.

DuBois, W.E.B. (1903). *The Souls of Black Folk.* A.C. McClung and Co.

Karenga (Maulana.). (2008). *Kawaida and questions of life and struggle: African American, Pan-African, and global issues.* University of Sankore Press.

Karenga (Maulana.). (2010). *Introduction to Black studies.* (4th ed.). University of Sankore Press.

Nelson, S. (Producer), Williams, M. (Co-producer),Seidlitz, A. (Writer), & Smith, M. (Writer). (2017). *Tell them we are rising: The story of Black colleges and universities* [Motion picture]. USA: Firelight Films.

Wapnick, E. (2017). *How to be everything: A guide for those who (still) don't know what they want to be when they grow up.* HarperCollins.

CHAPTER FOURTEEN

Black Male Gentleness

Justin Grimes, Virginia Tech

Black Men's Doctoral Educational Journeys

The issue of Black men not pursuing a doctoral degree includes many complex circumstances around eligibility for educational participation. Despite the increase of Black male baccalaureate awards from 5% to 8.5% over the past 40 years, the percentage of degrees conferred has only increased by 3.5% during this time span (NCES, 2015). Traditionally, statistics on Black men's persistence are used to portray Black male students' low enrollment because of disinterest. Even more, these statistics enhance the deficit narratives of Black male students, which leads to depictions of them in need of saving or instead of caring less about their educational pursuits (Tate & Bagguley, 2017). In contrast, data show that the fields chosen by Black men in college include the social sciences as well as the Science, Technology, Engineering, and Mathematics (STEM) fields (NCES, 2010). Some institutional leaders and students assume that Black men are not interested in pursuing careers where research is essential for success in their careers. Black men have increased their enrollment by 45% between 2002 and 2012 in the STEM fields (Bidwell, 2015). However, the numbers tell a partial truth that growth is happening, but it varies by field (Bidwell, 2015, p. 1).

The data clearly show that the issues of Black men's interest in pursuing a doctoral degree are reflective of a higher education system that minimally addresses the low enrollment and graduation rates for Black men overall. Beyond this information, discussions, and statistics on Black men's enrollment in higher education potentially highlight institutionalized problems that may not be thoroughly examined in today's educational landscape (Tate & Bagguley, 2017).

Black doctoral students face concerns that White graduate students do not face (Harper, 2005; Harper & Davis III, 2012; Johnson-Bailey et al., 2009). Even more, many graduate programs fail Black men with the lack of critical pedagogy that does not address systemic issues of cultural dissonance but reinforces notions of invisibility within institutionalized and systematic racism, rooted in White supremacy, that significantly affect Black students more than White students (Johnson-Bailey et al., 2009). Black graduate students describe their campuses as culturally insensitive, racially hostile, and dismissive of their needs (Harper, 2005; Harper & Davis III, 2012; Gildersleeve et al., 2012; Levin et al., 2013). Graduate educators speak of their goals for fostering spaces where critical analysis and thinking are valued, along with increasing the representation of voices across student populations (Harper & Davis III, 2012; Gildersleeve et al., 2012). However, Black men, like other racial minorities, not only serve as racial representatives but also help to educate White faculty and students about their challenging experiences, although their experiences often go unnoticed (Gildersleeve et al., 2012; Harper & Davis, 2012; Johnson-Bailey et al., 2009). Black men experiencing such acts share with others within their community, both on and off-campus, about the insensitive and hostile academic environments that facilitate their lack of fit within their programs (Harper, 2009; Johnson-Bailey et al., 2009). Therefore, institutional isolation cast on Black men pursuing doctorates at HWIs becomes translated into messages that HWIs are not welcoming environments for Black men.

Despite battling systematic and institutionalized racism, Black men's need to possess a sense of identity, wealth, and belonging makes education a viable option to defy social and economic reasons that mischaracterize their existence (Harper, 2009; Pope, 2013). Education has minimally served Black men as a positive avenue for skill development, improved employment opportunities, and finding kinship with other Black men (Pope, 2013). For many Black men, their motivation for more education helps dismantle notions of 'cultural absence' and shift notions about the worth and value of Black men in society. Black men's reason for pursuing doctoral degrees can have a rippling effect on their community with the increased chances for economic stability, visibility, role modeling of education as a viable option to circumvent institutionalized oppression, and greater participation in society (Pope, 2013). Also, Black men obtaining doctoral degrees increase the diversity of knowledge on Black men in academia by including their experience in discussions and research on underserved and undervalued student populations (Pope, 2013).

Summary of the Study and Participants

Black men's narrations have not been at the center of discussions about their experiences in education. Instead, educators have narrated deficit portrayals of Black men's experiences as being academically incapable, underprepared, and unmotivated to pursue graduate education. Educators often reinforce and replicate these narratives when working with Black men. Furthermore, these narratives become a part of research themes about Black men's failures, without examining Black male doctoral students' motivations for pursuing a doctoral degree (Cockley, 2015; Jett, 2010; McCallum, 2016). More research highlighting Black men's motivation to pursue a doctoral degree in education through an anti-deficit framework can help educators understand Black men's education past and future, and to restructure programs changes and recruitment efforts tailored to addressing the needs of Black doctoral students at HWIs (Cockley, 2015; Ivankova & Stick, 2007). The purpose of this research was to provide factors that influenced Black men to pursue a doctoral degree in education.

I was using Critical Race Methodology (CRM), which uses Critical Race Theory (CRT) to address issues of race and racism in all aspects of the research process, including the collection, analyzing, and presentation of data.

This study challenges the dominant ideology of Black men's experiences in education (Delgado & Stefancic, 2012). The design of this research study was to gather information and share through photos and narratives issues impacting Black men's motivation for pursuing doctorates in education. Data collection took place in two phases. Each of the seven participants self-identified as a Black man enrolled in a doctoral program in the College of Education (COE) at Bridgetown University, a Historically White Institution. These Black men identify with various roles as fathers, brothers, husbands, partners, bi-lingual, HBCU alum, and educators. The shared experience of the Black men includes that most were in their 30s, came from low-income backgrounds, and worked in education before starting their doctoral degrees full-time. The programs in which these Black men enrolled include Educational Psychology, Language and Literacy, Higher Education Leadership, Education Administration and Policy, and Applied Cognition and Development, with no one having reached candidacy before starting the study.

Black men selected and described five photos responding to prompts about their motivation to pursue a doctorate. After providing photos and descriptions, I used semi-structured interviews to guide a discussion exploring the factors that influenced each of these Black men to pursue a doctorate. Also discussed in the interviews were how race, gender, and racism impacted their motivation throughout their educational journey. I selected the research design so that I could write and record their experiences, gather participant's perspectives on motivation, and analyze the stories to identify emerging themes.

Black Male Gentleness

A significant theme that emerged in this study was a reconditioning of Black maleness and masculinity, where Black men's sub-othering experiences resulted in them presenting a gentler, non-violent version of themselves to be respected and validated throughout their educational journey. Some Black men pursuing doctorates are burdened with performing what I refer to as "Black male gentleness." Black male gentleness is the execution of several coping strategies, including the process of changing one's speech or talk, referred to as code-switching, self-silencing, putting others' comfort first, performing in costume, battling stereotype threat, and operating from a place of inauthenticity. Stereotype threat is defined by Steele & Aronson (1995) as "the risk of confirming, as self-characteristic, a negative stereotype about one's group" (p. 797). For example, Black men may spend intentional time in selecting their clothes to demonstrate business, non-threatening persona, to counter expectations of how Black men look in regard to their dress (costume). Black men perform gentleness as an extension of anti-blackness through professionalism and respectability politics, especially with faculty, peers, and other institutional stakeholders. Black men display signs of anxiousness and discomfort because, as Mark says he, "didn't know that you could be more relaxed in class." Anxiousness and discomfort are responses some individuals experience to the racism, which determines whose voices get power and

144

privilege, and the ways Black men are permitted to show up. Ultimately, if Black men in the academy fail to perform Black male gentleness, then anti-black policies and practices will punish them for not engaging in academic spaces the same way as their White peers. For example, Timothy talked about how his White peers get more respect and can disagree with faculty; meanwhile, he has "learned how to subtly disagree so as not to be confrontational, because the first thing as a Black man and you say you don't like something, they'll be like, oh my god, don't be angry."

The lack of safety Black men endure showing up in practicing a different version of authenticity happens because of racism and the centrality of white standards of beauty, language, and performance to require their assimilation. Since Black men felt moments of powerlessness, they conceived that performing Black male gentleness allowed them (1) to demystify stereotypes, (2) use counter storytelling to both addresses and respond to stereotype threat, (3) offer counter-representations of what it means to be a Black man, (4) and to honor a commitment to use their education and presence as a form of resistance for battling against social inequalities and inequities in their community. Because many spaces for Black men are uncomfortable, racist, violent, or divisive, Black men use gentleness as an actionable response to create comfort for themselves and others amid these issues. Also, Black men must use Black male gentleness to redefine for themselves what it means to perform masculinity, exercise agency, display vulnerability, and a struggle to find compassion for individuals who care about their needs. There exists a dualism in Black gentleness, which causes Black men to play the role of participant and victim, and as Mark says, it requires acknowledging:

You are representing the entire race. You are representing something bigger than yourself and … you want to provide a good representation so that you can demystify the stereotypes that are out there, so you don't uphold those stereotypes.

The stressful and consistent practice of Black gentleness required Black men to show up as actors participating in the act of improvisation. Dennis makes it clear that Black male gentleness is "a constant battle of validation and relevance and legitimizing." Black male gentleness is a part of pursuing and surviving in doctoral programs, which has become second nature for Black men's survival in the academy. As Timothy says, "survival should not be the ultimate goal, it should be the ability to prosper. But there are days, weeks; survival is what I'm going for."

Code-switching

One subtheme under Black gentleness is considering the use of code-switching, defined by the Encyclopedia Britannica (n.d.) as, "process of shifting from one linguistic code (a language or dialect) to another, depending on the social <u>context</u> or conversational setting," in the academy. Black men explained how they use speech in a certain way and use specific vernacular to be heard and respected. Black men felt they had to perform the subservient role of being friendly, but not too friendly; authentic, but with digestible

145

authenticity; and engaged, but not overly so. Black men had to learn what some refer to as "talking White," an idea rooted in anti-blackness and language bias where Whiteness is the standard for civil discourse. Moreover, speaking in Ebonics or African American Vernacular English (AAVE) (Rickford, 2020) might create issues for Black Men. For example, Timothy talks about having conversations outside of class with another Black woman about the impact racism has on his choice to speak freely and truthfully in the classroom. Timothy says that his classmate said to him:

When you are up here on the plantation, just realize you've got to take care of your business, and she would say things I thought, but I was like, I can't say this. But then she would just be like, boom; this is the way it is.

Timothy, like other Black men, found comfort with the interchange of code-switching between standard English speech and AAVE, but never in the classroom. Although encouraged by a Black woman to use their agency and voice to express their truth, Black men have this conflation of frustrations around choosing to be silent, self-censors, or speak from a place of confidence. Timothy, in his interaction with a Black female faculty member, reflected on how much enjoyment he felt, not having to code-switch with her. Timothy shared that he enjoyed the "intonations we used, and she didn't bat an eye. Whereas I have done that before and other people are like, oh, I didn't know you spoke that way." Therefore, Black men may choose to police their language and buy into a master-narrative that speaking in a version of Whiteness is the only way to gain White people's acceptance, even at the risk of their discomfort. As stressful as code-switching and tone policing are for Black men, they are attempting to navigate ways to speak authentically without the fear of being punished, misunderstood, or ostracized for speaking out of a norm.

Black Men Feeling a Lack of Inclusion

Often Black men burdened with the task of being gentle, have an undue responsibility to find spaces of inclusion, where they are valued and respected as whole human beings whose experiences differ from their White peers. I asked participants if they felt their program and Bridgetown were welcoming and supportive of Black men. Often the response was like Jason, who said, "I felt admitted, and it's the university role to make you feel welcomed." Black men feel like admitted into their program and institution, but they do not always feel welcomed or supported. No matter the posturing of messages of diversity and inclusion in the university mission statement, Black men felt it was their responsibility to find their fit within the institution because institutional members failed to prioritize holding the place for their needs.

Finding fit within the institution and classroom was hard for Black men. Black men interested in pursuing a doctorate often reflect how much space is given to White people to question their presence, and police how many opportunities Black men get in academic spaces. As Zander mentions, "I feel like there is an expectation that I prove why I have this seat. So, like why –

146

how do you get to sit in this room with these other White folks? Or how do you get to sit in this room in this program that is ranked, as a Black man?"

Black men feel like their voices and presence are not welcomed, and to consider how much space they take up. Feelings of not being accepted are rooted in assumptions that historically Black men have taken up either too much space or should not be given space. Mark summarizes the academy is not set up for him to be fully present, because "sometimes in higher education, you can be one of the only Black males in a class at times and so, therefore, having to, again, watch how you take up space."

Black Men in Costume

Black men's visual representation on a college campus was not found to be on a spectrum. The photo below provided by Glen (Figure 1), is a visual representation of the costume Black men pursuing doctorates must wear to resist stereotypes about Black men on college campuses.

Figure 1

Black Men

While there is no official dress code for doctoral students, Black men in this study dressed in business casual as a costume, also represented in Figure 1 Black Men, for several reasons. When asked his perception about the visual imagery of Black men and what their peers expect Black men on college campuses to look like, Glen said, "We look at African American men as athletes and entertainers." Glen was referring to both the roles and style of dress associated with Black college men (i.e., athletic clothing). Timothy re-emphasized the same point about the visual imagery of Black men, in his research on language, literacy, and children's books when he found "the only people that were successful were athletes." Consistently in photos, each of the participants chose a photo of themselves or others dressed in a suit, like the one above, which is counter to the perception of athlete or entertainer.
The symbolism in the photo provided by these Black men displays how Black men present themselves, sometimes as actors who put on costumes, as an

attempt to counter-narratives that White people should be afraid and alarmed by the presence of Black men. Black men in this study consistently referenced having to put on a suit as a part of their credentialing. Saying you are in a doctoral program is not enough; you must also assimilate to a White supremacist dress code expectation that Black men's peers were often not expected to follow. Black men's style of formal dress is historical, generational, and cultural. While most conversations on dress code policy issues with Black individuals center around Black women and hair, often, organizations are not considering how these policies reflect workplace diversity and inclusion (Pope, 2019). Inclusive organizations will think through the ways their dress code policies create further discrimination and implicit bias (Pope, 2019). Black men may experience these policies as hostile or challenging, especially within organizations that fail to consider unspoken expectations of Black men's dress. For a moment, think about events and/or offices where you have seen Black men. What did they wear? In your reflection, consider the dress of others, and compare the similarities and differences. Dress codes are maintained in Whites spaces and learned before entering spaces where racial understanding has happened. As a child, I reflect on experiences of dressing up for church, especially the big three: Christmas, Mother's Day, and Easter. Also, I remember conversations on how to dress for interviews, debutant balls, social gatherings amongst important people, conferences, and churches.

My clothing choices and style of dress, referred to as "my Sunday best," included a conversation around the importance of dressing in these clothes. While the intentions were good, the talks had gaps that failed to address Whiteness, racism, body discrimination, and cultural context. Event after event, I have assimilated to showing up with this standard of dress and felt guilty for rebelling against what I've known and wanted to wear.

Many institutional members reinforce to Black men a separatist standard of dress for Black men, by continually policing and questioning their choices of clothing when they are not in their costume. Participants and I have experienced entering a space, such as one's office or lab, not dressed in a costume and received messages such as, "you're so casual today or why aren't you dressed up." Black men's wearing of a costume served as an act of resisting notions of White Eurocentric standards of beauty and making it known that their acceptance and safety in doctoral programs are connected to deeply held racist visual imageries about Black men.

Authenticity

Within a majority White space, Black men internally struggle with being transparent and authentic, and with displaying a fraction of their authentic selves. Black men experience a constant policing around how authenticity is perceived and received. Mark mentions an experience he had with his peers in his master's program at an HWI that he expected to encounter again in his doctoral program; White women wanting to see a mirrored version of his personality both outside and inside the classroom:

One of the things that eventually my classmates brought up, they brought this up in class, that they really appreciated me outside of class, the person who I was outside of class, and felt like I wasn't being authentic in class.

Mark was shocked by their questioning of his authenticity, and felt compelled to defend not only his Blackness but to address the issues by saying:

I had to explain to them why. And what I mentioned was that I didn't want to be taken as a joke all the time, because I can joke a lot. But in a classroom setting, I felt like I needed to be professional, because if the teacher saw me, a Black male, cracking jokes or always being funny and things like that, how could the professor take me seriously?

Authenticity looks different for each person; yet, Black men are clear that White people respond to them, are highly contextual and connected to what they wear, say, and display.

Although authenticity is essential, questioning Black men's choices for being inauthentic, or for performing gentleness, is less about them ascribing to White norms, and more about the dualism in their gentleness, which allows them to show authenticity in multiple forms. For Black men pursuing doctorates, the focus extends beyond finding the motivation to battle racism. Black men are creating versions of authenticity that are intersectional. As Zander states, Black men in doctoral programs are "still trying to identify, prove myself as a student," because it is more critical to build authenticity in that role than personal. Authenticity shows up differently based on the person, context, and individual decisions of safety, and the historical context around who has power in the space. For some Black men, they responded like Mark, who says, "it makes sense for me to err on the side of being too professional than too casual." Zander addresses Black men's discomfort with having to create a pseudo-authentic version of them when he says Black men "feel this pressure to show up and be the best self all of the time." White people sometimes display a struggle to accept Black men as whole beings, which impacts Black men's versions of authenticity at HWI's. This issue is rooted in White supremacist uttering anti-blackness rhetoric around authenticity, where Black men's conformity and performance is more critical than their discomfort. What is unknown to White people is how motivation influenced these Black men's versions of authenticity and performance. As Black men, there has to be further interrogation around the dualism of authenticity/acceptance and comfort.

References

Bidwell, A. (2015, May). African-American men: The other STEM minority. *U News*. Retrieved from:
https://www.usnews.com/news/stem-solutions/articles/2015/05/07/african-american-men-the-other-stem-minority.

Cokley, K. (2015). A confirmatory factor analysis of the academic motivation scale with black college students. *Measurement and Evaluation in Counseling and Development*, 48(2), 124-139.

Delgado, R., & Stefancic, J. (2012). *Critical race*

theory: An introduction (2nd ed.). New York University Press.

Gildersleeve, R., Croom, N.N., & Vasquez, P.L. (2011). "Am I Going Crazy?!": A critical race analysis of doctoral education. *Equity & Excellence in Education, 44*(1), 93-114.

Harper, S.R. (2005). Leading the way: Inside the experiences of high-achieving African-American male students. *About Campus, 10*(1), 8-15.

Harper, S.R. (2009). Niggers no more: A critical race counter-narrative on black male student achievement at predominantly white colleges and universities. *International Journal of Qualitative Studies in Education (QSE), 22*(6), 697-712.

Harper, S.R., & Davis, Charles, H.F., III. (2012). They (don't) care about education: A counter-narrative on black male students' responses to inequitable schooling. *Educational Foundations, 26*(1-2), 103-120.

Ivankova, N.V., & Stick, S.L. (2007). Students' persistence in a distributed doctoral program in educational leadership in higher education:A mixed-methods study. *Research in Higher Education, 48*(1), 93.

Jett, C.C. (2011). 'I once was lost, but now am found': The mathematics journey of an African American male mathematics doctoral student. *Journal of Black Studies, 42*(7), 1125-1147. doi:10.1177/0021934711404236

Johnson-Bailey, J., Valentine, T., Cervero, R.M., & Bowles, T.A. (2009). Rooted in the soil: The social experiences of black graduate students at a southern research university. *The Journal of Higher Education, 80*(2), 178-203.

Levin, J., Jaeger, A., & Haley, K. (n.d). Graduate student dissonance: graduate students of color in a U.S. Research University. *Journal of Diversity in Higher Education, 6*(4), 231-244.

McCallum, C.M. (2016). "Mom made me do it": The role of family in African Americans' decisions to enroll in doctoral education. *Journal of Diversity in Higher Education, 9*(1), 50.

Morrison, C. (2017, May 30). Code-switching. Retrieved July 15, 2020 https://www.britannica.com/topic/code-switching

National Center for Education Statistics, U.S. Department of Education. (2010). *Doctorate recipients, by ethnicity, race, and citizenship status: 1976-2008.* https://nces.ed.gov/pubs2010/2010015/indicator6_24.asp.

National Science Foundation. (2015). *Survey of earned doctorates*. National Science Foundation. https://www.nsf.gov/statistics/srvydoctorates/#sd&tabs-1.

Pope, R.J. (2013). Reflections of a black male counseling psychology doctoral student: Lessons learned from APA division 45 commentary and the role of social justice for counseling psychologists. *Journal for Social Action in Counseling & Psychology, 5*(1), 103-115.

Pope, L. (2019, May 2). Learning Hub. *3 Tips to Keep Discrimination Out of Your Dress Code Policy.* Retrieved July 15, 2020 https://learn.g2.com/dress-code-policy

Rickford, J.R. (n.d.). What is Ebonics (African American English)? Retrieved July 15, 2020 https://www.linguisticsociety.org/content/what-ebonics-african-american-english

Steele, C.M., & Aronson, J. (1995). Stereotype threat and the intellectual test performance of African Americans. *Journal of Personality and Social Psychology, 69*(5), 797–811. https://doi.org/10.1037/0022-3514.69.5.797

Tate, S. A., & Bagguley, P. (2017). Building the anti-racist university: Next steps. *Race, Ethnicity, and Education, 20*(3), 289-299.

CHAPTER FIFTEEN

Ponderings and Reflections on Identity, Intersectionality, and Discrimination: A Call for Unity

Marquis B. Holley, University of South Florida

A Little Advice...

1. Drink water
2. Pray
3. Don't come for me

The Realization Of Me

The first time I realized my race was in elementary school, during our art class. I was in the first grade, age 6 or 7, and we were coloring our family/friends. A classmate told me that I had could not use the brown crayon, but only the black crayon. I asked them if they only used the white crayon when coloring themselves and their family/friends, which confused them, and I continued using the crayon(s) of my choice, as my family is a diverse and beautiful shade of several cultures and ethnicities. I consider this a grassroots description of me as a person today, as I value the perspective of others, but was raised to not bend to the pressures or opinions of others, no matter who or what they may be.

There were several outlets that helped define me from my childhood to the present day, including dance, poetry, songwriting, and a spiritual/personal relationship with God. Rather than ramble about who I am and where I am coming from, I wanted to take a different approach and use poetry to create the tapestry that is Marquis B. Holley. I base my approach to poetry on various levels and methods, but within academia, I use the methodologies of arts- based research, and Post Traumatic Slave Syndrome (PTSS) as beacons for clarity. DeGruy (2005) affirms that esteem means worth or value, which my writing aims to highlight. Furthermore, Leavy (2015) confirms that sometimes, we need to approach things differently. With poetry and other reflections, this will become more apparent through this journey, as I aspire to speak a message of unity, with a different lens for perspective building.

I Will...

I will walk when others choose to run
Rushing through life takes away all of the fun

Things make sense when you take your time
Worries flee, and fear departs, a soothing sound
comes like a wind chime

I will laugh when others choose to be upset
A merry heart brings health, and helps prevent a future regret
There is no need to be bitter about the small
When it is possible, if you stay positive, you could have it all

I will smile when others choose to frown
No matter what drama comes your way, don't bring
others down
When one removes negativity from the picture
Joy becomes a permanent fixture

I will give when others choose to not share
You don't have to reach into your pockets to show
that you care

A simple hello, a wave, compliment, or smile will suffice
It may be nice to be important, but it's more important to be
Nice

I will live when others choose to die
There is no time to have a pity party and ask "why"?
We must fight on and endure until the end
Abundant blessings will be ours, on this we can depend

I Will. I Will.. I Will…

Where there is a Will, there is a Way
A Word on Identity and Empathy

Discrimination has various meanings to various individuals, depending
on their race, ethnicity, gender, and class identity. And even when there is an
intersection between these for one individual, there is still a variation in
meaning when it comes to discrimination. The purpose of this chapter is not
to define those meanings, as that would lead to an almost never-ending
discussion, but instead, to persuade the reader that structural similarities exist
between different acts of discrimination. According to the theoretical
framework of Post Traumatic Slave Syndrome (PTSS) (2005), these
similarities are seen in the perceptions that intersect, regardless of race,
ethnicity, gender, or class identity. DeGruy (2005) is credited with developing

the concept of PTSS, which is a derivative of Post-Traumatic Stress Disorder (PTSD). Furthermore, one of the concluding points of PTSS (2005) is to begin the healing by sustaining and advancing future generations while acknowledging the traumatic past that slavery wrought upon people of African descent.

The topic of discrimination strikes a deeply personal chord in my life, as I have personally witnessed and been a recipient of discrimination based on all four categories. Also, as a Black man, I have been a spokesperson on equity and diversity within the workforce, everyday life, and now academia, for quite some time. It is part of who I am, and I do not consider it a load or burden. If someone is being wrongfully treated, we as humans have a responsibility to speak out for those without a voice, regardless of our or their race, ethnicity, gender, or class identity. History has shown us that not speaking up can cause tragic outcomes that can be felt for generations to come. That is why the PTSS another explanation is so relevant for society today. As Brathwaite and Orr (2016) remind us, "identity is never singular." Having a heart of empathy, but a stern determination to be in the corner of those that are underrepresented, mistreated, discriminated against, or just downright invisible to those in power is a social responsibility that we all must take on to heal wounds that have been left untreated for centuries. There is no day like today to commence this long, overdue, and much needed process. So, let's begin.

A Glimpse at Where We Have Been
and Where We Might Be Going

From a historical perspective, discrimination has worn many faces, yet served one purpose: to hold any selected under-represented minority back from succeeding in life. Historically, slaves were beaten, brutalized, mistreated, and more, which depictions we have today are based on data and documentation from the past and present. PTSS is passed on to their descendants. Once slavery was officially "abolished," a lack of empathy and mental health treatments, rehabilitation, or any restoration efforts continued to enslave the minds of the so-termed minorities, that is the Blacks in the USA, in such victim-blaming endeavors.

As the era of the Jim Crow laws during the Reconstruction Era proved that even when slavery was ended after the Civil War, there were still methods used to inhibit the progress of people of African descent. One of the main methods remained rampant discrimination. Laws that prohibited interracial marriage, to colored water fountains, segregated schools and hospitals, and provided water fountains for "coloreds" and more serve to highlight how discrimination was at the forefront all along. True, it could be argued that these are also examples of racism, but discrimination is nothing more than the first cousin of racism. Discrimination hinders regardless of race, ethnicity, gender, or class identity. As we are seeing in the 21st Century USA, history repeats itself, and much continues as if nothing has changed in spite of diversity and equity practices. Dr. DeGruy affirms this by declaring "It is from impacts of past assaults that we must heal, and it is from the threats of continuing assaults that we must learn to defend ourselves, our families, and our communities" (Leary, 2005, p. 100). History has proven time and again that discrimination regardless of which identity category is attacked, also creates intersections of identities and serves as a potential tool of destruction in the lives of those being discriminated. But if change takes place, and if those being discriminated against spoke up, historical perspectives could experience a dramatic shift. However, for now, we remain at the status quo.

It Takes
It takes strength to endure a test
Even when more drama seems to manifest
When you're able to take the good and bad in stride
The idea of giving up will have no choice but to step aside
It takes peace to know when to fight
Choosing to walk away will exude true might Extending an open hand
rather than a clenched fist Will truly evaporate an angering mist
It takes joy to produce the inner smile
Having a rich perspective will help you go that extra mile
For every time that you are mocked
Embracing the inner you will keep you rooted, and your enemies shocked
It takes love to help each other
Even if it's a glass of water for your sister or brother
The pure heart knows what it means to turn the other cheek And that there
is limitless ability in being meek
It takes all of this and more to be the best you can be
Step by step, the path you travel will become easier to see
Each day is a gift to begin anew
As a better, wiser, distinctive, You

Lifting up our Voices
Singing in a Chorus with All

Discrimination, as previously mentioned, has many meanings. Possessing a lens that is adjustable goes a long way in developing an understanding that has meaning. By peering through in a multiple meaning lens, individuals can identify issues such as discrimination. Jones et al. (2007) posit "little research has been conducted exploring self-authorship in the context of how students make meaning of their socially constructed identities, such as race and sexuality" (p. 5). This should cause an individual to seek a better understanding of where they fit in the spectrum of things. For example, if a student is being discriminated against for a student government position, because they are an African American female, who also identifies as pansexual, which group does this student ultimately fall under? Would the student need to choose in order to identify the root of the discrimination they are experiencing? Harnois (2014) provides another perspective, declaring "A commitment to gender equality, almost by definition, signaled a lower awareness of, and commitment to, racial equality, and a commitment to racial equality was similarly thought to decrease one's awareness of other forms of social injustice. It was as if, to view the world through the lens of racial inequality, one had to first remove her or his gender glasses" (p. 473). The tenets of PTSS would show the student to connect with discriminatory practices as a whole and decipher what methods can be used to fix the issue and possibly make the path a bit easier for the next person that follows in their footsteps. Furthermore, giving someone the option to better clarify their stance on an important issue such as class identity can prove essential on personal levels. And in this example, if little research has taken place, it could be safe to hypothesize that the structural similarities of discrimination could exist with individuals based on varying lenses of perspectives. If we root ourselves in a "multiple meaning" framework, which allows us to identify in more ways than one, we're making progress in changing the status quo to an ideal for positive, worthwhile change.

Discrimination, in terms of structural similarities, plays a major role in identities and equalities as well. A human being that has never been a recipient of discrimination in some form is either privileged to the highest order, or possibly numb to the realities that life brings to everyday people on an everyday basis. I wholeheartedly agree with the statement that "identity is never singular" (Braithwaite & Orr, 2016, p. 62). If one can admit there is no one way to identify the self, this encourages people to be okay with identifying at the intersection of more than one identity category. The acceptance of intersectionality can also give people a voice to speak for other affected parties to bring power and access to them. To have a voice that speaks for all affected parties brings power and access that is not normally found, regardless of the discriminatory practice being administered.

It is imperative to note that even from the base value, the intersections between race, ethnicity, gender, and class identity are evident, and the perceptions may possess the most clarity in this realm. For example, when the denied student inquires, about why they were not accepted into a graduate program, and the chair of the department states that the student is not the right "fit" for that particular program. In terms of PTSS, this is an all too familiar occurrence. People of color, African Americans in particular, are used to denials, and have learned to deal with it. However, that is part of the stress. Dealing with it. How long and how many times should someone just deal with it without having someone to talk with professionally about it before serious duress occurs? The struggle of always having to accept defeat even when one feels victory is within grasp can take a toll that may be too much to bear. This is how discrimination intersects and irrespective with which category or categories one identifies, it still brings color to the forefront. We see that we are losing the battle against discrimination when the intersections are no longer distinctive, but synonymous with exclusion, rather than inclusion. This is why it is absolutely pivotal to use our voice for effective and lasting change.

Some students that are not often acknowledged can feel targeted due to the color of their skin. Take ROTC members, for example, that attend higher education first, in order to obtain a rank upon graduation and a degree, rather than entering the military immediately after high school graduation. This example illustrates the intersect between race, ethnicity, gender, and class identity even within a group in higher education that is not always in the forefront. Additional research posits "Female and ethnic minority participants were more *likely* to agree that certain barriers would affect them, but the majority did not agree. Rather, their lack of certainty was significantly different from that of their male and Euro-American counterparts, who more often disagreed that given barriers would affect them" (McWhirter, 1997, p. 138). This example sheds light on how students of underrepresented populations are treated prior to arriving to higher education. If we're not examining the experiences of these students in particular, prior to their arrival at the universities or colleges, while continuing to overlook their experiences in higher education, how can we fully and truly grasp where they are coming from, and where they desire to go? PTSS supports this as well, as the lingering trauma that was passed down through generations still exists in the students today. As previously stated, I work with these students daily, and a high percentage of my students, well above 90%, are underrepresented minorities. I see in their work, discussions, interactions, and even more through the hardships of history, discrimination has dealt them an unfair and tough hand to play with, but somehow, someway, they make the most of it, and persist. As a member of an underrepresented population, with a similar background, I can affirm this determination.

Giving up is simply not an option in our communities, because history has proven that not many, outside of our communities, believe in us, thus self-preservation and communal support is what always makes or breaks us. That is the story of our lives, and it has been that way for centuries. As mentioned earlier, oppression is a first cousin of discrimination. Not only does it exclude underrepresented minorities, it enforces the exclusion, including excessive and violent, if directed to do so. This can be a very challenging experience for those being oppressed, especially if there is no break/relief in sight.

Hands

Come one, come all and see what they have to offer
Many were raised to keep their hands to themselves
But others have no problem sharing them
Hands... Where love can be found
Hugging a child after a long day at work
Embracing the love of your life before dinner
Giving Mom or Dad a high five before heading off to school
Hands... Where hatred thrives
Slapping, choking, or punching a spouse

Taking the leash off a dog, ordering it to harm, or even kill
 someone because they're defending their land
Tying a noose around someone's neck for a spectacle, all
because of the color of their skin Hands... Where peace loves
to dwell
Joining in unity, protecting another religious group while
 they pray for the world Holding an infant, rocking them to
sleep while singing a lullaby
Protesting with signs, raised fists, and megaphones
How can these hands be so gentle, yet so strong?
It's a tough task, but someone must see it through

So, the next time you or I look at our hands, may we acknowledge the power
they possess. They could build up, or they could tear down,
The choice is ours

Choices: They are Ours to Make or Break

It is my sincere hope that the readers were able to grasp a newfound
concept, or more than one, and apply it to their reflection of what terms like
discrimination, perceptions, gender, and more, mean to them. Overall,
discrimination harms all of us, regardless of race, ethnicity, gender, or class
identity. It is a social responsibility for everyone to stand up, to speak out, and
to be the agent of change that society needs for centuries-old wounds to heal.
Post Traumatic Slave Syndrome provides vivid examples and logic behind the
results of societal failings of the past, and how they continue to impact our
society today. If we do not want to continue to repeat that history, then the
time is now to be the light that shines in the darkness, and brings the wicked
past to the forefront, all for the purpose of righting wrongs that cannot be
undone but can be presented in order to prevent them from occurring once
again. The choice is ours. May we choose wisely, for the sake of our fellow
man and woman, regardless of race, ethnicity, gender, or class identity.

For Herbert & Rose...
His name is Herbert
A Husband, father, grandpa
He won his battle
Her name is RoseMary
She is stern, yet delicate
Black power lives on

References

Abes, E. S. & Jones, S. R. & McEwen, M. K. (2007). Reconceptualizing the
        Model of Multiple Dimensions of Identity: The Role of
        Meaning-Making Capacity in the Construction of Multiple

Identities. *Journal of College Student Development 48*(1), 1-22.
John Hopkins University Press. Retrieved March 26, 2019, from
Project MUSE database. http://doi.org/10.1353/csd.2007.0000

Braithwaite, A., & Orr, C. M. (2016). *Everyday
women's and gender studies: Introductory
concepts*. Routledge.

Harnois, C. E. (2014). Are Perceptions of Discrimination Unidimensional,
Oppositional, or Intersectional? Examining the Relationship
Among Perceived Racial-Ethnic-, Gender-, and Age-Based
Discrimination. *Sociological Perspectives*, (4), 470. Retrieved
From
http://ezproxy.lib.usf.edu/login?url=http://search.ebscohost.com/
login.aspx?direct=true&db=edsbl&AN=RN363541710&site=eds
-live

Leary, J. D., & Robinson, R. (2005). *Post traumatic slave syndrome: America's
legacy of enduring injury and healing*. Uptone Press.
Leavy, P. (2015). *Method meets art: Arts-based
research practice*. The Guilford Press.

McWhirter, E. H. (1997). Perceived barriers to education and career: Ethnic and
gender differences. *Journal of Vocational Behavior*, *50*(1), 124 -
140.
https://doi-org.ezproxy.lib.usf.edu/10.1006/jvbe.1995.1536

Pittman, C. T. (2010). Race and Gender Oppression in the Classroom: The
Experiences of Women Faculty of Color with White Male
Students. *Teaching Sociology*, *38*(3), 183–
196. https://doi.org/10.1177/0092055X10370120

All poems by Marquis B. Holley ©

159

CHAPTER SIXTEEN

Up 'Till Now, Racism, the Corona Virus, and Peace

Ronald Duncan, National-Louis University

When I finally took Lisa's class, I observed an attitude of hostility directed toward me. Her attitude toward me was completely different from the handful of times we had met previously. Before our first day of classes together, we had enjoyed social discourse, which led to a pleasant conversation in the Spring of 2019.

Her husband joined us in her office, where they began to craft a student-teacher relationship by showing me pictures of nieces and nephews. We talked and laughed about theatre and whether I should take magazine design or book design; I was excited to work with a person who shared similar interests. On the first day of class, I knew that as the affiliate professor in charge of hiring affiliate teachers, Lisa had bought every rumor, lie, and a bit of poison from other teachers with her, willingly because I was an outspoken black man. The opinions from others affected how she treated me for the first four to five weeks of course work. There is a saving grace here, however. I was able to alter Lisa's personal opinion of me slightly. Although her guard was up with me, she relinquished all the gossip and toxic rumors of me from naysayers and decided for herself to see the kind of person I was. At this point, Lisa had done more for my education than anyone else had previously in New England. I was amazed that someone was still willing to play the adult in the building and the supporting educator. I could tell she understood her duty as a teacher. After all, I worked diligently in the class, and despite everything, I managed to maintain a 3.9 GPA. No one could discount that I was creative and hard-working.

Before this particular class, discrepancy or random complication always followed me. For good or bad, nothing that I did before now ever seemed to be enough to satisfy anyone other than myself, a few family members, and close friends. Rejection and frustration had gone with me throughout my travels, theatrical career, Christian community engagement, and life-long learning. As an adult learner, I found that a couple of the educators upon my return to undergraduate study, as well as my current master's program, was wholly distanced as it related to students' best interests. These teaching professionals were a powerful demonstration of why not all people should ever consider leading classroom instruction. I had assessed these instructors individually until a few things began to occur throughout my second year of graduate studies.

One thing is sure. The pandemic has now taught me that nothing I had done was unprofessional, which provoked such irresponsible negligence in our interactions. I was just at the mercy of selfish people accustomed to playing dirty and getting their way. Two, the female teachers' attitude was also directly connected to the hyper-liberal student body and the greater college community. And three working in tandem: racism, hyper-feminism, and the LBGTQ

160

movements was at its best in New England. Never mind inclusion, they were only interested in a "yes and our way only" universe and fanatically opposed to anyone else's morality and principles. The saddest part is that I had to quit believing that these teachers were there for my benefit, and because of these people, I was able to look at racism in earnest. The thought that these movements that seek inclusion could house discrimination against blacks as long as they felt that no one was watching is rather disturbing.

I could see the four-hundred-year twisted mentality that would compel a folk to remove others from their land and enslave them, free them, and subsequently re-enslave them through a one-sided game of politics, policies, and erroneous laws tripled arbitrarily through the use of math and technology. As a man in Christ Jesus, I witnessed that racism, bigotry, discrimination, prejudice, all the words of hate added up to nothing more than Sin. It had as little to do with who I was or who the professors, or even who the everyday person was really. The impact those words have had globally didn't start with the generation of people currently inhabiting the globe. They were taught poorly by history. Led astray in the belief that they were somehow golden. That they were rich, and I was poor; they had talent while I had borrowed skills—all perishing materials.

I considered my life, every burnt bridge, or missed opportunity taken, given, stolen, or passed over because I have never bought into any of those ideals. The pandemic has also taught me that no one knows anything, that these people were never right, just in power and position, which is a far cry from any standard of unity or a bridge to such aims. *Grandmama didn't raise no fool*; that is, my grandmother never introduced me to differences in race or culture in a way that would place me low and them high, only God. I find it extraordinary that people tell and raise their children to be racists. My identity was never in my color, or my skin, only in *Yeshua*. People never believe language like this but thank goodness I am not usually the one that handles that. I was never what racism, Sin, attempts to declare that I am, and I'd walk out of a classroom or job long before I'd allow the enemy an attempt to lavish me with the ignorance of others.

The first time I had ever experienced racism was in my second year of undergraduate study in Chicago, IL—talk about culture shock. Even with Covid-19, a seemingly easily manipulated tool to reform and unite, rebellion is the mainstay of our everyday experience. As the coronavirus took center stage early this year, I'm reminded of how I got to my current living situation. It was in 2016 that I knew America's most incredible circus acts were not only heating up but that they would never end, and I do mean *never*. It was in prayer that the Lord finally removed the need and desire that I disliked from working in ungodly random stage and television productions. Prompted by the *Holy Spirit*, I returned to school to finish my undergraduate degree. In all honesty, actors, dancers, and singers generally aren't viewed as humans, but gypsies. However, I had always had a love of education, teaching, and learning.

Today there remains low quality and often inaccurate teaching lessons in public schools K-12 and higher learning. In my more than twenty years of teaching privately, I recognize that teachers are always ineffective when the lesson is more about who they are than who the student is. The best educators know the difference between racism, sincerity, and duty. For instance, the fact that there are racist educators only points to an unprofessional individual that took on a contract to educate children and older students without fully comprehending who'd show up for the class. They say that young children can always tell if people are being sincere or not. For educators who teach on any platform, sincerity is either hit or miss. A good teacher is someone with the developed sense of what works and what doesn't end the story. Children, teenagers, young and old adults wear every emotion on their sleeves, and I say this matter-of-factly because, as someone who has traversed and journaled through multiple industries, it's the model behavior all around. The racist professors in my current program don't have this commonsense. Even so, the coronavirus has helped me to find rest in all of this trouble.

After moving to New England, except for the dance studio directors who hired me fulltime, I knew no one else. I was grateful to secure a spacious studio apartment under nine-hundred dollars, a parking space with all utilities included. Thankfully, I still have my car, and I make sure to get the necessary maintenance yearly because with a two-hour train commute downtown, public transportation was out of the question. I discovered I'd end up paying less a semester than purchasing the college train and bus pass by driving to class in my car and paying for public parking. Twenty minutes in and out would be my routine, for I reasoned that the only reason I came to New England was for this program that offered me a decent fellowship to match. So, going out and partying or being out and about a lot was not my purpose. It took me a full year and a half to figure out that my experience and education had only been a conduit for racism and hatred. My refusal to participate in a culture of teacher's and student "pronouns" and same-sex bathrooms brought with it a thick cloud of resentment and hostility.

Indeed, my silent support for others' rights wasn't enough. My feeling of, "Hey, have your unisex bathrooms, men wear your dresses, and women become CEO's," wasn't enough. They failed to realize, like so many, that support and participation are two separate conversations. They targeted me because I never participated or marched with them in their efforts to change the world. I have my own beliefs; the Holy Bible tells me to live in the world, but not be of it. I know how to coexist. It's others who don't.

The animosity was so tangible that I could tell many hands, teachers, and students were around my throat. Someone else would dare to furnish the rope when I finally wrote the department of Justice at the College to get these vipers off my back. The situation softened but not even by a percentage. In response to the treatment and my walk to graduate in Spring 2020, I had elected to take an online course and one in-person session— Lisa's.

I was happy Covid-19 shut it down and put us all online. Folks have to work harder now at being messy and careless during the pandemic, they have to go out of their way to be terrible, and they are. I danced like King David danced because, at the very least, it meant that I did not have to have to sit in the faces of racist and hateful people. I could work in the privacy of my own home without having to worry about the weaknesses of ignorance. Thanks to the coronavirus's onset, there is a semblance of peace for me, and I am sure many others who want a break and a bit of rest from people who have OCD, self-control, and mental issues. People should rest from low wage labor, make more room for family, avoid mass murders in schools and public places, and perhaps see a drop in cops shooting kids at point-blank. Students can take a break from racist teachers or employers who use their positions to discourage well-meaning and hard-working people of color or not of color. The federal officials tell everyone to distance themselves and isolate, stay home, and stay well. Praise God.

Now that Blacks in America are ready scapegoats through the disorganization, BLM a new marketing strategy developed in schools all around the country. Suddenly, the colleges I've only known to subtly encourage a steady stream of racism, who pre-COVID 19 avoided all recognition of the issues faced for close to a millennium, are now somehow experts on dismantling racist rhetoric. I'd be all for it if I felt colleges and universities weren't jumping up to act as though they always cared about antiracist behavior if they weren't first concerned with potentially losing their federal accreditation status.

The hypocrisy is diabolical, to be sure, and still, I am grateful for the rest. To take a sigh of relief and know that there is nothing I can do to change people or how they ultimately and willingly decide to treat others. However, I can continue to work on myself, the inner man, which no one else seems to understand that that's how you change or improve yourself. It's not a webinar or a New York Times bestseller on meditation or practical living that will cut it or save them. Whether racism or hatred from family, enemies, other black people, whoever, I no longer have to be found by hateful people so quickly. Up till now, I thought I had to accept these things, and I do, but just not in person and certainly not in their classes or public spaces. The pandemic has taught me that no one knows anything at all. It has exposed the illusion of money and position where many still boast that it makes a person. Instead, the global catastrophe faced has cast a light on what unjust gains, pretentious and unquantifiable pretended places of hierarchy in the hands of people unfit to lead or govern genuinely looks like in the time of real crisis.

CHAPTER SEVENTEEN

Where Do We Go from Here?
Double Consciousness in Higher Education

Cameron Jernigan, A Southern State University

"It is a peculiar sensation, this double-consciousness, this sense of always looking at one's self through the eyes of others, of measuring one's soul by the tape of a world that looks on in amused contempt and pity. One ever feels his two-ness, an American, a Negro; two souls, two thoughts, two unreconciled strivings; two warring ideals in one dark body, whose dogged strength alone keeps it from being torn asunder."

William Edward Burghardt Du Bois,
"Strivings of the Negro People," 1897

The Water
A body of water is in constant ebb and flow
The tide moves towards and against the land, constantly
leaving a little bit of itself there
To the point that the water is unrecognizable, even it itself
Eventually it becomes something else, something it isn't,
something it never was
something it never intended to become

Eventually it becomes its worst nightmare
Instead of the clear, shiny, blue water kissed by the sun in
 the brightness of the day and illuminated by the moon in the
 darkness of the night
It becomes a dark, murky,
confused version of what it once was
Unclear of its identity in this ecosystem, its purpose, or its
 relationship with others

Regardless, it holds on to its (seemingly) true identity
Because it's still who it once was, right?
But the water doesn't realize that, as he changes,
 so, does his environment

With ebb and flow, everything changes
The land is different, the air is different
The people and things that inhabit this environment is
different

The space is fundamentally different
And as a result, the water becomes fundamentally different
The water struggles to reconcile these two worlds,
these two identities
He can never go back to who he was or the world he once
inhabited
Despite the struggles, he must find his place in this new
world
He must realize his purpose and his true self, against all odds
Where does he go from here?

***

The story of the water is my story, and his story, and his story, and his story, and his story. It is the story of all of us. It is the story of Black men, attempting to navigate this constantly unfamiliar space that is higher education. Two worlds, two versions of ourselves, two identities, two personalities meant to be one. Two people in one body, in a constant struggle of push and pull and ebb and flow. And in the worst of times? Conflicting ideals, voices, and stories, constantly grinding, grating, and pushing against each other. As Black men, we stand in a peculiar place in society. Both the survivors of centuries of oppression, violence, and intergenerational trauma and susceptible to perpetrating oppression, misogyny, and sexism, we walk a tightrope en route to ensuring equity for marginalized folx. At the same time, we have to balance the world, the community, and the culture we have been birthed from, while also having to make sense of this new world, new culture, and new societal expectations that we have not had to consider until now. When I made the decision at 20 to fully pursue higher education and student affairs as a career path, I was largely unaware of the challenges that would come with this decision, or the moral questions I would have to consider while on this path. It is a path I do not regret, but one for which I wished I had had more time to fully consider before walking. It is my story, and his story, and his story, and his story, and his story. It is the story of all of us.

••

August 2014 Just a few weeks prior, I had just completed a summer bridge program where I got a small taste of what being a college student would be like. I familiarized myself with the campus, I took an intro English and Math course, got acclimated to the social dynamics of college, and made a few friendships that lasted through college and beyond. Once completed, I had two weeks of rest, relaxation, and final goodbyes before returning for the Fall semester. And then, exactly a week before I was set to move into my residence hall on the 16th, Michael Brown Jr. was killed in Ferguson, Missouri on the 9th. Although I never met Mike Brown, and he was killed over 800 miles away from me, his death still impacted me, if for no other reason than that we were both young Black boys, born only months apart, on the cusp of manhood in a country colored by whiteness. As I prepared to embark on what would become a life changing, transformative four years, I thought about him often, and just how easily that could have been me or someone I know. Following the killing of Trayvon Martin, another Black boy that could have been me, and the ensuing trial, talking about violence against Black people was not something I was afraid of or with which I was unfamiliar. But once I left the small, mostly

Black, rural North Carolina town, things became a bit different.

Entering into a largely white university community of over 30,000 was an unfamiliar and daunting task for me at 17 years old. More than that, entering this community in the wake of such a public example of Black death and the nationwide protests that came as a result was jarring. Many people I encountered were apathetic at best, and hostile at worst, to the idea that Mike Brown's life mattered or that police brutality was a real thing that happened not due to the inherent violence of Black people, but due to racism. In a class of almost 4,000 incoming first year students, not much more than 100 of us were Black men. In 2013, the incoming class before did not even crack 100. Still, I soon learned the power and courage of the Black student population when protests for Mike Brown happened in the first week of classes. My first opportunity to see or engage in protests, it was a beautiful thing, and made me realize that the community I thought I had found during Summer Bridge did exist within the larger campus.

Still, this brief moment did not fully cause my concerns and feelings of marginalization to completely subside. Not long after the death of Mike Brown, I learned of the killings of John Crawford and Eric Garner, both at the hands of police. For the next nine months, I continued to exist and work to find my place in the sea of whiteness that at times felt like it was consuming me. I did what most Black students at Historically White Institutions do and have done for decades: I tried to find my chosen family and insulate myself from the violence. By the end of the year, I had found my people, got somewhat involved on campus, and had begun figuring out my place in the world. I had also seen armed Neo-Confederates come to campus to counter-protest Black and Indigenous students protesting for the removal of a confederate monument located on campus. So, in other words, balance.

Before I could step foot back on campus for my sophomore year, nine Black churchgoers in Charleston, South Carolina would be killed by Dylann Roof at Mother Emanuel AME Church. Less than a month later, Sandra Bland would be found dead in her jail cell in Waller County, Texas, three days after being pulled over for failure to properly cite a lane change. If that summer was any indication, constant Black death (and white people being apathetic to said violence and death) would be a recurring theme of my time in college, as well as my journey throughout the ivory tower.

***

July 2016 I am 19 years old. I was spending six weeks of the summer with 50 high school students as a counselor of Upward Bound Summer Academy, the summer portion of a college access program my undergraduate university held

166

for local area high school students. After not being chosen for a doctoral preparation program earlier that year, the director of the program thought I would be a good fit for Upward Bound and forwarded my resume. A few weeks later, I interviewed and secured the position. I had been considering student affairs and college access programs as a potential career path for some time, and this was my first real opportunity to get a taste of what that might look like.

After weeks of classes, professional development sessions, and the students loading the buses and going home every day at 4 P.M, we finally get a taste of around the clock supervision in the form of the annual Upward Bound Retreat. Three days of ropes courses, cabins, and bonding exercises. The night before we left for our excursion into the wilderness, I found out about the killing of Alton Sterling by Baton Rouge, Louisiana police officers. The day we left, Philando Castile was killed by police officers in front of his girlfriend and their child, during a traffic stop outside of St. Paul, Minnesota. As all but two of the 50+ students were Black or Latinx, I could not help but think about how, although Alton Sterling and Eric Garner were adults and my students were teenagers, it could have been them who were the new hashtags and viral death videos plastered all over my Twitter and Instagram feeds. It could have been their families and friends that had to come to terms with the death of a loved one at the hands of those sworn to protect them. But what I could not accept, and still work through fully accepting all these years later, is that if that happened to one of my students, there would be nothing I could have done to protect them.

Many of my students were the same age that Trayvon was, that Jordan Davis was, that Mike Brown was when they were killed. My youngest students, at 14, have lived longer than the 12 years Tamir Rice had before he was killed by police in Cleveland, Ohio. At the same time, I am considering whether or not to commit my time and effort to the pursuit of a career focused on the success and survival of students that look like me, I am also confronted with the realization that nothing I do can save them. White supremacy and police violence do not care how many accolades you have, how many degrees you have, how many successful programs you have put on, or how many fellow students you have mentored. They do not care about how many mentors or supervisors like me have counseled with them, encouraged them, motivated them, or ultimately helped them matriculated through college.

It was at this point where I came to realize that if I was going to commit myself to this path and journey of working with students, I had to fully shed from me the savior complex I had built within myself when forming my motivations for working in student affairs. As a Black man at a historically white institution, I wanted to work to ensure that many of the pitfalls, challenges, and violence enacted on me did not occur within the next generation of Black students. Years later, that is still my goal. However, only until I fully accepted that there was but so much I could do to protect the students I work with, from the pain enacted on them by the University and by greater society, could I truly begin to both protect them and arm them with the tools to protect themselves.

***

Sunday, January 26, 2020 I wake up sometime around 10 AM, and prepare myself for Sunday brunch at the Mexican restaurant I've been trying to visit for the better part of two years but to which, for some reason, just haven't been able to find my way. The majority of my weekend has been occupied, as I have been volunteering as a small group facilitator for a multicultural leadership conference my university held that Friday and Saturday. Aside from a couple of bumps in the road, it went smoothly and I am grateful for the opportunity to engage with students I don't normally work with in my assistantship and internship roles on campus.

The friends I am meeting up with were on the planning team for the conference and are relieved but exhausted after months of planning and finally, fruition. We all need a bit of a celebratory breather for a job well done, and brunch is the obvious answer. Finally, able to talk about something other than the conference, we discuss what is happening in the speck of free time outside of graduate school, and the job search of which we are all terrified. More than the pretty good food and drinks we share; it is the sense of community that I enjoy the most.

Following brunch, I need to run the usual Sunday afternoon errands around the city: grocery store run, a quick trip to Barnes and Noble, a manicure, etc. After a quick trip home to drop things off and change clothes, I hop back in the car to complete the most dreaded of Sunday afternoon tasks: homework. Because no matter what, as a graduate student working in student affairs, there's always work to be done. As I pull into the always crowded parking lot of my favorite coffee shop, I park my car and check my phone, realizing I have what feels like a million and one notifications to check, mostly texts and alerts from Twitter. And that's when it hits me.

Everyone from friends in my graduate program, to my brother, to my mom, have sent me either a text, Instagram post, or tweet about the supposed death of Kobe Bryant, the retired NBA player, and his daughter Gianna. After finding out that the reports are true, the rest of the day is a cloud. I try to continue in my normal Sunday routine, but it still feels off. The only moment of mental clarity is spending time with a friend later that night and engaging in the weekly ritual of watching our favorite TV show together. The next day, work is difficult. It still feels as if this is just an evil joke or some misunderstanding. For someone with so much life left to live to die so tragically is…always hard to a degree. However, it's not lost on me that the death of Kobe or GiGi doesn't mean the same thing to my colleagues or most of my students as it means to many of my friends and family. For many, Kobe's death is simply another death, and not a loss for a community or a generation.

Kobe's death was difficult for me for a lot of reasons. It was difficult as a fan of basketball for my entire life. It was difficult as a fan of the Los Angeles Lakers, the team that Kobe played for since the year I was born until his retirement 20 years later. It was difficult as someone that wants to be a father one day; the idea of not being able to protect your child in the final moments of your life is something I never want to feel. But more difficult than all of those things were reckoning with Kobe's death as someone committed to ending sexual and interpersonal violence, both in my professional work on college campuses and my life outside of work.

At the time of Kobe's death, I was a few weeks into an internship at my institution's Title IX office. It was the first leaf to sprout from a seed that was planted years ago when my interest in Title IX and intimate partner and sexual violence prevention was planted at a student leadership conference. Finally getting a chance to do this work is exciting and professionally challenging in the best way possible. To that same end, the nature of the work is mentally and emotionally taxing, for obvious reasons. But Kobe dying at this specific moment truly put in context the totality of his life, even the dark moments. For as much as Kobe can be celebrated for his time as a player, or even his involvement and commitment to girls' basketball following his playing career, he is still someone that was accused of and admitted to sexual assault. All of those things can and do coexist, but all must be acknowledged and considered when looking at someone's life.

The death of Kobe reminded me, more than anything, of the importance of the spaces I show up in and the conversations I have. When Kobe was accused of sexual assault, he initially made a statement that he perceived the encounter to be consensual. Later, he realized that it was in fact not consensual. I cannot go back and teach Kobe about consent, what sexual assault and violence are, or do anything else to prevent the survivor of his violence from being assaulted. What I can do is work to ensure violence like that does not occur again. I can work to gain justice for those when it does occur. Moreover, I can work to create a culture of consent, safety, and justice. As a cisgender heterosexual man, I understand that many men will listen to and accept the words of other men before anyone else. As a result, it is not only important but necessary that I have these conversations surrounding consent and sexual violence, and continue operating in spaces where few, look like me. It is not and never will be easy work, but when I decided to enter this field and engage in this work years ago, I knew that and accepted the challenge. This journey as a Black man in student affairs has never been easy, but if it was easy, our presence would not be needed. Let's keep working.

Swimming Through the Night

The night is dark and full of terrors
Wait...
Not just the night
But the day, and the morning, and the evening, and afternoon
... but especially the night

It doesn't matter

It's all dark
It's all terrifying
It all feels like night, no matter the time
It's all seen
It's all dark

It's like you're swimming in an ocean at night
Only the moon illuminates the midnight navy water
Except there's no moon
And it's all darkness

And all you can do to stay above water is swim
Just keep swimming, just keep swimming, into the darkness
The darkness that feels like it'll never end
The darkness that eventually envelops you

But still
You just keep swimming
Just keep swimming
Just keep swimming
Trying to find your way home
Wherever that is
Whatever that is

But I promise you this
You won't swim forever
Eventually there will be a reprieve
An opportunity for breath, for fresh air, for grounding
A second, or first, chance at life again
without the danger of drowning

Although the night is dark and full of terrors
And you feel like you're drowning
I promise you…
You won't swim forever.

References

Du Bois, W. E. B. (1897). *Strivings of the Negro people.*
Atlantic Monthly Company.

All poems by Cameron Jernigan ©

Blackmaled in Academia

PART FIVE

A Conversation in Black & White

A Conversation in Black and White

Max and Margrit

Introduction

Max and Margrit are fictional characters, alter egos, and extended metaphors...she is an "ally" and he an angry black man. Their conversation began a few years ago, before the murders of George Floyd and Brianna Taylor that sparked the nationwide protests over the unjust killings of blacks by police. These protests prompted white sympathy to racial relations that have been strained during the Trump years. The national mood toward race relations and reconciliation seems to have taken an abrupt change toward the positive, immediately after the Biden and Harris election. People are back in the streets, joyful and hopeful for change. Join them in the middle of the conversation.

Margrit: Max, don't you think everyone is tired of hearing about black people's problems, but they go along with the current social narrative? You'd think we'd moved into a post-racial world, because sophisticated people claim they no longer consider race a factor in relationships and jobs. We have become global citizens, by choice or not, and many accept diversity and multiculturalism as a given. You know, you'll be considered "just an old, angry black man," an anachronism, right? You know that people will say that many of the problems of race you talk about are just imaginary and the result of hypersensitivity or even white guilt of the liberal crowd. Are you sure there isn't some truth to it? After all, haven't people in this country put tremendous effort and resources behind anti-racist and inclusive initiatives, especially in academia?\

Max: Yes, all that you have said is true and yet many people still think it is negative, improper, and even unsophisticated to bring up the topic of race and its effects on relations. They say, "Oh, there you go with that again; everything isn't race-related," type of comments. It remains an unpleasant topic for many blacks and whites. They prefer to leave it in the past and never mention race, slavery, state-sanctioned oppression, and its ill effects, again. They'll only discuss its consequences on current conditions in the abstract. It's not as if they'll deny any ill effects but focus only on individual and historical efforts in the past to overcome an abstract adversity. The focus is only on the positives, how the nation has moved forward. They point to the heroic efforts of King and Parks, to successful family members, or to themselves.

Both black and white delight in discussing the "first" or "only" in their respective "positions" as signs of great progress. Blacks tell of how they personally dealt with prejudice, but it is to highlight their strength and advantage, and their exceptionalism; don't bring up their involvement in purely racial terms. They don't really want to be black; they prefer being African-American, it helps them to 'conversate' with whites at cocktail parties and hold their own in ethnic terms. Africana studies is the new exotic. Our good white allies tell of every minority or immigrants' struggle to succeed, and that the black experience was really no different; they relish stories of their ancestors' humble beginnings. That what they jointly encountered is a thing of the past. It's all over now, that no one is personally responsible for the past, so let it go. America is now great because we overcame it. There's no benefit in continuing to bring it up. Their proof is their kids are now able to go to school with anyone. They have friends of all colors and they are doing all right. They embrace diversity and multicultural efforts. Becoming a global citizen is the goal. That we are all equal as long as we are willing to work hard and play by the rules. Just be a good person. This mantra we hear from both black and white, brown and yellow. Well, who would argue with that?

Margrit: Yes, well that is the narrative that makes sense to people, who didn't grow up here and were not socialized in this unique brand of USA racism. Unless you have witnessed it, unscathed by early indoctrination, you will not believe the "American Dream" also dreamt by so-termed minorities remains more of a nightmare because the dream won't come true. But people here rarely recognize the reality of Black under-resourced communities. The myth of the American Dream for all remains.

Max: Next time you hear that point of view, look at the person; usually a middle-class clone. They don't deal with the effects of poverty and racism in the black community. They live in suburbia or an integrated, upscale urban enclave. They have run from the past and never looked back. "Ghetto blacks" are a foreign species to them. They will defend their lofty position with tales of donations to the causes, periodic community give-backs performed by their churches, fraternities and sororities, and their affiliations to HBCUs, NAACP, or other black social-cause organizations. If you point out obvious imbedded racism in their existence they will hate and disassociate you. The blacks are appalled, and the white "allies" resent having their hoods pulled back; they claim exemption and exceptionalism as well. Yes, well, I am now a pariah to be avoided.

Margrit: The early imprinting of beliefs about black people in USA is deep; so deep, people cannot and will not see what runs counter to all they know. It is amazing how North Americans can grow up in the same city, for example, and never even interact with one another across color lines…

Max: That's part of the American dream. To insulate. But the conversation is a little more awkward now with the killings of Breonna Taylor, George Floyd, and countless others, either by the hands of police or their black brothers. I make no distinction…a bullet is a bullet. Protesters have filled the streets. The middle-class whites plead innocence and ignorance; after all, they support "the cause." And the middle-class blacks just don't seem to get it; some refuse to admit it could have easily been them, that they are not exceptions, even in their white secluded havens. The black and whites are both, in large part, responsible for the conditions of the "hoods" they abandoned years ago. That they ran out on their brothers and sisters in the race to dis-integration. The whites showed their true colors and blacks devalued their own being in choosing to cloister with whites. More than any outcries of hatred and proofs of inferiority from the most vociferous of white nationalists, could the message of their worthlessness have been more heralded than by their abandonment of the black communities. Burrell (2010) offers this insight:

In our effort to prove our equality, we unconsciously chased the master's dream, adopted his values, moved into his neighborhoods, went to his schools, and danced to his tune. While in assimilation and survival mode, we had no time to consider the price we'd pay for leaving our communities and leaving behind so many who look like us. ... it has separated successful blacks from "disposable" blacks, those who simply refuse to "act right" and proper. (p. xiii)

That is why they are not relevant role models to those they left behind. That is why their values are being rejected, the source of the recalcitrance.

So, yes Margrit, I, for one, am tired of hearing about my peoples' problems. It is age-old. The episodic riots and marching will continue throughout each generation until there is fundamental change. I am hopeful that change will begin by including more black men in academia.

Margrit: Max, I still do not fully comprehend why people who are black are such a threat to the average person who is white, here in the USA with its professed values of equality and freedom. Of course, class and race go hand in hand here; but still, the existence and behavior of this one group of North Americans is so "intimidating" that the average white person will silently support racist behavior; continue not to speak up when their colleague or student is clearly mistreated, whispered about, or obviously discriminated ... So, how do you define being Blackmaled?

Max: The act of being Blackmaled defies a simple definition. Sometimes it looks like murder by police because they felt threatened by a black man handcuffed behind the back or running away; bogus 911 calls by white women on a black man bird watching in the park; being tracked and hunted by two white men while jogging on a suburban street. Other times its presence can be inferred through interaction with the public, such as, the clutching of purses, or just being avoided in public spaces. It is the combined effect of inductive, deductive, and abductive reasoning by all members involved in the interaction. More often than not, it results in faulty reasoning or illogical conclusions toward its object: black males. There are many instances of this phenomenon; black male lives are snuffed out while conducting everyday activities, including just being in one's own apartment (i.e., the Botham Jean/Amber Guyer incident), because they are considered a deadly threat, based solely on their perceived "menacing black-male-ness." There are too many contemporary instances to list but are well documented in the media. But I offer one recent event specific to academia: A black, male, adult student at Ball State, named Mustafa Benson, had police called on him in a college classroom, by the professor, because he preferred to remain seated. Obviously, there is no safe space to be black and male. It's a lived experience. Deny all you want.

Margrit: So, being blackmaled means you cannot escape the mere color of your skin that signals all those traits associated with black maleness, because the social narrative is so deeply carved into the USAsian psyche? But how does that translate to the academy and why do you deem it so significant in academia, which is but a microcosm of USA society where you are blackmaled anywhere, just for being, really?

Max: Let me try to define it by an observation. Tell me, why is that when black men are hired, they're considered affirmative action hires and perceived as less qualified, but when white women are hired under the same initiatives, they are not perceived as so? And why are white women even covered under this statute? Because of black males. President Johnson's executive order's original intent was to redress an injustice done to black people by whites, so how can a white qualify? It was later expanded to include other so-called minorities and women. The cruel irony is that they now have the jobs intended for black men, and further participate in the same exclusionary hiring practices the white males use to exclude all women and minorities. Many of these same white women will claim "they don't see color" or harbor racial prejudice, or even to be allies, but the hiring results scream otherwise; just check the faculty lists. Perhaps she really doesn't see color because she doesn't have to, except when she thinks she may have to sit next to a black man as a peer. Or, when she finds herself alone with a black male on an elevator, clutching her purse. Then the subtle hints emerge; "he looked at me funny, I don't feel comfortable around him, your evaluations are low, you are not a good "fit" for our department or student body, we've had lots of complaints, I'm not at liberty to say, there's insufficient enrollment for your class, we've decided to go in a different direction this semester." You never get to address these concerns directly; the dean or chair is unavailable, or it was a committee decision. They snake you.

Margrit: How do *you know* you know when it's being done? Explain that, because, clearly, the reaction by white folks is often that you are "paranoid," or even worse, that you are "playing the race card...".

Max: There's an adage attributed to Oliver Wendell Holmes that states "even a dog knows the difference between being kicked and being stumbled over." It's through an abductive reasoning process that one can draw this conclusion. Being Blackmaled might not always be apparent at first, but it is always evident in the end. Does that answer the question of how one knows?

Margrit: I mean, ok, yes, I can relate to how one knows...as an immigrant. I *know* when I was being ostracized, even when I have not been outright called a "Nazi Bitch."

Max: Overt racial discrimination was carried out individually and collectively in this country for a set period; institutions, codes, and laws facilitated its existence. So, when the formal legal and institutional supports ended, when did the habitual collective and individual discrimination end? For those who claim it was a thing of the past that maybe their grandfathers practiced, and the present generation is exempt from residual effects, I would again ask when did it cease? Maybe when they ran to the suburbs? Do they honestly believe that they are exempt from individual, collective, and institutional forms in so short a period? How and when did that happen? I

176

would like to know. That must have been one heck of an overnight transformation! Maybe, they can teach others who are still influenced by the past but haven't yet transformed. And while they're at it, maybe they can teach those others not to discriminate based on gender, age, income, religion, etc. as well. Or maybe they believe that doesn't exist either. So, to me, the proper question is: given the long history, how can we not expect to have some vestiges held over and how and where do they manifest? Consider that modern corporations have invested enormous sums on organized change-management strategies to effect organizational culture with limited success. How well has academia scored on this metric?

The other dimension of this discrimination is that the 19th century immigrants to this country so readily adopted racism and oppression in the new world. The massive wave of European immigration occurred after slavery was abolished. They supposedly came here for freedom and opportunity not available in their home countries. While it is true that most of them never owned slaves or participated in the antebellum structural supports, they readily participated in discriminatory, exclusionary, and terrorizing tactics to prevent blacks from organizing and developing into a free and competitive workforce (Litwack, 1962). They and their descendants essentially displaced and dislocated the black labor force in this country. So yes, they never owned slaves and are therefore not responsible for that institution; they were however, co-conspirators in one of the darkest periods in American history from 1870s to 1950s against blacks: including lynching, Jim Crow, forced segregation, labor riots, and all other overt acts of violence against black aspirations.

Though overt discrimination has tapered, their descendants still practice many of these cloistered, exclusionary methods in contemporary workplaces. This is not ancient history; this was something their great-grandparents, grandparents, parents, and possibly they participated in…and now I'm to believe they have no vestiges of this heritage? These tired, poor, huddled masses yearning to breathe free, this wretched refuse landed on this teeming shore willing to fully participate in barbarous acts of inhumanity on black men. These were not the finest from the shores of Europe. The masses were persons of "mean and vile conditions;" some even distinguished themselves as grave-robbers and cannibals (Zinn, 1980). Hypocrites all. I abhor the stories of their struggles to make good in America. I prefer the truth. This is a description of the early English stock that peopled the colonies: "…one among them slew his wife as she slept in his bosom, cut her in pieces, salted her and fed upon her till he had clean devoured all parts saving her head…" (Zinn, 1980 p.24).\

Margrit: Of course, most people will shrink from such atrocities and find one reason or another to explain it, at minimum, as isolated incidents by mentally ill individuals. What I see is a society with locally-born and foreign-born individuals that for generations has not been willing to confront the extent of cruelty, atrocities, and terror bestowed upon black people in this country. So, I must interject that you ought not generalize against a category of people, in your argument saying "all" immigrants. You'd be doing the same thing you accuse the racists of doing, then. That groups of people stick together makes sense to me. I like to be among people who share my language and culture; and, at the same time, I have no concerns about other groups doing the same, including Americans who are black. Institutionalized processes maintained the racist practices of hiring, and immigrants were selected over black Americans, yes that certainly happened as research has shown … when you work and live within immigrant communities, however, you find racist attitudes, too, surely; but you also find solidarity with Blacks among immigrants across the board, just like you do in the rest of society. Violence and exploitation happened against immigrants, too. And I fully know it is so taboo to note such acts against "others" when talking about the white and black race issue in this country. In no way is that meant as a comparison of sufferings; however, if this country is to ever confront what was done here for a few hundred years and continues in many forms today, then it ought to begin with looking at all the incredibly barbaric behaviors that prevail. Has the USA changed since the days of slavery and Jim Crow, and how?

Max: Immigration was voluntary, slavery was not. Immigrants can return home. They arrived to exploit opportunities rigidly denied to US-born blacks. I say at the very least that makes them ungrateful guests. According to Frazier (1957),

> "The picture which white Americans wanted to present to the world was that although Negroes had been enslaved and had suffered many disabilities since Emancipation, on the whole they were well off economically, had gained civil rights, and had improved their social status. Therefore, what had happened to them during slavery, which was after all a mild paternalistic system, should be forgotten along with other injustices which they have suffered. Moreover, their economic position was superior to that of other peoples of the world, especially the colored peoples." (p. 4)

This is the lie told and sold to the immigrants and helped them to justify their attitudes and treatment of blacks; the lie is still perpetuated with each succeeding wave of immigrants, foreign-born blacks included. I recall a conversation with a young man from Nigeria studying in this country. He was warned by white academics to avoid black Americans and told the standard lies of how blacks do not take advantage of the great American system. Of course, the Nigerian believed them and acted accordingly, treating U.S.-born blacks with disdain.

Many contemporary whites plead innocence and ignorance to complicity in a system of white superiority grounded in slavery and maintained by institutional structures of which they are a functioning part. For instance, they will claim they never held slaves. Foster (1884) describes this condition:

> "it is a common but mistaken opinion that to constitute one a slaveholder he must be the claimant of slaves. That title belongs alike to the slave claimant and all those who, by their countenance or otherwise, lend their influence to support the slave system. If I aid or

countenance another in stealing, I am a thief, though he receives all the booty.

A man may commit theft or murder alone, but no solitary individual can ever enslave another. It is only when several persons associate together and combine their influence against the liberty of an individual, that he can be deprived of his freedom and reduced to slavery…nor is the nature or criminality of his offense altered or affected by the number of persons connected with him in such an association. If a million people conspire together to enslave a solitary individual, each of them is a slaveholder, and no less guilty than if he were alone in the crime."

This logic indicts every individual in combined association who supports the current systems of inequality in the academy: white, black or otherwise.

Margrit: Well, that is why I keep saying, this entire country needs to confront what has not been talked about; what people claim to know nothing about; what people can push aside as not having participated in and so forth. There are, particularly in the so termed liberal academy, instances daily in which one could take responsibility for maintaining equality and freedom for all … and speak up when racist behaviors occur, or processes are not questioned … Why that isn't happening is beyond my comprehension. Despite the deep socializing about the Black man that happens here in USA, wouldn't people see blatant injustices and discrimination, and even the micro-aggressions? Especially among the self-proclaiming, liberal allies?

Max: We both know of instances where the recent black graduates of programs could not get adjunct positions in the school from which they graduated, while white graduates in the same cohort did. They all graduated from the same program, had the same professors, and were otherwise similarly qualified in backgrounds and experience. Obviously, it was a collegial preference for the white candidates. A type of homosocial reproduction. You have witnessed multiple instances of overt discrimination against black males in hiring practices at all levels in the academy. You witnessed it when you were on the search committee for a dean. Three or four candidates were narrowed for consideration to interview; all but the black candidate was brought in to interview. The committee could offer you no explanation nor was justification ever provided. This is a form of mob-ocratic rule disguised as shared governance.

You also witnessed it with me. I was one of two finalists, highly qualified with ten years of teaching experience and three degrees in the discipline for a teaching position in an adult education degree program, yet the white male was hired possessing an unrelated degree in French Feminist History. That's how I know.

Margrit: Yes, and that makes me add that when this discriminatory practice is pointed out by a White faculty member, the collective collegial wrath is instant and permanent. Perhaps, that is what keeps many from speaking up or standing with Black students and colleagues …

Max: My experience is not unique. Carter G. Woodson, with a master's degree from University of Chicago, couldn't get a job at Harvard where he earned his PhD. He was good enough to study there, but not work. More irony? He established the scholarly *Journal of African-American History*, the Association for the Study of African-American Life and History, and Black History month, which we celebrate as a national observance. The same is true of W. E. B. Du Bois. Both not good enough for Harvard? Why blacks flock there bewilders me; why would Skip Gates want to head a Black Studies Department in a place that rejected Woodson and DuBois? Why not give that glory (and research funding) to an HBCU? I suppose we still need that white man's validation.

So, by the time this black man applies for a position his education, credentials, and experience are discounted by people who often have never even had a job outside of academia. The sum of their experiences lies in jobs delivering pizza or painting houses while working the summers during their college years. The real question is what qualifies them to judge a black man's abilities? Particularly when many have never worked or lived in a black community and are deathly afraid to even travel through a black or brown neighborhood. Just recently a noted white female professor from a prestigious state university in New Jersey put out a request on an adult education listserv to "point" her to articles and book chapters on how to be an anti-racist adult educator, to use in her course for adult educators. There are so many racist assumptions built into this request it would take a separate chapter to explain them all. What's even more horrendous is the nature of the eager responses she received from the members on the listserv, both white and black, all wanting to show how informed they were on this new brand of "pedagogy." When you search the department, which she chairs, it's all white female and one young black female. You think maybe she needs more than a few articles? This is the type of classic insult "innocent, well-meaning, clueless" professors commit against blacks, but do so much harm. It is no palliation of her offense to say she is opposed to racist practices. If she is opposed to it why is she involved in it? Why does she aid and abet the racist system? The fact of her opposition to it only serves to enhance her guilt, since it proves that she is not unconscious of the wrong she is doing. Even to begin to explain "the why" to her would involve trying not to offend and protecting her white "fragility." Do you see why we're so exhausted? One obvious solution is to just stop being racist, yes? Moreover, what makes her think blacks can tell her how not to be a racist? Maybe if she just examines her own cesspool it will become apparent? First, hire more black professors, especially males. We are the objects of such derision that all the articles submitted will certainly have the black male as the spoken or unspoken threat that, in her mind, justifies the racism she practices. Don't the current killings and protests attest to this fact?

And then to add insult to injury, they use the same affirmative action initiatives originally intended to help a black man used against him to hire a "minority" in his place. No offence to my Black African, Brown, and Yellow brothers and sisters, but why and how do you qualify for my affirmative action?

Africans, Asians, Mexicans and other so-called minority immigrants have their own issues with whites, I concede, but they shouldn't be lumped under a rainbow umbrella. This just dilutes the issues and solutions and lets the whites off the hook with a one-size-fits-all remedy. Should we band together, perhaps, but solutions are not monolithic. Besides, each of the aforementioned do have their own country, language, culture, and heritage to which they can return. In fact, many of them do after they've earned their pot of gold. US-born black males have no such recourse.

Margrit: Well, again, it seems to me that the very acknowledgement is lacking that a systemic approach for keeping Black males on the bottom rung of the socio-economic ladder; however, such acknowledgement is fundamental to posing the issues and implementing solutions. There is division among Blacks, among Whites, among leaders, among preachers, among politicians ... name any group... in which members share a category, and you find no unified understanding of what we need to address. So, naïve as you may call it, until this country puts the hatred and vitriol into abeyance, and, so to speak, sits down together to listen and hear, ain't nothing gonna change cuz the powers-that-be benefit and do not want it to change. And those powers-that-be include individuals from across the rainbow and socio-economic status...
All those alleged efforts in Academia for inclusion and diversity initiatives, the massive efforts and money spent, even the creation of special departments and high-level executive appointments are doomed to fail because they are not sincere. Why do I say this? Well, sit with me in faculty meetings, and then sit with me behind the closed doors of faculty members, and you will find the disingenuity with which Black faculty members and students are treated in public and then ridiculed in private ... And, dear Max, this is done by both, Black and White individuals.

Max: You know there's an internal debate about the efficacy of mandatory "diversity and inclusion efforts" in university hiring, with faculty both supporting and opposing these initiatives. The debate reflects a tension between faculty who see efforts to promote diversity as an intrusion on their hiring prerogatives and a lowering of standards, and those who see opening their departments to historically marginalized candidates as a means to advance the institution's mission. Either way, it is money wasted, because when you look at the faculty or administration rosters there is a sea of white faces. Don't you think well-informed black men would have qualified and applied for these openings even without diversity initiatives? The fact that there **is** an initiative and that blacks still didn't get hired speaks to the intransigence on the part of the hiring body to open its ranks to black men, despite all claims to the contrary. Or else, the hiring bodies are totally incompetent in that function. Maybe even both. But logically, why is a federal mandate necessary if discrimination in hiring practices doesn't exist? The success of these efforts, as I see it, only increases the ranks of white women and non-US born people of color in slots that could have been easily filled by native-born black men. Any thinking person should conclude that diversity and inclusion initiatives are a clever way to dilute any direct efforts to hire black males. Perhaps the way out of this morass is to allow the basketball and football coaches at these institutions to recruit and hire black scholars in the same fashion they do black athletes. They're able to find black talent without a diversity mandate; they want to be competitive; they want to win.

But, more specifically as it relates to our adult education profession, from my perspective, there is a direct relationship between and intersection of adult education, social justice, and white supremacy. Historically, the idea of social justice and adult education as connected and opposed to oppressive systems, including white supremacist systems, is the mantra by many so-termed radical adult educators in the US. I assert that the practitioners of Adult Education, irrespective of color, are not as sincere in their actions to prevent discrimination as their writings might suggest; that they are hypocrites and work actively to suppress the aspirations of the blacks they profess to serve.

Margit: Ok, here I need more detail. My main question is "why would they work to suppress aspirations?"

Max: For example, one current exploitative action which offers lucrative funding and publishing opportunities to boost their careers is the fad of studying incarcerated black men, whom they would be reluctant to hire as colleagues when similarly qualified. I can give you names. Now, who's playing the race card?

And as far as black men not meeting the mark, I suggest you read *Men of Mark: Eminent, Progressive and Rising"* (Simmons, W. J., & Turner, H. M. (1887).

> "I wish the book to show to the world--to our oppressors and even our friends--that the Negro race is still alive, and must possess more intellectual vigor than any other section of the human family, or else how could they be crushed as slaves in all these years since 1620, and yet to-day stand side by side with the best blood in America, in white institutions, grappling with abstruse problems in Euclid and difficult classics, and master them? Was ever such a thing seen in another people? Whence these lawyers, doctors, authors, editors, divines, lecturers, linguists, scientists, college presidents and such, in one quarter of a century?" (p. 7)

There are plenty of qualified black men capable of teaching in the academy. They know they must be overqualified to get even the lowest of adjunct positions, but many never get the opportunity to interview. They are judged ineligible by opaque screening criteria. Yet, you know there are significant numbers of whites who are hired and given tenure according to traditional academic criteria who prove to be mediocre teachers and unimpressive scholars.

Many black men are currently returning students gaining additional credentials in hopes of future employment. As students, they also have experiences that are not valued by the traditional credentialing models. Even when offered opportunities to access credit through prior learning assessments and alternative credentialing models, the white assessors, are ill-equipped and unqualified to evaluate the learning outcomes embedded in black experiences

(Williams, 1972). And rarely are the white assessors qualified to extract and evaluate the learning through the different modalities that these experiences were gained and expressed. The traditional standardized tests and the writing of "papers" is insufficient to capture their authentic, non-traditional richness; and often the expression of such is unpleasant and offensive to white sensibilities. Yet, you want them to get those student loans and fill up your course sections. And when they don't complete, you say they weren't college material anyway.

Margrit: Oh, actually it goes even deeper than that, Max. In higher education, as much as in the K-12 world, black students are swiftly labelled and then counseled into being LD or otherwise disabled. In my experience, the staffers at the centers for students with disability are just as complicit in labelling students without providing adequate assessment and accommodations. Faculty are not trained nor even supported in assisting students, even when a disability is legitimate. Faculty members, who asks for support to learn how to modify instruction appropriately, are told by center staffers that they do not provide such assistance. Given the generally subpar public schooling Blacks receive in marginalized communities, particularly in urban areas, with teacher un-versed in teaching methods and community cultures. Children are quickly placed into special education/needs programs, and this carries over to higher education, too. This goes for any school in a segregated neighborhood. I have seen these practices in Latino as much as Black communities, too. It's all a matter of the hidden curriculum and victim-blaming. Needless to say, just follow the money! Education institutions receive funding for their services; Black students are the selected clients in this scheme.

Max: Yes, as students they encounter many mediocre white professors that don't meet the mark, yet these professors maintain a sense of superiority in their positionality and application of "standards and rigor" to admit black students. The illusion of racial progress and equality justifies an individualistic, survival-of-the-fitness mentality among the professors, who then fail to provide the supports and accommodations needed for the type of students entering with known deficits often coming from poor quality public school systems…yet, in true Darwinian fashion, they admit them and charge exorbitant fees and tuitions, all while denigrating these students that support their elite, parasitic lifestyles. They, being afraid of appearing illiberal or discriminatory, fail to give the necessary corrective feedback and delude the students into thinking their work measures to standards. Because they have low expectations for these students, the students fail to measure up in real-world tests and are viewed as even more deficient with their useless degrees. But they pump them up with glowing reports of their results and pimp them out in their program marketing and showcases as if they are top students to keep the enrollment pipeline filled. This racist caricature and impersonation of *ed-u-ma-ca-ted nigras* are widely accepted tools of white supremacy; AE is complicit in perpetuating this *meme* in the academy.

And Margrit, since you mentioned "special" in your comment, let me give you a brief history of why "special" schools were created for blacks by enlightened folk in the early to mid-1800s. According to Woodson (1936), the special schools for blacks were established and segregated because of the peculiar circumstances of the institution of slavery. Since many of the blacks to be trained were adults, they could be given the same studies that were assigned to children, but because of their life experiences they could accelerate their learning and complete the course requirements in less time than children. He further states,

> "…there were certain things which the Negroes had not been permitted to learn as slaves whereas other persons in school had mastered such by experiences earlier in their careers. In addition, the Negro in his peculiar situation had to learn to work efficiently at the limited occupations open to him." (p. 329)

Would be that such enlightened folk would permeate the academy today regarding black men. But instead, we have charlatans that continue the policy of mis-educating the black man through inferior schools and rendering any academic occupations unavailable to him.

Margrit: Yes, see, you answered my question about why individual White professors and institutions maintain this mis-education. Of course, the attitude of superiority is bestowed, for most faculty members, with the terminal degree. Moreover, in my experience, the paradigmatic assumptions about the Black man are so solidly carved into the USAsian psyche that one can easily continue to fool oneself into believing one is helping the ones less "intellectually endowed." And, as I said before, subpar schooling is to blame as well when students are not prepared for higher education pursuits. Seems to me those are reasons why it is it so important that black men are hired into the professoriate because they may understand these realities?

Max: The real question is why is it so important that black men be excluded? Because whites will not accept the leadership of black men. The universities recruit black and brown students from these historically marginalized communities as part of their market strategy. Maybe some affirmative action/diversity considerations are at play, but it's a money-making, market-driven opportunity for the university, nevertheless. One can anticipate that problems will occur, for both student and university; these students don't necessarily arrive with the middle-class values, cultural expectations and habits, or foundational education required for college success; many have been isolated from the mainstream. And the faculty is not prepared to accept these students with educational deficits. They both, the black students and white faculty, will need compensatory supports for success. This is the quintessence of special needs education. This should be obvious to any thinking being, particularly a so-called intellectual. If the people and situation were considered normal mainstream, there would be no need for the "affirmative action;" they'd be like any other applicant. In his chapter on *The Education of the Negro Prior to 1861*, Woodson (1936) states that:

"Owners of slaves were induced to join the general movement for the emancipation of slaves on the condition that they would be trained for the duties of citizenship and not become a public charge. They were to be educated not only to work at occupations but also to administer a household, to teach their less fortunate fellows, to organize churches for further religious instruction and spiritual salvation. This education, then, was of a higher order than that which was intended merely to render efficient service in the employ of a master class." (p. 329)

Even slave masters recognized the need for some form of compensatory training to overcome the deprivations of enslavement. So, if today's students are also uniquely and institutionally handicapped, then the teachers and structural supports should align to this uniqueness. Again, this should be obvious. For example, when you 'rescue' an abused pet, that came from horrid conditions, it needs special care and consideration for recovery, in fact, it may never fully regain normalcy. Fortunately, humans have better prospects for full recovery, especially with proper intervention. We know that many of these black men come from similarly horrid conditions and from the failed inner-city schools that systematically miseducated them and exhibit the learned failure habits and behaviors of victims of abuse and mental illness. So, who taught them? Often, they were female, black and white, constructivist teaching clones that failed to provide them the necessary skills to succeed. Then, the black students arrive in college to face the same liberal-professing clones who taught their K-12 teachers that same failing, constructivist philosophy. Then to add insult to injury, these professors think, because they've participated in some grant-funded "ghetto" research, they understand the problems of the black community, and that white, middle-class valued, ivy-league solutions should be applied to every situation. These students need professors that can relate, particularly US-born black male professors. How can whites teach and respect someone they are afraid of and are unwilling to have as classmates, neighbors or colleagues? How can they teach someone they abhor and consider repulsive to them? How will black students be expected to respond to such instruction?

The power relationship is a set up for failure. For example, remember the case of a Ball State University black student, Sultan "Mufasa" Benson, who declined to switch seats in the middle of his marketing class, and the professor summoned the police? Fortunately, his white classmates spoke up in his defense and de-escalated the situation, or he could have been killed on the spot. What is even more infuriating is the professor, Shaheen Borna, is an immigrant from Iran. How is it he can get a job, but a US-born black man can't? Now the university plans to spend additional money, that could have been spent on student supports, to train this so-called professional on how to manage a classroom and avoid discrimination. Oh, stupidity runs deep throughout the system. One hopes they'll find a qualified black man to train Borna on appropriate teaching methodologies. One can also hope this incident will highlight the need for the University to hire more US-born black men to teach. White male leadership is being contested in government, business, and education, hence the push for more diverse representation at the top. But the overrepresentation of black women in leadership positions in the black community and education is not being equally challenged. Why? Because black women will naturally defer to white male authority. It is deeply rooted in slavery. So, this aggregate placement of black female leadership directly serves the interests of whites. I call it the replacement theory because nothing changes. One may say it's chauvinistic, but men are the natural leaders and people respond accordingly; the response to black men in leadership is typically negative and combative, except among other black men. Consider the country's Blacklash over Obama in charge; but they swallowed the shenanigans from Trump, under the guise of "style." White males seem conditioned to resent black professors teaching them and black males often resent white men teaching them, as well, but for obviously different reasons. Black male K-12 students typically resent being taught and told what to do by women, especially white women who either disdain or patronize them, who comprise the bulk of inner-city teachers. That's why they fail; why they are perceived as dangerous and land in special education or jail. They will naturally respect and take direction and discipline from black men; gang leaders are black men. Black women follow Obama as a messiah, elevate their black male preachers, and yearn for black male leadership within the communities. They will do the same in the classroom and work hard if he's a real man. They don't seem to respond as positively to Africans and gay men. They follow white men because they are women and naturally defer to males by nature, even the dykes. A critical mass of real black men in the academy will greatly diminish racist acts. I guarantee it.

So, if you want to segregate your students and faculty in all white private schools it's your prerogative. If you think that preserves your way of life, so be it. God bless you. But not with tax dollars, exemptions, or subsidized student loans. As long as your education institution is subsidized by taxes and government subsidized grants and loans, sons of US slaves get a job. Period. This goes a long way toward notions of reparation, restoration, or rehabilitation. If you don't care to work beside me, you are welcome to exit the academy with the same speed you did the inner city. But history has shown that exiting has negative consequences for both of us. Recent history has also shown the benefits of cooperation and blending of talents, such as, in the areas of sports and entertainment. It's time to throw off the medieval notions of academia and the inbred faculty franchise. We need the talents of all members, we need fresh thinking on the problems facing the community, we need to channel the energy currently dissipating in prison cells, street corners, and meaningless existence. We need real black men in education.

Margrit: In my country of origin, there was such a strong belief in this amazing progress that has been made for black people. For the longest time, the USA has generally been considered an example of a melting pot where everyone can partake in the American Dream. One is quickly pointed to the Civil Rights Movement; the many laws enacted then; the incredible caring and outpouring of good will during the protest marches in the 1960s; the abundance of quotes by Dr. Martin Luther King, Jr.; not to mention a whole four weeks of highlighting achievements of slaves and their descendants during the annual Black History month. Clearly, with the recent initiatives, such as the protest and the BLM initiatives, white America is proud of its solidarity with its black citizens. Social media is filled with images of "me and my best black friend" and peppered with ridiculing videos of tirades by Karens. And this spilled over into the international arena. Many white professors are liberal-minded and consider themselves allies. What do you think?

Max: Just as the new, hot language among the intellectual set is anti-racist pedagogy and promoting critical race theory as the panacea. They are now proclaiming themselves as allies. Wypipo, really? I see this proclamation as just another farce. As just another attempt to co-opt the moment. Another way to jump on the bandwagon. To publish. To teach. It's all just self-aggrandizement.

I would suggest the term sympathizer for the person who aids my cause. Sympathizers do not join the fight; they might provide assistance in some form, but do not fight or engage directly. An ally joins directly in the fight. They don't staddle. They become an enemy to my enemy, as well. There is no neutrality. They don't hide. They put everything at risk. They choose sides and accept the potential for loss. Let me illustrate with an old tale:

A Chicken and a Pig lived on a farm. The farmer was very good to them and they both wanted to do something good for him.

One day the chicken approached the pig and said, "I have a great idea for something we can do for the farmer! Would you like to help?"

The pig, quite intrigued by this, said, "of course! What is it that you propose?

"I think the farmer would be very happy if we made him breakfast."
"I'd be happy to help you make breakfast for the farmer! What do you suggest we make?"

The chicken suggested, "ham and eggs."

The pig, very mindful of what this implied, said, "for you it's just a cackle, but for me it's a total sacrifice!"

So chose your words carefully. You can't chicken out and run when the going gets tough. That would be termed cowardice. So obviously, there are few true allies. Otherwise, there would be either more black males in academia or more white casualties on the battlegrounds. I see neither.

Margrit: It goes back to the herd mentality and to fear. In academia, speak up about, stand with a black colleague or student, and challenge implicit bias or outright racist acts by a white faculty member, and you are ostracized quickly from the herd. It happens so silently but so thoroughly, you don't even know what hit you at first, mostly because of the polite but two-faced behavior.

After all, liberal folks wish to maintain their image. The risks are clear and high. If you wish to survive in academia as a "white ally," you better have a finely honed strategy, know how to play off what I call the "ideological arrogance" of self-proclaimed liberal professors, and know how to circle your own wagon. And even then, dear Max, you need to be ready to lose the battle for tenure, advancement, and even your job. Those fears keep most of us trekking along with the herd.

Max: How to talk-the-talk **and** walk-the-walk

I would like to see the field of adult and continuing education revisit and return to its core mission; what the profession of adult and continuing education should be doing and why. It seems we have strayed in unproductive paths of navel-gazing over the last few decades under the guise of "critically informed practice." Albeit most contemporary perspectives involve some combination of quality life, work, and individual focus, but the original, overarching goal seems to be that of transforming the citizenry from undesirable into a desired state. Well, we have a whole group of black men sitting in prison ready to be transformed, but into what? It's an old question. It's the negro question.

James Weldon Johnson states that "what Americans call the Negro problem is almost as old as America itself." (Johnson, 1928)

> "For three centuries the Negro in this country has been tagged with an interrogation point; the question propounded, however, has not always been the same. Indeed, the question has run all the way from whether or not the negro was a human being, down-or-up to whether or not the Negro shall be accorded full and unlimited American citizenship. Therefore, the Negro problem is not a problem in the sense of being a fixed proposition involving certain invariable factors and waiting to be worked out according to certain defined rules." (p. 399)

Johnson continues:

> "But there is a common, widespread, and persistent stereotyped idea regarding the Negro, and it is that he is here only to receive; to be shaped into something new and unquestionably better. The common idea is that the Negro reached America intellectually, culturally, and morally empty, and that he is here to be filled—filled with education, filled with religion, filled with morality, filled with culture. In a word, the stereotype is that the Negro is nothing more than a beggar at the gate of the nation, waiting to be thrown the crumbs of civilization." (ibid p. 409)

In this new millennium that attitude toward black men persists. One of the biggest challenges facing our field is integrating the formerly incarcerated black men into society. This requires mission-oriented approaches much like that of the newly freed slaves. A new Reconstruction of sorts. Many of the problems of the black community and therefore the men incarcerated from those areas stem from the Great Migration periods of 1910-30s and 1940s-70. Those sons and daughters of slaves, sharecroppers and laborers in the south were enticed by better living and working conditions, but most compelling was escaping the soul-killing Jim Crow to migrate north. The war industries called

188

for labor and they answered. They filled the cities that were already teeming with immigrants in squalid conditions. They settled in the "black bottoms" of the north. The corporate racketeers exploited their labor and pitted them against the Bohunks and newly-forming white unions. The cities failed to plan for this influx and corporations were allowed to use and dispose of this heap of labor pool in the same fashion they were allowed to dump their heaps of toxic waste to pollute cites, and then abandon the cities and factories with impunity (e. g., Flint, Michigan water). Seeking lower wage costs and higher profits, they finally abandoned the country altogether. This discarded people waste was left to fend for themselves in the cities without resources. The middle-class sold out and abandoned them along with the buildings; the schools deteriorated along with the neighborhoods. Despair took the place of hope. American dreams of better lives became stunted. Drugs and crime would be the inevitable path. Rather than hold the corporations accountable, the politicians colluded to add prisons to the complex. To add insult to injury corporations colluded to further rob the coffers of the blighted areas through TIF schemes and other tax-financed incentives to wring the remaining dollars from these "opportunity zones."

Corporations that were complicit in creating these conditions should be required to return the living wages that were stolen to those qualifying to learn and work toward permanent employment re-entry within industry. That is a true corporate responsibility. Exploit opportunity, maybe resources, but not people. It's well known that the inception of certain gangs in Chicago and LA, for example, were drawn from youth with rural origins from the south. They formed these gangs to protect themselves from assault as newcomers to the block, and from schools and businesses that would exploit and abandon them. The academy has an opportunity and an obligation, if they receive public funds, to provide a path back to legitimacy for this population. The public schools failed them the first time. Education policy created the school to prison pipeline. Prison cannot be the only publicly-funded response-to-intervention. Classrooms ought to be an available alternative to the street. Alternative programming is a start in that direction. Alternative teachers are also the answer. Black men teaching black men. White teachers and systems are largely responsible for the black men trapped in the conditions that seeded the prisons. How can they be the answer? It's not considered unusual to have all white male teachers and students; neither should it be for black men.

Black men that have been formerly incarcerated require an educational environment that differs from the traditional, including the professors. The design requires a multi-faceted approach (e.g., Dr. Robert L. Williams' 10-point plan). Professor Benneth Lee (Co-founder, National Alliance for the Empowerment of the Formerly Incarcerated-NAEFI) provides a backdrop to these considerations:

"One has to understand the notion of multiple cultures when dealing with the formerly incarcerated. There's the culture of the home they came from, the culture of the streets, there's the gang culture, there's a drug culture, and a prison culture to deal with."

What traditional teacher is academically prepared for that? How can a white suburban clone relate? If she can't handle him in the classroom between the ages of 8-16 without referral to special education for "intervention," how can she possibly deal with him 20 years after his release from prison? How will she help him to master academic culture?

Then there's the issue of America's educational institutions owing a debt to the sons and daughters of slaves that built them and in which the white inhabitants prosper. For example, the nation's second oldest institution of higher education, among others, was built with slave labor:

> "From its beginning, the success or failure of William & Mary relied on the labor of black people who worked tobacco fields in Virginia and Maryland. King William and Queen Mary specified in the charter that the institution was to be funded with…the said revenue of a penny per pound, for every pound of tobacco aforesaid, with all its profits, advantages, and emoluments, to apply and lay out the same, for building and adorning the edifices and other necessaries for the said college,"

(Cook, 1982) Royal Charter Collection, Special Collections Research Center, Earl Gregg Swem Library, William & Mary.

The college acknowledges the use of slave labor to fund and to maintain the campus throughout a 170-year period, by erecting a monument. Really? The Lemon Project. That's the payback? The place is crawling with white professors. I counted 53 professors in the education department, one black male, and three black females. I guess black men are hard to find unless willing to labor for free. Obviously, their affirmative action, diversity and inclusions efforts are time and money wasted. This, in a public state college that receives 11% of its funding from state taxes.

I leave you with these words from DuBois:

> "…but the bulk of the work of raising the Negro must be done by the Negro himself, and the greatest help for him will be not to hinder and curtail and discourage his efforts. Against prejudice, injustice and wrong the Negro ought to protest energetically and continuously, but he must never forget that he protests because those things hinder his own efforts, and that those efforts are the key to his future."

References

Burrell, T. (2010). *Brainwashed: Challenging the myth of Black inferiority*. Smiley Books.

Cook, M. (1982). An Exhibit of Treasures and Autographs from the Earl Gregg Swem Library's Manuscript Collections. Royal Charter Collection. Special Collections Research Center. *Earl Gregg Swem Library, William & Mary*.

Du Bois, W. E. B. (2008). *The souls of black folk*. Oxford University Press.

Foster, S. S. (1843). *The Brotherhood of Thieves: Or a True Picture of the American Church and Clergy*. William Bolles.

Frazier, E. F. (1957). Black bourgeoisie: The book that brought the shock of self revelation to middle-class Blacks in America. *Nova Iorque: Free Press Paperbacks*.

National Alliance for the Empowerment of Formerly Incarcerated (NAEFI). Personal Communication. https://naefimentor.wixsite.com/naefi

Johnson, J. W. (1928). *Race prejudice and the negro artist*. Harper.

Litwack, L. F. (1962). *The American labor movement* (Vol. 44). Prentice Hall.

Simmons, W. J., & Turner, H. M. (1887). *Men of mark: Eminent, progressive and rising* (No. 247). GM Rewell & Company.

Williams, R. L. (2008). A 40-year history of the Association of Black Psychologists (ABPsi). *Journal of Black Psychology, 34*(3), 249-260.

Williams, R. L. (1975). The BITCH-100: A Culture-Specific Test. *Journal of Afro-American Issues, 3*(1), 103-116,

Woods, A. (2020). Cops Called on Black Student at College with History of Racism. NewsOne. Retrieved on September 12, 2020 from https://newsone.com/3900249/cops-called-on-black-student-at-college-with-history-of-racism/

Woodson, C. G. (1936). *The African background outlined: Or handbook for the study of the Negro*. Association for the Study of Negro Life and History, Incorporated.

Ortega, R. (2020) White professor apologizes after he called campus police on black. student who refused to move to a seat in the front of his class. MailOnline. https://www.dailymail.co.uk/news/article-7925201/White-professor-apologizes-calling-campus-cops-black-student-wouldnt-seat.html

Zinn, H. (1980). *A people's history of the United States: 1492-present*. Routledge.

Blackmaled in Academia

PART SIX

View from within the ivory tower

One Moment at a Time
Thoughts on How to Stop Institutionalized Racism in Academia

Gabriele Strohschen, DePaul University

Berlin   -   Chicago

Then a child I played among the ruins
They held no threat
We jumped from bombed out buildings
Onto mattresses below
The rubble the grown-ups had created
From our city was our playground
Now grown-up ruins wall me in
There is familiarity in this wretchedness
A new city, a new county, four decades later
And the same environment exists here
Children jump from rotting buildings
But into the hopelessness of their lives

© 1985 Strohschen
Performed during 1991
Urban Metaphor Tour
The Chicago Überlyriker
Erfurt, Germany

Origins
How I Learned to Make Choices

I am a member of the generational cohort designated in "the post war generation" Germany. In other cultures, it has been combined with the Baby Boomer cohort. A child of survivors of World War II, I grew up in an environment that held more questions than answers. Mine was a child's lifeworld that saw the aftermath of war and hate; that saw adults struggle with physical and psychological damages inflicted upon them. It was a world struggling in the wake of hegemonic oppression and the results of individuals' and countries' ethnocentric and expansionist goals. These adults were born in the 1920s, children of the survivors of WWI. In childhood, they experienced the darkness of post-War I with its poverty, disease, and violence. Then had followed their elders' and their leadership's propaganda in the 1930s. Few of their parents recognized the Third Reich's early regime's greed for power, the quest for forced territorial acquisition, the desire for riches, or the proposed self-aggrandizement and self-righteousness of an "Aryan race." They were the children of survivors of a world war, too; and many of their parents yearned for the old days; for the Kaiser; for the pride they had once felt for their fatherland. They were ready to be believe in it again.

Their children, the survivors of WWII, grew up to become my family members. They surrounded me during my formative years. As children and teenagers, my parents, aunts, and uncles had gone along with what they had been taught since birth. My father went to war at age fifteen. Yet, the horrors of war and the violence of imprisonment; the rapes, sodomy, and tortures of girls and women; and the starvation during the occupation of Germany by the Allieds along with the realization of truths that emerged during the war and after the fall of the Third Reich put questions to them that they continued to deal with in their adult years. They dealt with these questions, if not openly with actions, then internally in agony for the rest of their lives.

As a child in the 1950s in Germany, I, too, began to live with questions. Mine was a childhood lived in utter flux. We lived among destruction and poverty in a post-war and cold-war world. In Berlin, we lived in the houses that remained after the bombings. They were pockmarked by the impact of grenades and bullets. Our apartment lacked one outside wall. As children, the ruins were our playground and we jumped from bombed out buildings, for fun. Broken was normal. The everydayness of shattered spirits was all around us. There was no concept of or assistance for PTSD for our elders who had soldiered through WWII; or for the women and children that had been violated by Allied soldiers. We accepted the impact of war and post-war trauma in our elders' behavior. We were taught "to get over it" when we ran home with bleeding knees to seek comfort. We learned that problems were to be solved, tenaciously --- by yourself. My family embraced the psychological and physical war injuries of uncles and father, back home from concentration camps and war prisons. My family stoically suppressed trauma about brutal violations of our mother, aunts, and grandmothers. My family and the family of my peers had been a part of a mass hysteria, the extent of which they did not know until after the war. And when they did know and did question, the equivalent of a local precinct captain of the National Socialist Party had ways to subdue them. And when they didn't succeed, brutal force, even murder, was the secret police's (GESTAPO) resolution. Sheer brutality silenced people.

We were their children and grandchildren, who learned to accept the incapacitated, to take physical handicaps for normal, to endure outbursts; but we also learned to stand up for ourselves, mostly because we were the underdogs, the recipients of all the ways in which our elders coped with and stumbled through their post-war lives. Left to ourselves as children while our elders rebuilt our City brick by brick, we urchins roamed those post-war streets. In our child world, we banded together during city escapades that often meant getting into trouble by those elders. But we peered into their aching, tortured souls in search of seeing how to best navigate out of trouble in our all too often hostile environment. What we learned as naïve children taught us to look and see what was under all the debris, under the rocks and ashes of our city, under the silent screams and agony in the eyes of our elders, under the rage or apathy that hid fears of those around us. We were extremely curious and not afraid to search for information. Much later we also learned to speak up, to question critically, to protest, and to defend.

In our teens, now the era of prospering days of the Wirtschaftswunder (economic miracle) during the 1960s, we witnessed assassinations, political unrest, the building of walls, and the further division of our world into East and West. Division among people was not just created with barbed wire and concrete walls in my City, but also with hand-held weapons, mines, and automatic shooting devices. And with propaganda with a different theme. Division also cocooned minds within the invisibility of unexamined ideologies. Behind the invisible and visible walls, among the tangibles and intangibles, we began to question. In our schools, I was introduced to the atrocities of war in a matter-of-fact, historical context; rich in visuals of concentration camps; filled with cacophonies of propaganda speeches. We had to confront the past of our country.

From early childhood, imprinted by this post-war reality, through the *Sturm und Drang* years of my teenage-hood in the tumultuous 1960s, my experiences were instrumental in shaping my world views, my values, and the way I approach others. Having grown up in rubble, the material as much as the emotional one around me, I had learned that one must confront situations and learn about the people in them. I had learned this was important because only if one sought and advocated for equitable solutions for all, could any one of us survive and thrive. The strength of us, the children of the survivors of war, came with physical and emotional resilience. Persistence during the juvenile struggle for empathy, fairness, and collaboration among this comm unity of us little 'underdogs' was pivotal for survival as a child in that broken world … the only choice we would have to make, we had learned, was whether to act without fear, no matter the consequences, or to allow that ruined world to make us a victim. I chose to take risks.

Beginnings:
The Lessons Learned and From Which to Learn

My experiences and insight and the way the world spoke about us taught me much about insidious governmental systems, indeed. It taught me, how easy it is to generate prejudice and escalate it to mass murder of any people, with regular folks standing by... immobilized by their fear; brutalized into submission; and even of their free will for many pathological reasons. Superiority of a color or religion or ethnicity was the lie that works. In Germany's Third Reich, being "Aryan" and proving our lineage of white ancestors was the key. After the war, it was easy in Germany to confront these "Nazi tactics" and the holocaust. After the war, it was an open discussion in which the whole world partook, unfolding with media-displayed photos of concentration camps and witness accounts; of feverish-glistening blue-eyed faces of impassioned orators of the Hitler entourage.

It damned a whole country. It failed to unearth the initiation of it all and complicity of world leaders in this whole affair. The orchestration of what happened in Germany in the envisioned but not realized Third Reich was solidly grounded in political and economic power of white supremacist conductors. History has unveiled this. What it has not made so visible, is that the same tactics continue to convince people who look like me into believing their superiority; teaching us to hail whichever chief du jour. The real horror is that the supremacy with its unique brand of racism continues in this country, despite what we have learned about the alleged roots of a difference in "races" that feed such prejudices. The US brand of racism is ever more sinister because it comes from a deeper, psychological complex of lies, denials, dissonance, insecurities, fears, perversions, contradictions, colonial mindsets, mob behaviors, murder, etc., all based on simple outward appearance. So, for me, the first lesson I learned upon arriving on these shores of liberty and justice for all, was that what I learned in my home country about our National Social Party era and the post-war realities; namely, that superiority propaganda costs all of us dearly here in this land of the free; and the legacy of white supremacy (Baldwin, 1969) not slavery will fracture this country, if it not already has.

The second lesson I have learned was painful at first and far less theoretical. I learned what it is to be a white woman when coming to this country. That is a long journey to describe and might require another chapter, at least. Suffice it to say, that learning what it really means to be white is crucial for us *wipipo* in US society if we are serious about changing systemic racism. My skin color alone gave me access in academia to survive even the vitriol and hatred I earned from colleagues for being a "nigger lover," that is, when I was not being called a "nazi" in the halls of academia. But my white skin also allowed me entry into the secret chambers where the conversations are held... for a while. It turned out to be rather useful in my work.

The Moment

There are pivotal moments in one's life when one encounters incongruence between what one sees in one's environment that immediately contradicts one's deeply-held beliefs. One can choose to move on and ignore the inner sense of discrepancy and remain silent. Or one can seize the opportunity in the moment to acknowledge such incongruence, feel it deeply, and move fearlessly forward to act in good faith with one's values. Such a moment happened to me when coming to Chicago in the mid-1980.

When a fellow graduate student and long-time community activist took me driving through Chicago's West Side back in the 1980's, I sat in awe in the car peering at the broken people and buildings we passed. In stark contrast to the Latino/a communities within which I worked teaching English as a Second Language, this West Side area was devoid of business, street vendors, and beautification attempts. I likened the difference between the immigrant communities and this neighborhood where black people lived to one of switching from color TV to a black and white telescreen version once we crossed over Western Avenue into the West Side. While in the Latino/a immigrant communities the hustling and bustling was one of commerce and family activities with festivals and art events and street vendors hawking their wares; on the West Side, it looked simply 'post war' to me. My awe came welling up from a deeply felt familiarity with what I saw, namely a physical environment that I knew; a flash-back to post WWII Berlin, where I grew up; where bombed out buildings still stood; where sidewalks were broken; where men hung aimlessly at the corner; where few flowers bloomed; and where street urchins ran unbridled. This I knew. Words of astonishment about such a sight came only after my long, stunned silence; after all, in Berlin we had been supported in rebuilding the lives and the city and we had been able to do so with the help of these North Americans, one of the Allieds. How then, four decades after WWII, could such a post-war environment exist in the USA? That's when the poem wrote itself, and it wrote me straight out of my silence.

That one first moment was significant in defining the rocky journey in academia I chose to take, when I began walking the walk. That moment on the West Side became pivotal in the choices I was to make in my life work. I say life work because I did not so much become engaged in a career as I chose, and reluctantly so in the beginning, to stand with those who were pushed back into hopelessness by and in USAsian society's institutions, such as academia. And in our US society, such hopelessness is perpetuated and propagated, particularly in its microcosm of adult education, which is said to be the purported social justice and liberal education 'division' of academia. Hopelessness is deeply engrained into the collective psyche here, taught in a hidden curriculum to the so-termed minorities. This hopelessness is inherent in black and white people with respect to racism. Much of 'black America' is turning more and more against itself in the wake of a failed civil rights movement and the destruction of the black family and community infrastructures since then. And most of 'white America,' including academicians, is more and more obeying the thoroughly engrained approach of avoiding confrontations, foregoing critical analyses, fearing bone-hard honesty, and avoiding directness in communications. Supremacy reigns in that white American doesn't think it can benefit from being in community with

198

black Americans. Moreover, indoctrinated so deeply with the sense of superiority over students, and especially black students, seldom if ever are academics called out for racist behaviors. I used to think my colleagues didn't know better when discriminatory acts became apparent to me. In fact, a part of me was really wishing that to be the case, i.e., the unintentionality, the subconscious-driven acts, the 'harmless' micro-aggressions of their racist behaviors. But I don't believe that any longer. Perhaps, I was able to realize that the US brand of racism is grounded in generations-deep socialization, because I grew up without such socialization. Nonetheless, one drive through the West Side alone will show you truth. One search on the Internet will show documentaries of decades ago, that address the "black issue." The problem, however, is – it is a white issue. White politeness reigns in group gatherings, whilst vitriol is reserved later for private settings. And the few good-hearted people give up. These traits of the USAsian mentality --- albeit a bit stereotypical, especially because this is not a homogenous society--- wittingly and unwittingly support the unique brand of institutionalized racism and adolescent kind of sense of supremacy in the USA.

The White Problem

Make no mistake about it: no matter how many protest marches are joined or how many photos are posted with "my best black friend," or how many webinars on how to become anti-racist are being attended on Zoom these days, behind these scenes, 'white America' at best overreacts to prove it is ok with 'black America;" at worst it enshrouds itself in the American Dream, a myth upheld when believing the preamble of the constitution. The Great American Dream propagates a cut-throat positionally for people to take as much as they can; and it has people believe that everyone can "pull themselves up by the bootstraps." Homosocial reproduction is alive and well behind the white veils and wailings of the academy, too, however. It is most fashionable and rewarded when white faculty speak and publish about racism. However, it is not accepted for a white professor to speak up against micro-aggressions, or blatant acts of discrimination, or unfettered individual racist acts when committed by colleagues against students and against colleagues who are black. Make no mistake about it, I have seen it. The indoctrination runs deep, and I have yet to meet an academician who does not reject being called racist. Even the kind discussions of 'positionality' in the teaching-learning complex fail to name the issue as one including pure white superior attitudes.

My intent with this glimpse into my *Schlüsselerlebnisse* (key experiences) above and analysis of experiences in this country are not to play one-upmanship nor to arrogantly separate myself as 'better than' from my USAsian counterparts nor to show how knowledgeable I am about Blacks. My intent is to frame my soul-felt recommendations for white (and some black) sister-and fellow academicians to find our way out of our paradigmatic assumptions and homosocial reproduction, that result in externalized racist behaviors, which are then normalized by and in academia. In turn, this creates a closed system of systemic acceptance of processes and behaviors. My motivation is simple: In the decades that have passed since my first ride through the West Side of Chicago, too little, if anything, has changed for the better! The USAsians who helped to rebuild my country of origin; who fed us during the blockade; and who became our best allies for a long time; these very USAsians could not help to rebuild the West Side? How then could I in good faith keep from speaking up about the violence, rapes, killings, homelessness, discrimination, miseducation, mischaracterization, and hunger that keeps breaking so many USAsians, simply because of the color of their skin? How can it be that these USAsians could work with the Nazis, the ultimate blatant white supremists, if you will, but have not worked with Americans, who are black in their own country? How can it be that there is so little recognition of the benefit of working together with Blacks in all areas of commerce in this free enterprise system? Why would an entire nation continue this brand of racism, in its institutionalized, systemic manifestations? It is a 'white problem' for us to solve not a 'negro problem.'

Reflection: How I Learned to Unlearn

That 'first moment' on Chicago's West Side holds a very particular significance in my choices. Although there were more moments that had me look and see; listen and hear, it was that one first moment that set the trajectory of my attitudes and actions in my work in academia. It continues to guide me, because in that moment, I connected to an environment and to people, both of which simply held sufficient familiarity that I was curious and fearless to learn more. This familiarity made me able to stave off being indoctrinated into the unique USAsian brand of racism (for the most part,) after I learned that I was white. To me, the Black man and woman posed no threat.

Aside from any other designation that defines a person, we are each a human being. As such, we go through our life in stages of psychosocial development. In that, our environment does imprint us in significant ways; our quest may well be more alike despite outward differences. Here in Chicago, I found that I am very much the person I always was, but my environment pegged me in a different way. In the USA, at this point, I was suddenly thrown back into having to define and defend my identity. I have seen white colleagues around me struggle with such moments of having to face the reality of they are perceived by others. I have seen them retreat into what has been engraved, somewhere in the depth of their psyche since childhood. I felt, I could not function in my work if I didn't learn about this country's kind of racism and what 'those black people' saw when looking at me. As educators of adults in academia, we ought to know ourselves first and foremost to gain the necessary emotional intelligence to guide other adults to learn and transform what they determine they need to accomplish, and how.

I must thank "my" black students and colleagues for embracing my quest and putting up with quite a bit of uninformed, offensive, and too many questions… Moreover, had some of them not decided to become my allies, my first steps in walking the walk might never have taken place. Perhaps, the most

200

important message to truly get here is that we wipipo in the academy need to stop claiming we are culturally sensitive, or we understand, or we are sympathetic, or we are so learned about the Black reality. What we ought to do is learn to know our Selves and maintain authenticity of who we are. From such a Self, we can then treat students and colleagues with respect, justly, and fairly. And when we see others doing otherwise, we would not be able to remain silent. We would understand that we all lose, when we behave otherwise, and we would walk not just talk…

Self-Knowledge

Freire told us, "[…] the educator must not be ignorant of, underestimate, or reject any of the 'knowledge of living experience' with which educands [students] come to school." (2004, p. 58). All too often, educators have not critically examined their own lived experience, investigated their Selves, and inquired into the goals and subject of our profession in relationship with one another.

Illumination of one's pathways and passages clarify the process of moving from the known to the unknown; a concept that runs deeply through the ideas and work of Freire and many other writers in our field, who purport critical reflection as a means for self-awareness raising (e.g., read your Brookfield, Gergen, Giroux, Daloz, Stanage, Vygotsky). Self-awareness is a simple concept, the importance of which educators readily accept in their practice of writing articles, and at times in their teaching and learning. Just think of the myriad ways educators incorporate 'reflection' into assignments. This concept is a precursor to delineate and strengthen one's professional identity and choose group belonging. Freire's concept of conscientization speaks to awareness, action, and organization (2001, p. 19) and shows a straightforward movement from individual change to communal change. Can individuals support communal (or social) change without having completed critical self-examination on their values and assumptions? Surely, we will answer, "no." However, just how do we approach this personal, ego-transcending self-awareness raising in the moments we are challenged with understanding a greater, shared or maybe even universal truth, i.e., a truth or reality that includes the truths and realities of those "other" from one's Self? What principles might guide this process? How do we become what Aronowitz and Giroux (1985) first termed a "transformative intellectual?" Can we possibly manage systemic changes when we, individually, have not yet critically analyzed our values, understood our feelings, and examined our behaviors and actions? And if we are not clear on our actions or inactions as a member in a community, how can we possibly continue blaming a "they" when things go awry in the society in which we live? Institutionalization of ~isms is created and maintained by people.

In this so-termed democracy that is built on some impressive ideals that are detailed in the values underlying the Declaration of Independence and Constitution, popular beliefs are deeply engrained in the USAsian systems. Yet, our awareness is centered on the Self and not on those ideals; ideals to be pursued by all, with all, for all. And although this awareness of the self is an important step in the direction of transformation toward such ideals of interdependency in *Gemeinschaft* (Fechner, 2008), within USAsian society, we get caught up in a circular movement of experiencing only what we have already projected to be or become our truth. We cling to the Dream, and we don't want to see the Nightmares.

In 1975, Krishnamurti opened a vast panorama for considering such thoughts on transformation, "To understand oneself there must be the intention to understand – and that is where our difficulty comes in" (p. 43). Although he agrees that for transformation of the world, transformation of the self is necessary (p. 44), he claims, "the fundamental understanding of oneself does not come through knowledge or through the accumulation of experiences, which is merely the cultivation of memory. The understanding of oneself is from moment to moment; if we merely accumulate knowledge of the self, that very knowledge prevents further understanding, because accumulated knowledge and experience becomes the centre through which thought focuses and has its being" (p.46). The difficulty in our training, schooling, and socializing into mind-centered thinking is that it strengthens how we have already defined the existing "me" by societal labels with its myths, stereotypes, and racism. Krishnamurti would explain that we do so through the projection of desires, which we then manifest in our experiences; with such desires being the democracy's ideals of equality and justice for all, for example. In other words, when we consciously and cognitively, with our knowing mind, seek peace, inner stillness, justice, understanding, altruism, prosperity, knowledge or any other such valued ideals, all of which are part of what is typically considered important in individual and social transformation, we are strengthening this existing self in its now heightened awareness. Yet, with radical critical reflection to analyze our values and subsequent actions, we have the possibility of a "moment-to-moment" creation of Self, or *trans*-formation, authentically.

Transformation: How to Stop Blaming 'Institutionalized Racism'

Changing discrimination of Blacks, stopping the blaming of black students for our shortcomings as educators, refusing to devalue the scholarship by black colleagues, ceasing to hide behind rigged hiring process to avoid hiring black colleagues, refraining from claiming cultural sensitivity, quitting our silence … that is not learned by reading about racism in the abstract. Transformation, if desired, starts with confrontation; with examining our values and coming to grips with our feelings; and acknowledging our short comings as well as strengths as much as those of others. And then we need to take what we learned during our radical reflection for a spin around the block. Period.

> **White Male Faculty Member**: *"Oh, of course I don't grade them down because they write how they speak, you know, Ebonics. That's their culture and I let them write their papers that way."* – I called his a racist attitude.
>
> **White female Student**: *"Dr. G., that Jamal is so loud in class, he intimidates me."* – I told her to get to know Jamal as they are peers in the course.
>
> **White Female Faculty Member**: *"I never drive through that neighborhood. zSure, it's shorter to get home from the university, but I take the expressway. I mean, just look at those students we have who live there."* – I asked her to come along to a community meeting on the West Side with some of our students.
>
> **White Male Student**: *"Dr. G., we can't hold our social justice class session in that soul food restaurant. That's in a dangerous neighborhood."* – I picked the student up to go to the meeting. Our group talked at length about the community issues with patrons.
>
> **Black Male Student**: *"Dr. G., oh man, you didn't have to call out that professor on her racists crap."* – I had to because I can.
>
> **Black Female Student**: *"Dr. G., No, you didn't, are you serious? You're asking us about the 'those itchy wigs' black women wear? Don't you know that is not something to talk about"* – but we did.
>
> **Black Male Faculty Member**: *Hey G, I agree with you that we should have interviewed the black applicant.* – Then why didn't you speak up in the search committee meeting when I brought up this issue?
>
> **Black and White Committee Members:** *"If we change the admission policy to use essays and interviews instead of SAT scores, we will get all of those poorly prepared students."* – Are you implying we would get too many applications from students in poor, black communities with sub-standard schools? Stunned silence; then a wild and lengthy discussion; the intent unveiled; my motion to accept the admission option carried.

To arrive at a so-called 'non-racist' attitude is not that difficult when we stop basing our action on the color of another's skin. Given our 'positionality' as white professors we have such power to support a fair, equitable, equal, and supportive environment for all students and colleagues. If we know our craft, if we study learning theories, if we understand instructional design, and if we can leave our ego at the front door, many of those issues wouldn't even become issues. Unfortunately, few of us know how to facilitate learning.

When we seek a sort of *one-approach-fits-every-moment* model to self-awareness, to living in community with a diversity of people, and to teaching, ell, then those possibilities are thwarted. We then fall short of becoming aware of social issues or the pain and injustice experienced by our fellow human beings and also our behavior, because we are not in relationship with others. , We forego grasping the whole of a situation; one, that includes more than our own, pre-programed, and encoded take on reality. We cling to our paradigmatic assumptions about the values of equality, equity, and inclusion of all members of our society, so deeply believing all is well; there with our heads in the sand. And we look away when our students fail to adhere to expectations (which are all too often irrelevant to the learning tasks at hand or their needs); we remain silent when our colleagues are mistreated; and we end up just blaming the victims of a racist academy. As academicians we ought to hold ourselves to a much higher standard than dancing around behind a shield of institutional DEI efforts, basing our superiority on being a white, while clutching our terminal degree as proof.

Our little Self has to peer into three buckets of issues to begin a confrontational sorting work of our values, feelings, thoughts, and actions toward ending our racist behaviors in the academy. And, most importantly to become audible advocates for system changes. This listing is intended to give some prompts for critical reflection on items, issues, causes we ought to consider.

Clarification of Values and Goals

- Seek clarity as to why we teach
- Examine how we navigate academia and why we are doing what we are doing
- Identify and examine our institution's goals and where we stand about those. Then help to dismantle that system
- Acknowledge our prejudices ... we all have them. At least start there.
- Stop pretending that we do not know about the fundamental issues - books, movies, songs, documentaries if nothing else have been around for decades even if we never drove through a black neighborhood
- Stand up and speak out. There may be many more silent colleagues than you think who may stand with you; but don't cry if they don't
- Start a movement to gather strengths for what must be done in our respective environments; or join one; take action. (Happold, 2017; Strohschen, 2014).
- Walk the Walk of our proclaimed values of DEI and speak up/do something when we experience the incongruence of what we say and what we see being done to our black students and colleagues. It's not enough to just help one through.
  Accept that not everyone will like you for it; suck it up.

Exposure to "Those People" and "Their Communities"

- So, what if we live in segregated parts of a neighborhood? We can build relationships with a community without being intrusive, act like a savior, or conduct research about "them"
- Don't assume black students and colleagues have less to offer than other students or colleagues
- Contact a community organization and build real relationships. Take our course sessions into the community. We teach a course on social justice but have never even driven through "that" neighborhood? Built honest, mutually beneficial relationships
- Admit our curiosity and accept potential fall-out from our questions. Most people will respect authenticity; it is worth the few times we will be called racist... or worse. But let's build our relationships first just like we would with anyone

- Stop pretending we do not know of the issues with institutionalized racism. Take a look at the documentaries to examine our professorial arrogance

(e.g., Fraser, & McGowan, 1988). Let's learn before we assume, call ourselves expert, and give webinars on how to be 'anti-racist.'
Accept that not everyone will like you for it; suck it up.

Knowledge of the Teaching Craft and Commitment to Our Job

- Just be honest about our shortcomings in instructional design and teaching methods and go about learning more
- Value different modes of providing evidence of learning
- Collaborate on developing competences and evidence thereof with our students
- Become genuine about loving students; read our Dewey; or go train dogs
- Commit to our profession:
- Stop running other business at work – do our job
- Don't favor our research over improving our teaching skills
- Actually, do work at the university and be available for our students; get to know our students but stop prying into their personal lives or treat the students like soap opera entertainment during discussion in class --- or during faculty meetings
- Stop using the professional development funds for vacations
- Set up clear and equitable processes that treat students as adults; ground ourselves in learning theories; accept that teaching isn't preaching, or worse, having chats in a circle only; make a lesson plan
- Check our positionality and ego at the classroom door
- Quit being politically correct but stretch toward respect and acceptance for others
- Be your Self, authentically
  Accept that not everyone will like you for it; suck it up.

Closing Thoughts

In the beginning was the deed. J. W. von Goethe
It is not enough to be compassionate. You must act. Tenzin Gyatso

To change our actions and interactions with sister and brother human beings, we begin by learning what we need to unlearn. We have internalized much; mostly deeply engrained beliefs upon which we act. When we begin to engage with "others" and honestly reflect on what we see, what we hear, and what we feel, we will encounter incongruence between what we experience in such exchanges that contradicts what we have been taught to believe to be true. Most likely, we may feel a bit lost and say stupid things. Who hasn't blurted out how much they like soul food or that they are color blind or they just love that new hairdo when in the company of a black person. Yes, it will leave us uncomfortable. Essentially, we have little if any experience with being in mixed company, and inevitably, we see color and we feel the inevitable unfamiliarity of knowing how to act. It goes both ways, by the way. But this is the needed first step toward unlearning the homo-socially re-produced vision of an allegedly 'commonly shared opportunity' and equality in our country. If as white professors, we do not even know about the reality of our black colleagues and students or engage with them authentically, then let us at least stop shrouding ourselves in non-racist glamor and priding ourselves about our culturally sensitivity, cuz we ain't got it.

My upbringing and the world around me then taught me to stand for truth and justice in my adulthood. It was easy during the 1960s because speaking up and marching was a rather impersonal act, done in the safety of like-minded folks, protected by the herd. Standing up and protesting racist acts in academia when those perpetrating the acts are our colleagues, well, that herd will quite quickly turn on you. Yes, doing so, though, is not easy, pleasant, or rewarding most of the time. I had to "suck up" - the drama of a vicious tenure battle; a lost job for siding with a black student who was about to be dismissed by a black colleague for unbelievably untrue gossip about him by his white peers; ostracism from the colleague herd; catty gossip from "the mean girl" colleagues (oh my, a white girl fraternizing with black male students, you know what THAT means!); cyber-stalking by a colleague; being chastised for 'making' a female colleague cry after calling out her racist demeanor about a black male student's alleged sub-par thesis because he wrote about the significance of Black church and she thought this was a trivial topic; and being labelled an un-collegial "lone ranger" by a dean in her attempted denial of my tenure. I actually took that last one for a compliment because between being called a nazibitch or a niggerlover, I learned to circle my own wagon and realized the power my white skin gives me. Those are realities for standing up for values and ideals that are written right upon the very mission statements on our walls in the halls of academia; for allying with the people who were violated by academia and the men who were blackmaled by it. Mine was, and continues to be, a road I make by walking… It's not really so much of a hard choice anymore as it is simply how it goes when one commits to uphold those values. An unexpected twist in my story is that once I started walking that walk, it was Blacks who walked next to me, behind me, and in front of me. My black students and colleagues and I had become allies; and it was amazing what we accomplished in spite of the racism barriers in academia. But, we have not been able to topple the system. Racism is alive and well in academia and is supported by complicity of all the silent academicians.

In the decades that have passed since my first ride through the West Side of Chicago, too little has changed, it even got worse! How then could a so-called learned one in academia keep from speaking up, from doing something, from at least learning to recognize the realities within which black males must function in our world and lend a hand? How can a so-called learned one not be willing to act with and for others in pursuit of ending oppression, marginalization, and disenfranchisement of black males in academia? How then could a so-called learned one in academia reap the benefits of position, status, and income and mis-educate students and mistreat colleagues, who are black? Is it really enough to help behind the scenes? It is time for both: for the 'good' white professors to do what we must in good faith and aligned to the

206

proclaimed values in our university's mission statements; and for all of us to stop pulling the bodies out of the river one by one and instead go see why they are being thrown in in the first place. Starting at the roots, a radical change means to create a new system. Together, we really can stop blackmaling our peers and students. Real change will come when we recognize the play by the powers-that-be and cut the marionette strings all together.

Consulted Sources and References

https://cmarlinwarfield.com/the-bodies-in-the-river-a-story/

https://www.youtube.com/watch?v=yoKLoSC52Lg&feature=youtu.be

Baldwin, J. (1969). James Baldwin Discusses Racism on the Dick Cavett show. Retrieved from https://www.youtube.com/watch?v=WWwOi17WHpE

Fraser, A., & McGowan, R. (1988). An episode of KPIX-TV's People Are Talking Features. Retrieved from https://www.youtube.com/watch?v=VHL7glIcP4o

Davis, A., Ture, K., Hamer, F.L., & et al. (1973). *Black Leaders Discussion feat*. A Black Journal Special Program. Retrieved from https://www.youtube.com/watch?v=MojDoeloUTc

Happold, M. (2017). *DePaul's Secret Zine Scene*. 14East. Retrieved from http://fourteeneastmag.com/index.php/2018/10/05/depauls-secret-zine-scene/.

Peck, Raoul. (2016). *I am not your Negro*. Vintage International.

Strohschen, G., & Elazier, K. (2007). The 21st Century adult educator: Strategic and consultative partner. *Assumption University Journal 1*(1), 42-53. Bangkok: Assumption University Press.

Strohschen, G., & Elazier, K. (2020). Metagogy: Toward a Contemporary Adult Education Praxis. In K. Pushpanadham (Ed.). *Teacher education in global era: Perspectives and practices*. Springer International.\\

Strohschen, G. (2020). By Means of Critical Theory: Informed Emancipatory Education – An Essay on Realities an Possibilities. In V. Wang (Ed) *Transformation and Adult Education*. IGI Global. https://www.igi-global.com/chapter/by-means-of-critical-theory/252802 .

Strohschen, G., & Lewis, K. (2019). *Competency-based and social-situational approaches for facilitating learning in higher education*. IGI Global.

Strohschen, G. (2014). The Community Connexxions Project: A University's Civic Engagement Approach to Bridging Racism and Classism in Urban Chicago by Examining Identity. In Efrat Tzadik, Ram Vemuri, and Rob Fisher (Eds.). *Proceedings of 7th Global Conference Interculturalism, Meaning and Identity*. 18th March –20th March. Prague, Czech Republic. Paper delivered at: Interculturalism, Meaning & Identity: A Diversity Recognition Project. March 2014. Prague, Czech Republic.

Strohschen, G. (2012). In Black and White: Transformation through Examined Selves. In Boden McGill, C.J., & Kippers, S.M. (Eds). *Pathways to Transformation: Learning in Relationship.* (pp. 207-221). Information Age Publishing.

Williams, John. A. (1967). *The man who cried I am.* New American Library.

Blackmaled in Academia

PART SEVEN

The Final Blow

Infinite Rounds

Blayne Stone, University of Wisconsin-Madison

Infinite Rounds

Like a tree on the verge of falling
My foundation is tired and weak

But

I will not fall because they are watching
Ring Side
From cracked phone screens
Barber chairs and window fronts

They are afraid because I am a contender
Heavy – weight
It will be a slugfest

They pronounce my name wrong

As I enter the ring
You address me as the other Black guy
Even though we look nothing alike

Ding
Ding
Ding

Jab, cross, jab
Cross, jab, cross
Move
Block
Jab

Slip
Slip
Pivot

Block block
Rapid body shots
I throw punches hoping to crack skin like slave whips once

used
You
Will not get me on the ropes

I have to go the distance
For myself
My ancestors
And those that will come after

Jab, left hook, right hook
Slip
Rolling with it
I throw punches that make slave owners souls quiver

Can't stand still
We were born in the twelfth round
Jab, uppercut, cross
Now
We
Can fight back

And I intend on going toe to toe

Move
Block
Slip
Pivot
Double jab, cross, left hook

I swing to connect
As dog teeth once punctured my people's skin

A top dollar chin
                          At the slave auction
Fight fiercer than a Tasmanian devil

Nose bleeding like slave blood your forefathers took
Eyes swollen

I wait for the bell
But I know it will never come
Block

Dip
Left Jab
I throw punches to hurl you back like fire hoses

Jab, cross, left shovel hook

Move
I want these punches to break you

Broken like the virginity of Black women
raped by their masters
Crying in their husband's arms
Who legally cannot defend them

Gasp for air like Eric Garner and George Floyd
I hope the cameras capture every punch I throw

Every punch I throw is to break you

An all-out war

Freeing more minds than Harriet ever imagined
You cannot camouflage freedom

Distractions
I'm Swinging

Swinging
Swinging

To break these chains
Inflect this pain

Deteriorate you slowly

Like racism institutionalized

Move
Pivot
Uppercut, uppercut, uppercut
Your feet are barely on the ground
These punches will lift you

To treetops where the souls of many still hang

Jab Jab
Block
Pivot

You won't find freedom underneath these stars
This unconscious state may awaken you

Throw in the towel
Can be heard on all levels
Of the filled arena

One voice overpowers their chants
Keep going
King

Black gloves
       Send burning blows to your core
       Heat like the crosses left in front yards

Something you can't ignore

I hope they hit like bombs

       Blow you steps back
           And allow you to see
           The souls of four little girls
           That still can't rest in peace

Black trunks Graceful
Choreographed Moves

They will still assert that I have more to prove

I entered the ring a Black student
And will leave as a Black professor
Maybe today is the day
I will finally defeat and destroy our oppressor

Black men were born to go infinite rounds.

Biographical Statements by the Authors

Alan Acosta, Ph.D., is a passionate higher education professional whose work focuses on supporting college students in their identity development and helping them to become ethical global leaders. He currently serves as Acting Senior Associate Dean of Students at Clark University, supervising the Office of Residential Life and Housing, student conduct, and supporting the diversity, equity, and inclusion initiatives of the university. Prior to Clark, Alan spent almost 14 years at Florida State University in a number of roles. Alan believes in the power of education to uplift communities and change lives, which drives and centers the work he does.

Mr. John Anderson is an educator, mentor, and thought-leader with over 25 years of experience and impact, working with people from all walks of life. He is a lecturer of sociology at Ball State University, where he teaches courses on race, globalization, and urban sociology. He is also completing a Doctor of Education degree in Adult, Higher, and Community Education at Ball State University. His dissertation examines how African American students find an African sense of self, belonging, and community through Purdue University's Black Cultural Center. Mr. Anderson's educational journey in higher education has meant that he has studied at every level and has completed six programs of study to date.

Vashon H. Broadnax is a native of Louisville, Kentucky. He currently serves as an academic advisor in the Miller College of Business at Ball State University. Vashon is pursuing an EdD in Adult and Community Education, with an interest in diversity, equity, and inclusion in higher education. Vashon is an experienced, student affairs professional and researcher with progressive experience working in both public and private institutions of higher learning; with experience working in small, midsized, and large institutions of higher learning.

Lawrence Bryant, PhD, MPH, RRT, BSW, AAS is a member of the Cobb/Douglass Behavioral Workgroup. Dr. Bryant brings a plethora of experiences dealing with substance use disorders through clinical practice, policy, and research. He has been successful in developing and implementing a statewide strategic plan for the state of Georgia in response to the opioid and prescription drug overdose epidemic. As a part-time Assistant Professor at Kennesaw State University, Health Promotion Department, Dr. Bryant has received funding from the Georgia Department of Public Health to do a needs assessment in support of the Statewide Strategic Plan for Opioid Abuse. Dr Bryant just received certification in contact tracing and plans to utilize this knowledge to train others in this technique. Dr. Bryant continues to publish in the field of public health and holds dual positions in both public health and psychology at Capella University. Dr Bryant is also a registered respiratory

216

therapist, fighting on the front lines of the Covid-19 pandemic in the field of pediatrics.

DaShawn Dilworth is a recent graduate from the Higher Education Master's program at Florida State University. He currently serves as a qualitative researcher, studying the capacity of political learning and democratic engagement among college students. His research interests include studying campus environments and their impact on Black students and staff, Black college student development, and the overlap of community engagement with identity development of college students.

Dr. Adeyemi Doss is Assistant Professor in the Department of Multidisciplinary Studies at Indiana State University in Terre Haute, Indiana. His research interests are shaped by the growing trend towards producing scholarship that focuses on issues confronting African American men and boys. His research raises important questions regarding black subjectivity, modes of black spatial mobility, and embody resistance.

Myron C. Duff, Jr. is currently the Associate Director of Multicultural Recruitment at Franklin College in Franklin, Indiana. He is passionate about adult learners, community building, social justice, the issues concerning Black males, and calling out and addressing systematic racism. He holds a Bachelor's degree in sociology from Ball State University, a Master's degree in higher education administration from Miami University (Oxford, OH), and a PhD in Urban Education Studies (Adult Education minor) from Indiana University Purdue University Indianapolis.

Ronald Duncan earned a BA from DePaul University, a MA in Writing, Literature, and Publishing from Emerson College, and is currently a Doctoral Candidate in Postsecondary Education at National-Louis University. His lifelong experiences, coupled with current events, have played a significant role in his decision to impact and inform social justice through higher learning and instructional leadership.

While being Blackmaled, **Dr. K. B. Elazier** has managed to teach courses as an adjunct professor for Hampton University, Southern Illinois University, and DePaul University. Despite his experience as a certified, K-12 special educator; developing and administering School-to-Work programs for the Chicago Public Schools and the Illinois Department of Rehabilitation Services; conducting professional development seminars for teachers of the Paul Simon JobCorps Center in Chicago and Adult Educators for the State of Georgia, he remains unemployed in academia. As a Master Trainer, he has conducted corporate train-the-trainer seminars throughout the United States and Canada, and provided training program evaluations in Africa, Thailand, and for UNESCO in Afghanistan. He is also a published co-author of several professional journal articles and book chapters.

Dr. Frederick Engram Jr., is Assistant Professor of Instruction at the University of Texas at Arlington in the Department of Criminology/Criminal Justice and the Center for African American Studies (CAAS). Dr. Engram's research engages how the invention of race and racism created the framework for the United States and is the impetus for the current racial climate. Dr. Engram applies this understanding to interpret and highlight the role of racism in higher education and the criminal justice system. His research areas of interest are structural racism (institutional and systemic), oppressive systems, hbcus, pwis, white supremacy, white manning, and white privilege.

Steffen Gillom MA, is a therapist, conflict resolution specialist, professional mediator, diversity consultant, TESOL educator, and conference trainer. In 2019, he was elected as a delegate for Senator Bernie Sanders and awarded Vermont Business Magazine's 40 under 40 'Rising Star' Award. Most recently, the bulk of his activism work is through the NAACP, where he currently serves as President and Founder of the Windham County Vermont Branch of the NAACP. Steffen also serves as the only Black voting executive committee member for the Vermont Democratic Party. Steffen holds a BS in Political Science (2013) from Southern Illinois University, Edwardsville and a MA in Peacebuilding and Conflict Transformation from the School of International Training (2015). He is currently pursuing his Ph.D. in Marriage and Family Therapy from Antioch University, New England.

Dr. Justin Grimes completed his Bachelor's degree in Computer Information Systems with a minor in African American Studies, and a Master's degree in Workforce Development Education with an emphasis on Human Resource Education, all from the University of Arkansas at Fayetteville. He completed his Ph.D. in Counseling and Student Personnel Services (College Student Affairs Administration) at the University of Georgia. Justin has over 12 years of experience working in Student and Academic Affairs, teaching, customer service, recruitment, and consulting. As a scholar, Justin's research centers on mentorship, successful dissertation completion strategies, the impact of racism on college students, motivation, and embracing identity and differences. He has received several awards both as a student and professional for outstanding leadership, service, and mentorship.

Dr. Anthony L. Heaven is higher education scholar-practitioner who specializes in diversity/inclusion work and development/fundraising. He is a proud graduate of both Stillman College and the University of Texas at Austin. His work experiences span student services, development, and donor relations. He currently serves as the Associate Director of Development for the Sally McDonnell Barksdale Honors College (SMBHC) and the Division of Diversity and Community Engagement at The University of Mississippi.

Marquis B. Holley is an Ed.D. Candidate in the Educational Innovation Program at The University of South Florida. His dissertation focuses on the barriers to the full implementation of policies designed to advance Black and Brown faculty, staff, and administrators in Higher Education. His research interests include Arts Based Research (ABR) and Post Traumatic Slave Syndrome (PTSS), along with Equity, Diversity, and Inclusive-based initiatives in society.

Cameron Jernigan is a Higher Education/Student Affairs professional and writer originally from and currently based in North Carolina. He is a 2020 graduate of the Higher Education program at Florida State University, where he completed his Master of Science, and is a proud member of the LifeNet. Prior to this, he obtained his Bachelor of Arts degree in Communication from the University of North Carolina at Chapel Hill, graduating in 2018.

Denzel Jones Ph.D., LMFT, is Assistant Professor of Couple and Family Therapy at Antioch University New England and a licensed marriage and family therapist. Prior to this appointment, he received his B.S. in Psychology from Campbell University (2013), an M.A. in Marriage and Family Therapy and a Certificate in Expressive Arts Therapy from Appalachian State University (2015), and a Ph.D. in Couple and Family Therapy from Kansas State University (2018). His primary research interest is on identity development across time and social processes that impact identity with a secondary research interest in relationships education. Additionally, Dr. Jones engages in multiple professorial, clinical, supervisory, scholarship, and community engagement and service roles.

Dr. George Ligon, IV is Research Associate and Mathematics Specialist at edCount, LLC, where he manages the assessment development and alignment evaluations of large-scale state assessments. In addition to this work, Dr. Ligon is the Principal Researcher and Consultant with Equitable Education Solutions, LLC. He has worked with more than seventy U.S. school districts and international education agencies as an education consultant. Dr. Ligon's research explores the influence of education policy on the performance of economically disadvantaged Black students attending persistently low-performing schools. He believes all students can achieve great heights. However, policymakers must employ appropriate policies, structures, and supports to redress the factors that influence poor student outcomes, like opportunity gaps. According to Dr. Ligon, "If Black people are the touchstone of American democracy, social stratification indicates that either democracy has failed us all, or it is doing what it was intended to do."

Blayne D. Stone, Jr., is a doctoral student in the School of Education at the University of Wisconsin-Madison. He is also a research associate in Wisconsin's Equity & Inclusion Laboratory (Wei LAB). Blayne received a B.A. in Liberal Arts with minors in Business and Communications and an M.S.

Ed. in Higher Education Administration from Florida International University, and an M.A. in Human Development Psychology from Cornell University. Blayne has work experience in residential life, summer bridge programs, Greek life, and multicultural affairs. In addition, he has worked with foster care and at-risk youth for several years. Blayne's research interest advocates for equality and justice for former foster care youth of color that aspire to attain a post-secondary education.

Professor Emerita Dr. Gabriele Strohschen completed her studies at Northern Illinois University in Educational Leadership and Policy Studies. She works in Chicago's historically disenfranchised communities and joined DePaul University as director for the graduate programs at the School for New Learning in 2003. Dr. Strohschen conducted action research, program design and evaluation, and teacher training in Germany, Czech Republic, Kenya, China, Mexico, Thailand, and around the USA. In Afghanistan, she completed a program evaluation project for the Afghan Ministry of Education's Women Literacy Project, funded by UNESCO, with Dr. Elazier. Currently, she collaborates with community residents, organizations, institutions of higher education, students, artists, and activists in social justice projects, virtually around the world and locally at her Pilsen Storefront in Chicago.

Dr. Headley White is Associate Professor in Secondary Education in the College of Arts Humanities, School of Education at Bethune-Cookman University. Dr. White taught in both rural and urban secondary schools, before taking his talents to the college level. He believes in the continued effort to level the playing field professionally and academically for historically underrepresented and marginalized groups. His personal quote "In an era of blunt instruments, one needs to be a Swiss Army knife!"